WORD AND WITNESS

UNDERSTANDING THE BIBLE II

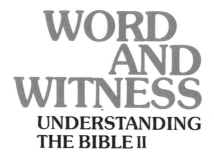

WORD AND WITNESS

UNDERSTANDING THE BIBLE II

By Foster R. McCurley, Jr.

and John Reumann

Edited by James L. Barkenquast

Division for Parish Services   Lutheran Church in America   Philadelphia

WORD AND WITNESS PROGRAM

The lines of hymns, reprinted on p. 33, are taken from the *Service Book and Hymnal* and used by permission of the Commission on the Liturgy and Hymnal.

Map of Palestine on p. 118 is taken from *Luke/Acts in the Today's English Version*. Copyright © American Bible Society 1966, 1971. Used by permission.

"Wooden's Pyramid," p. 148, © 1973 by The New York Times Company. Reprinted by permission.

Quotations from Luther's *Small Catechism* are from *The Small Catechism by Martin Luther, in Contemporary English,* copyright © 1960, 1968 by Augsburg Publishing House, Board of Publication of the Lutheran Church in America, Concordia Publishing House; and are used by permission.

Quotations from *The Book of Concord* are from the 1959 edition translated by Theodore G. Tappert and copyrighted by Muhlenberg Press, Philadelphia, Pennsylvania.

Except as otherwise noted, Scripture quotations in this publication are from the *Revised Standard Version Common Bible,* copyrighted © 1973 by the Division of Christian Education of the National Council of the Churches of Christ in the U.S.A., and used by permission. Brief phrases from other versions are identified in the text.

Other Scripture quotations are from *The New English Bible.* © The Delegates of the Oxford University Press and The Syndics of the Cambridge University Press 1961, 1970. Reprinted by permission.

Cover and book design by Johanna Sperl

Photo credits: p. 2, Hicks, courtesy of The Brooklyn Museum; p. 45, Leon V. Kofod; pp. 60, 69, 89, 92, 126, 162, 181, 185, 192, Religious News Service; pp. 112, 151, John Reumann; p. 194, Camerique.

Printed in U.S.A.

CONTENTS

PART V
GOD'S FUTURE REIGN

PART VI
THE GOSPEL IN THE EARLY CHURCH

PART VII
ONE GOSPEL, MANY FORMS

PART V God's Future Reign

The Peaceable Kingdom on page 2 is
one of about one hundred paintings by
the eighteenth-century Quaker Edward
Hicks on this theme. Based on Isaiah
11:6–7, it portrays the day when the
kingdom of the Messiah would become
a reality on earth. Hicks' primitive but
vivid and imaginative imagery was intended to proclaim a confident hope
in a reliable future as pledged in the
Scriptures.

17. The Day of Yahweh

HOPE TAKES SHAPE

Maybe it was because the reign of God in Israel's wordly existence seemed so incomplete, marred as it was with such tragedies as the division of the monarchy and the fall of the Northern Kingdom, and the subjugation of the Southern Kingdom, to say nothing of the constant bickering between the two while both survived. Perhaps it was due to a realization that God's reign must extend far beyond the recognition and confession of Israel to include the whole universe. Whatever the reasons, the biblical witnesses looked beyond the immediate situation to the future when God would establish himself as King and Creator of a new age and reign in glory.

This new time to which the Old Testament points was not to come about as a result of gradual growth. It was in no way conceived to be the end of a process in which the world and its contents would become better and better and finally evolve into a golden age. Indeed, if anything, the Old Testament portrays a view which points in the opposite direction. After the grandeur of the Davidic-Solomonic Empire of the tenth century B.C. life seemed to run downhill. Instead of the old glory there was tragedy; in place of freedom there was confinement—political, economic, and even moral—because of an increasing legalistic structure.

Hope, though it waned at times, never died. The mediators of God's Word preached in various ways that one day the Lord would execute some dramatic event that would begin his kingship over everyone. Indeed, this expectation must have begun quite early in Israel's history and spread among the folks of the marketplace, the fields, the washing wells, and the court. They believed that by some mighty act the Lord would come one day to claim rightfully everything as his own. Of course such a deed included his destruction of the evil forces which opposed him with their counterclaims. In the minds of the people those forces were primarily Israel's enemies.

4

FIRST THERE WAS AMOS

The first preacher among the prophets to address the people with this idea of the day of Yahweh was Amos. Though a southerner from Judah, Amos preached exclusively, it seems, in the Northern Kingdom of Israel in a time of national optimism (about 760–750 B.C.). His message was essentially one of judgment. He interpreted the day of Yahweh in a manner quite different from his audience:

> Woe to you who desire the day of the Lord!
> Why would you have the day of the Lord?
> It is darkness, and not light;
> as if a man fled from a lion,
> and a bear met him;
> or went into the house and leaned with his hand
> against the wall, and a serpent bit him.
> Is not the day of the Lord darkness and not light,
> and gloom with no brightness in it?
> (Amos 5:18–20)

The verses that follow explain that the Lord takes no pleasure in the formalities of religious expression if there is no heartfelt commitment which results in justice and righteousness (v. 21-24). For this reason God will make "the day" one of darkness for those optimistic Israelites who had thought that because God was "on their side" they could simply sit back and watch his judgment descend on everyone else. Not so, said Amos. God's judgment comes on you as well when he acts "in" or "on that day."

> ". . . He who is stout of heart among the mighty
> shall flee away naked in that day," says
> the Lord (2:16).
> "The songs of the temple shall become wailings in
> that day," says the Lord God (8:3)
> "And on that day," says the Lord God,
> "I will make the sun go down at noon,
> and darken the earth in broad daylight" (8:9).
> "In that day the fair virgins and the young men
> shall faint for thirst" (8:13).

Or, with a turn of the phrase, the prophet spells out another reason for such judgment on Israel:

> "Hear this word, you cows of Bashan,
> who are in the mountain of Samaria,
> who oppress the poor, who crush the needy,
> who say to the husbands,
> 'Bring, that we may drink!'
> The Lord God has sworn by his holiness
> that, behold, the days are coming upon you,
> when they shall take you away with hooks,

5

> even the last of you with fishhooks.
> And you shall go out through the breaches,
> every one straight before her;
> and you shall be cast forth into Harmon,"
> says the Lord (4:1–3).

Thus, while the precise expression "the day of Yahweh" occurs only sixteen times in the Old Testament, the same future and decisive act of the Lord is meant by such phrases as "that day" or "the days are coming."

THEN OTHER PROPHETS

Amos was first to introduce these terms into his prophetic preaching midway through the eighth century B.C. in order to announce judgment upon Israel (along with other nations); he was by no means the last.

> In that day man will cast forth
> their idols of silver and their idols of gold
>
> . . . .
>
> to the moles and to the bats,
> to enter the caverns of the rocks
> and the clefts of the cliffs,
> from before the terror of the Lord,
> and from the glory of his majesty,
> when he rises to terrify the earth.
> (Isaiah 2:20–21)

Indeed, following Amos's lead, later prophets preached about the Lord's day and God's impending judgment in ferocious battle terms. A passage from the end of the Babylonian Exile (about 538 B.C.) inserted into the Book of Isaiah contains this oracle concerning Babylon:

> Hark, a tumult on the mountains
> as of a great multitude!
> Hark, an uproar of kingdoms,
> of nations gathering together!
> The Lord of hosts is mustering
> a host for battle.
> They come from a distant land,
> from the end of the heavens,
> the Lord and his weapons of indignation,
> to destroy the whole earth.
> Wail, for the day of the Lord is near;
> as destruction from the Almighty it will come!
>
> Behold, the day of the Lord comes,
> cruel, with wrath and fierce anger,
> to make the earth a desolation
> and to destroy its sinners from it.
> For the stars of the heavens and their

> constellations
> will not give their light;
> the sun will be dark at its rising
> and the moon will not shed its light.
> (Isaiah 13:4-6, 9-10)

Likewise, the prophet Jeremiah included in his preaching the oracle concerning the army of Pharaoh Neco, ruler of Egypt:

> "Prepare buckler and shield,
> and advance for battle!
> Harness the horses;
> mount, O horsemen!
> Take your stations with your helmets,
> polish your spears,
> put on your coats of mail!
> Why have I seen it?
> They are dismayed
> and have turned backward.
> Their warriors are beaten down,
> and have fled in haste;
> they look not back—
> terror on every side!
> says the Lord.
>
> Advance, O horses,
> and rage, O chariots!
> Let the warriors go forth:
> men of Ethiopia and Put who handle the shield,
> men of Lud, skilled in handling the bow.
> That day is the day of the Lord God of hosts,
> a day of vengeance,
> to avenge himself on his foes."
> (Jeremiah 46:3-5, 9-10)

We find this same view of this day of the Lord as a time of disaster and bloody judgment in the preaching of Ezekiel in the early sixth century B.C. (7:1-27; 30:1-5) and before that between 630 and 625 B.C. in the denouncements of Zephaniah (1:7-18).

A DAY OF JUDGMENT AND DARKNESS

The imagery of the Lord doing battle as a mighty warrior who causes his enemy to panic and flee in the midst of terror (Jeremiah 46:5) and who uses the heavens to envelop his unfortunate enemy in darkness (Isaiah 13:10) calls to mind the ancient holy wars of Yahweh when the judges ruled in Israel.

In the days of Joshua the Lord fought against the five kings of the Amorites, throwing them into a self-destructive panic and then pelting them with hail stones from heaven (Joshua 10:1–11). In Samuel's battle against the Philistines, the Lord "thundered" and so sent the enemy fleeing in panic (1 Samuel 7:10–11). And we have already seen God's use of darkness and water to destroy the Egyptians at the Red Sea (Exodus 14). It seems obvious that the description of the Lord doing battle with all sorts of enemies "in that day" derives from this old notion of Yahweh's holy wars. By reaching back into the historical past, the Old Testament witnesses found the means to proclaim the future judgment of God upon the forces of evil.

A DAY OF RESTORATION

But what is to happen on the day of the Lord is not judgment alone! After judgment upon Israel, and in some cases judgment upon another nation through Israel, "on that day" the Lord will restore his people. Or at least a remnant of his people. Even the Book of Amos concludes with two day-of-Yahweh passages which promise restoration. Although the conclusion may not have come from that "prophet of doom" himself, someone saw fit to end his preaching with two promises for the future. The second describes the fullness of restoration in the land.

> "Behold the days are coming," says the Lord,
>   "when the plowman shall overtake the reaper
>   and the treader of grapes him who sows the seed;
> the mountains shall drip sweet wine,
>   and all the hills shall flow with it.
> I will restore the fortunes of my people Israel,
>   and they shall rebuild the ruined cities and
>   inhabit them;
> they shall plant vineyards and drink their wine,
>   and they shall make gardens and eat their fruit.
> I will plant them upon their land,
>   and they shall never again be plucked up
>   out of the land which I have given them,"
>   says the Lord your God.
>
> (Amos 9:13–15)

Here the Lord promises the rebuilding of ruined cities; vegetation and fruit so plentiful and fast growing that the farmers will hardly be able to keep up with the harvesting; abundant wine from fertile vineyards; and an end to destruction and exile.

Another feature in the kingdom to be established is the restored Temple. Isaiah 4 provides one description, along with a reference to the "remnant" issue.

In that day the branch of the Lord shall be beautiful and glorious, and the fruit of the land shall be the pride and glory of the survivors of Israel. And he who is left in Zion and remains in Jerusalem will be called holy, every one who has been recorded for life in Jerusalem, when the Lord shall have washed away the filth of the daughters of Zion and cleansed the bloodstains of Jerusalem from its midst by a spirit of judgment and by a spirit of burning. Then the Lord will create over the whole site of Mount Zion and even her assemblies a cloud by day, and smoke and the shining of a flaming fire by night; for over all the glory there will be a canopy and a pavilion. It will be for a shade by day from the heat, and for a refuge and a shelter from the storm and rain.

(Isaiah 4:2-6)

Like so many passages dealing with the day of salvation, this one contains the picture of a fruitful paradise. (See Isaiah 30:23 ff; Jeremiah 31:12; Ezekiel 34:29; 47:12; Isaiah 41:17-20; Zechariah 9:16 ff; 14:8; Malachi 3:11.) It reaches beyond the response of nature to the old signs of the Lord's presence among the people, the cloud by day and smoke and fire by night (Exodus 13:21-22). These will become protective instruments for the Temple and the congregation assembled there for worship. Thus the Temple of Jerusalem plays a central role in the kingdom of God which will be inaugurated "on that day."

AND A DAY OF *SHALOM*

Such broad-sweeping portrayals of the "paradise life" lead directly to the conclusion that the day of the Lord when God establishes himself unequivocally as King is the beginning of *shalom*. *Shalom* is that condition in which men and women are free to live unrestrained and unhindered by restrictions. *Shalom* means living life to the fullest, participating without difficulty in the life of the community, experiencing a devout and close relationship with God. All this seems to fit the descriptions of that restoration which will occur on the day of the Lord and beyond. Thus the kingdom of God or the new age for which people waited was seen as a part of this world. It was to be a time of material and spiritual plenty, of joy, of protection, and long life.

Moreover, this state of *shalom* in the new age to come would include nations other than Israel. To be sure, Israel—specifically Jerusalem—was the focal point for God's relationship with the Gentiles, but the latter would also come to learn his will.

> It shall come to pass in the latter days
>> that the mountain of the house of the Lord
> shall be established as the highest of the mountains,
>> and shall be raised above the hills;
> and all the nations shall flow to it,
>> and many people shall come, and say:
> "Come, let us go up to the mountain of the Lord,
>> to the house of the God of Jacob;

> that he may teach us his ways
>   and that we may walk in his paths."
> For out of Zion shall go forth the law,
>   and the word of the Lord from Jerusalem.
> He shall judge between the nations,
>   and shall decide for many peoples;
> and they shall beat their swords into ploughshares,
>   and their spears into pruning hooks;
> nation shall not lift up sword against nation,
>   neither shall they learn war any more.
>
>   (Isaiah 2:2–4)

This beautiful and powerful passage, repeated at Micah 4:1–3, expands the earlier descriptions of "the latter days" to include a universal pilgrimage to Mt. Zion. There all nations would learn God's law (that is, his instruction), submit to his judgments, and abolish war. Peace among nations! Harmony among the peoples! Worship of the Lord in every land! Even the concept of *shalom* becomes larger. This is what the reign of God will be like. So different will life be in the future kingdom that no other term would suffice but "new creation."

> For behold, I create new heavens and a new earth;
>   and the former things shall not be remembered
>   or come into mind.
> But be glad and rejoice for ever in that which I
>   create;
>   for behold, I create Jerusalem a rejoicing,
>   and her people a joy.
>
>   (Isaiah 65:17–18)

The passage goes on to describe the lack of distress, the long life of children (but not eternal life), fruitful vineyards and the enjoyment of them, meaningful labor, abundant posterity, even harmony among hostile animals. Now the picture of *shalom* is so vast that a new heaven and a new earth will be required to contain it. Still, this hope to come does not call for the ruination and dismissal of all material things. On the contrary, along with the new heavens a new earth will appear at God's doing, and material blessings will abound! Again, God the Creator will reign!

The prophets looked to specific historical events as God's means of bringing about his "day" and his resulting reign. They linked the fateful day to God's impending judgment on the Egyptians or the Assyrians or the Babylonians or a long list of others, including Israel and Judah. Frequently the prophesied judgments came and went and life went on much as before. So the people looked forward to the next big event on the world scene. And when that was over, they peered ahead to the next—and the next. In other words, the day of the Lord was constantly being pushed into the future because the expected results, the historical happenings, were not fulfilled.

10

Thus it is striking that this promise of God to reign in the future over a kingdom of universal *shalom* persisted among the prophets. It reflected the confidence of Israel that the reign of God would one day include all people. Such a time would come only at God's own doing!

It shall come to pass in the latter days
that the mountain of the house of the Lord
shall be established as the highest of the mountains,
and shall be raised above the hills;
and all the nations shall flow to it, . . .

(Isaiah 2:2)

References and More Information

Biblical references: Isaiah 2:2-4, 20-21; 4:2-6; 13:4-10; Jeremiah 46:3-12; all of Amos, but see especially 2:16, 4:1-3, 5:18-24, 8:3, 9, 13; and 9:13-15; Zephaniah 1:7-18; Zechariah 9:16 ff.

Metzger, Bruce M. and Isobel M., editors. *The Oxford Concise Concordance.* See the following entry: peace

Richardson, Alan. *A Theological Word Book of the Bible.* New York: The Macmillan Company, 1962. See the following entries: choose, determinate, peace

18. The Birth of Apocalyptic

The longing for that glorious day of Yahweh—which he would bring about to fulfill but not end history—became more and more a remote dream in many parts of Israel. Little wonder! Hundreds of years of history did not seem to warrant the idea that things were getting any better. On the contrary, it seemed that Israel walked a downhill path of oppression and disaster. The longer history continued, the worse life would be.

The splendid years of the Davidic-Solomonic Empire had been short and were long gone. That glory began to fade into memory the day near the close of the tenth century B.C. when the monarchy split into north and south. In the eighth century, Assyria overpowered both factions, bringing an end to the state of Israel and subjecting Judah to vassalhood. As the seventh century receded into history, Judah enjoyed a few years of freedom and influence under Josiah, but soon found itself a vassal, first of Egypt and then of Babylon. As a penalty for rebellion in 597 B.C., Judah was devastated, her leading citizens in exile in Babylon. Ten years later, after a second rebellion, Jerusalem was leveled, and the sacred Temple reduced to a pile of rubbish. When the Persians took control in 538 and offered the exiled Judaites opportunity to go home, few were interested. As beneficent as the Persians were, Judah remained a vassal state. That relationship ended in 331 B.C. when Alexander the Great made the territory of Judah part of his Greek Empire. For the next one hundred fifty years various factions warred for control of the land, only to give way eventually to the powerful Roman Empire with its special brand of authority and requirements for allegiance.

How could the people of Israel continue to hope that God's plan would unfold into fulfillment in history? History appeared to be nothing more than one disaster after another. Without confidence in history and God's action in history the people resorted to a different kind of theological expression—apocalyptic.

FIVE MARKS OF APOCALYPTIC

Apocalyptic is a Greek word which means "to unveil." It has to do with unveiling the secrets of the cosmos which are revealed only to a select few. Following are several distinct characteristics of apocalyptic.

An apocalyptic revelation comes in various forms, but most commonly through bizarre visions which can be interpreted only by those individuals to whom the secret code has been given. This is the first and major characteristic of apocalyptic.

The second has to do with the future. Apocalyptic works describe the future as the time when God will suddenly intervene in history, destroy virtually everything which now exists, and establish a heavenly kingdom. Apocalyptic writers are regarded so inspired as to be able to describe vividly the fate of the wicked and the bliss of the righteous. They are also supposedly able to determine when the end is coming on the basis of a divine world plan which has been foreordained.

Third, apocalyptic views history in a very mechanical way. It follows the "game plan," and people are rather passive as they wait to see what will happen next. It does not reflect belief in a personal God who acts in history. Rather, things simply occur by predetermined plan and people wait for the terrible day.

Fourth, the world and its inhabitants are regarded as evil and becoming increasingly more so. Since people do not act but merely wait and watch to see what will happen next, the world becomes progressively worse, and no one does anything to better the situation.

Finally, as a consequence of all this, apocalyptic proclaims two worlds or ages which are directly opposed to each other, the present age of evil and the time of bliss to come. That future scene is other-worldly rather than earthly and filled with the children of light rather than the children of darkness. Thus there are various forms of dualism.

APOCALYPTIC AND PROPHECY

The summary above helps us to see how sharply apocalyptic contrasts with the typically prophetic way of thinking and viewing life, past, present, and future. A comparison of the two throws the strangeness of apocalyptic into even clearer perspective.

1. The prophetic view of history regarded Israel as a nation that saw itself as saved, elected, and made a covenant partner of God. The basis for such a self-image lay in God's unfolding activities in the past. Each generation, by identifying itself with the past communities who were delivered and chosen, also became a people with whom God continued to act as a covenant partner. There was nothing mechanical about the relationship. God acted to judge and to save his people in the midst of whatever situations the people found themselves.

This view contrasts sharply with apocalyptic. There the emphasis is not on the personal dealing of God with Israel but rather on the divine plan for world empires which would work itself out along a cosmic time line. Apocalyptic's concept of history as a world plan depersonalizes the Lord of history known in the preaching of the prophets.

2. The prophetic view of history saw God acting in it. History was the unfolding of a plan or purpose in which God would lead events toward his desired goal—that time when all people on earth would come together at Mt. Zion, giving praise to Yahweh and seeking to learn his law. Even in the wild-eyed new creation of Isaiah 65—66, the new will be earthly. People will still die, but they will live longer (a hundred years!); justice will prevail for all; food will be abundant on the earth.

In contrast, apocalyptic sees at the end of the road the destruction of a world which is becoming more and more evil with each passing day. Only with its obliteration can a new spiritual age come into being.

3. The prophets spoke clearly to and about the situations in which their audiences found themselves. They "told it like it is." They described the problems, named the villains, and announced publicly what God had revealed he would do. Again, in contrast, in apocalyptic, the divinely inspired wrote about his own situation in veiled images of animals, statues, or even past times and long-dead people. Only the gifted few could interpret what would happen next according to God's mechanical plan. And their message was shrouded in allegory.

In ancient Israel and in our day as well the apocalyptic flourishes whenever times are bad and confidence in history and in mankind is lost.

Thus it is clear that in apocalypticism history was not the arena of God's activity with his people. There was no positive value to history at all; it served only as the arena in which evil evolves into destruction. Hence, in ancient Israel and in our day as well, apocalyptic flourishes whenever times are bad and confidence in history and in mankind is lost.

THE BOOK OF DANIEL

Although there are small sections of various Old Testament books which reflect apocalyptic style and thought, only the Book of Daniel is classified as apocalyptic. The story is set in the time of the Babylonian exile in the sixth century B.C., but the book was actually written to address the times of persecution under Seleucid King Antiochus IV Epiphanes (175–163 B.C.). The author started writing sometime after 167 B.C. when the Maccabees rose up against the Syrians. The reference to the "little help" received by the faithful in their time of testing is probably an allusion to the unenthusiastic response given to the Maccabean leaders (Daniel 11:34). Moreover, the reign of Antiochus IV is rather accurately described with the sole exception of his death—an error which probably indicates the book was finished before he died in 163. So we can conclude that Daniel was composed sometime between 167 and 164 B.C.

The book consists of two parts. Chapters 1—6 contain stories of Daniel and his friends in Babylon; Chapters 7—12 report Daniel's visions of the future of the kingdoms of the earth. Thus only half the book contains apocalyptic features. The two halves are linked by the insertion of Nebuchadnezzar's dream in the first section at Chapter 2.

With the exception of Chapter 2, the first part of the book is concerned with one fundamental point: the faithful and pious Jew who finds himself threatened by temptation and harm will be protected if he holds firm to his faith in God and does not compromise his allegiance to God's requirements. This is demonstrated in the first chapter; Daniel and friends refused to eat the king's delicacies but flourished nevertheless by eating only kosher food. In Chapter 3 the friends were tossed into a furnace which was so hot the attendants died from standing too close. The three friends were unharmed because of their refusal to indulge in idolatry. In Chapter 4, when Daniel said that the king's dream meant he would not only lose his kingship but also go mad, no harm came to Daniel. On the contrary, he received a promotion. The handwriting-on-the-wall incident in Chapter 5 tells of that same fearless allegiance to God on Daniel's part. And in Chapter 6, Daniel, thrown into the lions' den, emerged unharmed while his guards were mauled to death. Thus, every chapter provides one more episode which testifies that Yahweh will protect those who remain faithful and pious. Such ones in Israel had nothing to fear from Antiochus IV and his hatchet men. God would deliver the steadfast.

It is the dreams and visions, however, which illustrate the method and message of apocalyptic. Nebuchadnezzar's dream in Chapter 2 and the vision of the four beats in Chapter 7 provide good examples of the way apocalyptic works.

Nebuchadnezzar's dream

Troubled by dreams, King Nebuchadnezzar summoned magicians, sorcerers, enchanters, and "Chaldeans" to describe to him his dream and its meaning. When they admitted that they were unable to comply with his wish, the king ordered all the wise men throughout Babylon to be killed. One of this unlucky band was an exile from Judah named Daniel. The young Jew gained a special audience with the king and detailed both the contents of the dream and its meaning.

In his dream the king had seen a mighty image standing before him. Its head was gold; its breast and arms, silver; its belly and thighs of bronze, and its legs of iron. Its feet were partly clay and partly iron. Here is how Daniel explained its meaning:

> "You, O king . . . you are the head of gold. After you shall arise another kingdom inferior to you [silver], and yet a third kingdom of bronze, which shall be a fourth kingdom, strong as iron, because iron breaks to pieces and shatters all things; and like iron which crushes, it shall break and crush all these. And as you saw the feet and toes partly of potter's clay and partly of iron, it shall be a divided kingdom; but some of the firmness of iron shall be in it just as you saw iron mixed with the miry clay. And as the toes of the feet were partly iron and partly clay, so the kingdom shall be partly strong and partly brittle."
>
> (Daniel 2:37–42)

The dream provides a clear and simple presentation of history marking the course of events in four world empires. Each is more inferior than its predecessor until the coming of God's kingdom puts an end to the series.

The first empire was clearly that of Nebuchadnezzar, the Babylonian (or more properly, Neo-Babylonian) Empire: "You, O king . . . are the head of gold." The fourth seems to point to the achievements of the Greek conqueror Alexander and his successors, which was a divided empire. The second and third, therefore, must be the rule of the Medes and the Persians. Daniel 5:28 tells us that the Neo-Babylonian Empire was given to the Medes and Persians, and 8:20–21 that the Medes and Persians were overthrown by the King of Ionia, that is, Greece.

According to the author of Daniel, the end of the succession is near his own time, 167–164 B.C., for he and his audience are living in the days of the fourth and last empire. Such a realization prompts two observations. First, the coming end is not due to the nature of the Greek or Seleucid Empire, it is just that the cycle has run its fixed and foreordained course. Second, the question of the precise time of the end is left open, but it is near at hand.

The four beasts

The vision of the four beasts at 7:1–28 portrays the same series of empires and their fate. Daniel had a vision in which he saw four beasts come up out of the sea. The first, which looked "like a lion," was the Neo-Babylonian Empire. The second, "like a bear," was the Median Empire. The third, representing the Persian Empire, looked "like a leopard." And the fourth, horrible beyond description, was the Greek Empire. This last beast had ten horns representing various kings, with "a little one" added to denote Antiochus IV Epiphanes. Then "one that was the Ancient of Days" appeared, the royal figure of God the Judge, and soon the fourth

16

beast was slain and the dominion of all the others was taken away. As the vision continued, "one like a son of man" appeared before the Ancient of Days, and to him was given dominion over all peoples and nations. His kingdom was proclaimed as eternal and indestructible.

The interpretation of this vision is offered in verses 15–18 and in different form in verses 23–27. The "one like a son of man" is a corporate figure representing "the saints of the Most High." These saints are apparently those faithful and pious Jews who withstand the persecution under Antiochus IV and who will be rewarded with authority in the kingdom to come. That villian will prevail "for a time, two times, and half a time" (7:25) or for three and a half times—a number used elsewhere in Daniel (12:7) and in the New Testament Book of Revelation (see Revelation 11:11; 12:14; also 12:6 where the 1260 days represent three and a half) as a time of trial and of waiting for the coming of God. At any rate,

The nature of these visions shows clearly that they must be interpreted historically. That is to say, the writer had in mind not events on some day in the twentieth century but events in his own time; he tried to address the Word of God with his own understanding.

once again the end is near, and the people wait in hope for God to establish his own kingdom and his own reign.

The nature of these visions shows clearly that they must be interpreted historically. That is to say, the writer had in mind not events on some day of the twentieth century but events in his own time which he tried to address with his understanding of the Word of God. It was persecution and trouble between 167 and 164 B.C. which caused the Book of Daniel to be written, and it was to that situation that the writer addressed his message with all the devices of apocalyptic literature. Seen in this way, neither Daniel nor any other book can be used today to predict the end of worldly history on the basis of forced analogies between the "secrets" of apocalyptic and contemporary events. To do so would be to deny that the Word of God is spoken to a specific audience at a certain time and place.

OTHER OLD TESTAMENT APOCALYPSES

The seeds of apocalyptic were sown long before 167 B.C. Hence we find that apocalyptic sections appear in other books of the Old Testament. For example, during the Exile of the sixth century B.C. the prophet Ezekiel and his disciples used images and concepts that introduced apocalyptic to the people of Israel. The famous prophecy against Gog of Magog at Ezekiel 38—39 is one example. With Israel living secure in its borders the leader of a powerful army will suddenly appear. God will bring his forces out of the far north to conquer Israel, but in the manner of his holy wars of old, the Lord will cause the earth to quake and Gog's army will panic and destroy itself. By this victory "the nations shall know that I am the Lord, the Holy One in Israel" (39:7).

Like the later apocalyptic visions, this passage must be interpreted historically rather than as a prediction for "the late great planet earth" to be fulfilled in our time. While the name of the long-gone Magog remains a mystery, Gog is probably the seventh-century King Gyges of Lydia (known in Semitic writing as Gugu and Gug) who waged war in Asia Minor against the powerful Cimmerians ("Gomer" of Ezekiel 38:6) and terrorized weaker nations. The mighty Gog became legendary, and it is in such legendary fashion that the author of this passage speaks to his audience about the day of the Lord on which he will defeat the overwhelming enemy, just as in the days of the old holy wars. To suppose, as some present-day interpreters do, that the *Meshech* of 38:2 is contemporary Moscow, that the Hebrew word *rosh* (meaning "chief" prince) in the same verse should be changed to *rush* (for Russia) and to further identify that country by its "northern" location in relation to Israel—all in order to argue that an imminent Russian invasion of Israel will mark the end of the age—is not only without evidence; it is based on pure conjecture and coincidence of similarities among sounds. But worse, it assumes that the prophecy had no real meaning for the people of Ezekiel's day. If it did not, then it was no proclamation of the Word of God at all. *The Word is always addressed to a particular situation in the life of people.*

Several centuries after Ezekiel, sometime in the fourth or third centuries B.C., a poet of apocalyptic bent composed a series of songs, poems, and sayings, which became Chapters 24—27 in the Book of Isaiah. This little "apocalypse of Isaiah," inserted into the preaching of the eighth-century prophet, has many of the characteristics identified at the beginning of this chapter. The overriding message is that the present world of distress will be replaced by a new age of bliss for Israel and for all people after Yahweh ends the old with a cosmic catastrophe. Several individual units stand out in this apocalypse.

There is a banquet to celebrate the day of the Lord:

> On this mountain the Lord of hosts will make for all peoples a feast of fat things, a feast of wine on the lees, of fat things full of marrow, of wine on the lees well refined. And he will destroy on this mountain the covering that is cast over all peoples, the veil that is spread over all nations. He will swallow up death for ever, and the Lord God will wipe away tears from all faces, and the reproach of his people he will take away from all the earth; for the Lord has spoken.
>
> (Isaiah 25:6–8)

The dinner guests include nations from far and wide who come to Israel for the Feast of Booths (see Zechariah 14:16). The meal is the means by which God will bring all peoples into fellowship with himself as he establishes his kingdom on that day (see also Matthew 8:11). Such a celebration marks the end of the utter disdain which the peoples hold for the long-persecuted nation of Israel. And it also signals the end of death.

The hope for the end of death is sharpened somewhat by a promise of a resurrection from the dead. Apart from Daniel 12:1–3 that idea is found nowhere else in the Old Testament.

> Thy dead shall live, their bodies shall rise.
>   O dwellers in the dust, awake and sing for joy!
> For thy dew is a dew of light,
>   and on the land of the shades thou wilt let it fall.
>
> (Isaiah 26:19)

In this poet's preaching, the day of the Lord will surely accompany God's victory over his enemies. In highly mythological fashion the apocalyptist announces:

> In that day the Lord with his hard and great and strong sword will punish Leviathan the fleeing serpent, Leviathan the twisting serpent, and he will slay the dragon that is in the sea.
>
> (Isaiah 27:1)

This passage is particularly striking because of its similarity to one of the ancient Canaanite poems of Baal found at the city of Ugarit:

> If you smite Lotan, the fleeing serpent,
> Destroy the serpent tortuous,
> Shalyat of the seven heads. . . .[1]

Doubtless Lotan and the biblical Leviathan are the same. So are the first two descriptions of the serpent. *Fleeing* and *tortuous* are identical words in the two Semitic languages. But the biblical writer uses the mythological image in a new way. No longer does the destruction of Lotan/Leviathan belong in the precreation past or in the natural cycle of the seasons, as did the Baal stories in ancient Canaan. Now, the victory of God over that fearsome monster, the symbol of evil, will occur in the future and specifically "on that day." This is the apocalyptists's description of the last battle in history.

One more battle description clearly identifies the result of the Lord's victory:

> On that day the Lord will punish
>   the host of heaven, in heaven,
>   and the kings of the earth, on the earth.
> They will be gathered together
>   as prisoners in a pit;
> they will be shut up in a prison,
>   and after many days they will be punished.
> Then the moon will be confounded,
>   and the sun ashamed;
> for the Lord of hosts will reign
>   on Mount Zion and in Jerusalem
> and before his elders he will manifest his glory.
>
> (Isaiah 24:21–23)

The cosmic victory of God over all who oppose him will provide the basis for his reign as king and for his glorious manifestation. Thus just as in his historical victories over his foes at the Red Sea (Exodus 14) and in Babylon (Isaiah 52:7–10), just as in his hymnic victory or salvation in creation (Psalms 96 and 98), so now in the apocalyptic victory over the forces of evil, God will reign as king. This is the gospel of apocalyptic: God's kingdom will come soon!

THE LESSONS OF THE APOCALYPTISTS

A final word about apocalyptic. It is important for us today to realize that only a fraction of the many apocalyptic writings of late Judaism are a part of the Old Testament. There is only one full book and a few chapters here and there in prophetic texts, usually from the time of the exile or later. To know that helps us to see that negative attitude toward history and the lack of confidence in God's work in history was not the normal attitude found in the Old Testament. The idea of an impersonal God and a mechanical view of history runs contrary to the whole biblical perspective.

But these apocalyptic writers had their good points too, especially the moderates among them. They saw that one cannot identify God's kingdom with the kingdoms of the earth. They understood that the history of the world would not evolve into the kingdom of God, and that his kingdom would come only by his own hand, his own intervention, his own will. Thus, the apocalyptists knew that the kingdom of God was not of this world. What they failed to realize, however, was that the kingdom would take place *in* the world. They lost the idea that God's rule is in the present as well as in the future, and so they really would not have understood a carpenter from Nazareth announcing, "The time is fulfilled, and the kingdom of God is at hand; repent and believe in the gospel" (Mark 1:15).

References and More Information

1. James B. Pritchard, ed., *The Ancient Near East: An Anthology of Texts and Pictures,* Vol. 1 (Princeton: Princeton University Press, 1958), p. 108.

Biblical references: Ezekiel 38–39; Daniel; Isaiah 24–27

Metzger, Bruce M. and Isobel M., Editors. The Oxford Concise Concordance. See the following entry: Daniel

Richardson, Alan. *A Theological Word Book of the Bible.* New York: The Macmillan Company, 1962. See the following entry: hope

19. The Kingdom and the Messiah

A KING FOR ISRAEL

The reign of Israel's first king, Saul, had little significance religiously for the tribal confederacy of Israel. In fact, in many ways Saul was more of a charismatic leader—like such judges as Gideon and Samson—than a king. Nevertheless, king he was acclaimed in a purely political way so that Israel would be like the nations around her (1 Samuel 8:5). The move to kingship came so quickly that Israel had no cultic or religious ideas to back up the change. Israel had religious rites within its loose confederacy to take care of the appointments of various personnel, but nothing to accompany Saul's accession to kingship. In truth, the new monarch along with his kingdom could not really be harmonized with the old traditions.

Kingship for Israel's first man on the throne was really a matter of political necessity quite separate from cultic or religious institutions and thinking. As a result, his potential as king was undermined from the very beginning. Whenever he stepped beyond his political bounds and presumed to disregard distinctions between cult and monarchy, he was promptly rebuked by the prophet-seer-judge Samuel and, of course, by Yahweh himself who eventually withdrew his spirit from the unfortunate Saul (see 1 Samuel 15:10–35; 16:1–14).

In effect, Saul was a failure as king not because of his own shortcomings, but because through no fault of his own his kingship lacked religious foundation. If this kind of rule had prevailed among Saul's successors, Israel would probably have returned to its former confederation and relinquished kings entirely.

THE DAVIDIC COVENANT

As for David, it was largely his military and political maneuvering which brought him to the throne of Judah and eventually of Israel as well in his new capital city of Jerusalem. At first David's power existed solely in his own exceptional ability to arrest political decline and disorder. He fortified

This relief from a temple wall at Karnak in Egypt portrays a group of Phoenicians cutting cedars of Lebanon. It was sculpted about 1300 B.C. Three hundred years later King Hiram of Tyre sent timber from these famous cedar groves for King David's palace at Jerusalem.

his city; he built a palace with the help of foreign craftsmen; he soundly defeated the Philistines; and he brought the sacred Ark into his capital (see 2 Samuel 5—6). When David had firmly established himself, the Lord pledged through the court prophet Nathan that the new king's dynasty would endure forever. " 'And your house and your kingdom shall be made sure for ever before me; your throne shall be established for ever'" (2 Samuel 7:16).

In this way David's kingship acquired what Saul never knew, a religious or theological foundation on which the government was constructed. The Lord chose or elected David through the prophetic spokesman Nathan, and thereby did his reign gain the sanction of religion. Kingship was no longer a separate political institution, but an integral (if not major part) of the religious understanding of the people of God.

This religious significance of Yahweh's election of and promise to David cannot be overstated. In David's farewell speech at 2 Samuel 23:1-7 the failing king describes his relationship with Yahweh thus:

> "Yea, does not my house stand so with God?
> For he has made me an everlasting covenant,
> ordered in all things and secure"
>
> (v. 5)

The Lord made a covenant with David in which God promised an enduring dynasty. That covenant of divine grace provided the foundation for David's kingship over Judah and Israel.

Yahweh's covenant is the essential difference between the kingship of David and that of Saul his predecessor. Saul's rule was a matter of immediate necessity in the face of the Philistine threat, but David was appointed to royal authority by the oracle of Yahweh's prophet and backed by a lasting covenant. This new covenant, however, initiated a radical new understanding of Yahweh's relationship with his people. In the old tribal confederacy Yahweh was the ruler of his people; in the new royal covenant, David served as the elected representative of divine rule. In the old confederacy of tribes Yahweh's relationship with the people was quite direct; in the new royal covenant Yahweh related to his people through a specific dynasty.

In some texts of the Old Testament, the continuance of a Davidic heir seems to depend on a king's faithfulness to Yahweh's ordinances.

> "If your sons keep my covenant
> and my testimonies which I shall teach them,
> their sons also forever
> shall sit upon your throne."
>
> (Psalm 132:12)

What appears to be a conditional statement, however, is preceded by one which demonstrates that the promise of God is unconditional.

> The Lord swore to David a sure oath
> from which he will not turn back:
> "One of the sons of your body
> I will set on your throne."
>
> (v. 11)

Another psalm makes the point even more explicit. After repeating the oath to David in verses 3-4 and again in verses 28-29, Psalm 89 continues:

> "If his children forsake my law
> and do not walk according to my ordinances,
> if they violate my statutes
> and do not keep my commandments,
> then I will punish their transgression with the rod
> and their iniquity with scourges;
> but I will not remove from him my steadfast love,
> or be false to my faithfulness.
> I will not violate my covenant,
> or alter the word that went forth from my lips.
> Once for all I have sworn by my holiness;
> I will not lie to David.
> His line shall endure for ever,
> his throne as long as the sun before me.
> Like the moon it shall be established for ever;
> it shall stand firm while the skies endure."
>
> (v. 30-37)

It is not the conditions placed on the kings but Yahweh's promise which is the significant element in this election of and covenant with David. Here, as with God's covenant with Abraham (Genesis 15:7-21), the promise is unconditional.

That promise was tested severely in the eighth century B.C. when the Assyrian Empire was reaching westward toward Canaan. In an attempt to block Tiglath-pileser's advance, the king of the Northern Kingdom of Israel and the king of Syria plotted to replace Davidic King Ahaz with their own crony, a certain "son of Tabeel" (Isaiah 7:6). But speaking through the prophet Isaiah, the Lord gave Ahaz a sign. A young woman is pregnant and is about to bear a son, and she shall call his name Immanuel. By the time he is old enough to distinguish good (tasting food?) from bad, the lands of the two plotting kings will be deserted. That sign, addressed to Ahaz as "O house of David," assures even this miserable and faithless king (see 2 Kings 16:1-4) that the coup will not work. Yahweh will keep the Davidic kings on Jerusalem's throne.

THE ROYAL PSALMS

As one might expect, such a religious or theological understanding of kingship prompted the writing of a number of psalms. The psalter includes an entire collection of "royal psalms," covering such a range of kingly matters as coronation, marriage, warfare, and duty. This collection consists of Psalms 2, 18, 20, 21, 45, 72, 110, and, as we have already seen, 89 and 132. The most interesting are the two which were composed on the occasion of the king's coronation on Jerusalem's throne, Psalms 2 and 110.

Psalm 2

The second psalm begins with a description of the chaotic political and international scene which follows the death of the monarch. Hostile neighboring rulers and vassals begin to plot their independence.

> The kings of the earth set themselves,
>   and the rulers take counsel together,
>   against the Lord and his anointed, saying,
> "Let us burst their bonds asunder,
>   and cast their cords from us."
>
> (v. 2–3)

Along with this action sparked by the event, what captures attention is the descriptive title given to the king. He is called "his anointed." To put the title back into its Hebrew word is to spell out *messiah*. In other words, "an anointed one" is a *messiah,* usually a king. Even Saul was so named by David (see 1 Samuel 24:6). *Messiah* is the king who rules on the throne, and the word is not so much a title as a description of one whom the Lord has appointed by anointing.

In any case, God greets such rebellion against the messiah on Jerusalem's throne with uproarious laughter. He knows that he need only speak and they will destory themselves in panic. The security of the Jerusalem king is assured when the cultic priest (or prophet) speaks for Yahweh.

> "I have set my king
> on Zion, my holy hill."
> (v. 6)

The king then speaks of the relationship between the Lord and himself.

> I will tell of the decree of the Lord:
> He said to me, "You are my son,
>   today I have begotten you."
> (v. 7)

This announcement spells out the relationship between the Lord and the crowned king in several ways. First, the announcement of God, "today I have begotten you," indicates that on coronation day itself (not on the day of the king's physical birth but on the day he is crowned) the king becomes a "son of God." "Today" is the key to understanding when and how this relationship takes place. Second, the short declaration "You are my son" was a formula used throughout the ancient Near East as a technical and legal expression of adoption. A man or woman needed only say these words to a child in order to make the adoption binding. Contrariwise, the negative expression of the formula meant disownment.

Thus, Yahweh's election of and covenant with the Davidic kings takes the form of a father-son relationship by virtue of adoption.

This image, by no means confined to Psalm 2, provides one of the basic ideas for the "messiahs" of Jerusalem.

> "He shall cry to me, 'Thou art my Father,
>   my God, and the Rock of my salvation.'
> And I will make him the first-born,
>   the highest of the kings of the earth."
>   (Psalm 89:26–27)

Even the oracle of Nathan which announced to David the promise of Yahweh for an everlasting dynasty identifies the Lord's relationship to David's successor with these words: "I will be his father, and he shall be my son" (2 Samuel 7:14).

The belief that the very human kings were adopted by Yahweh on the day of their coronation stands in sharp contrast to the view of ancient Egypt that the king was himself divine. It is also quite unlike the Mesopotamian notion of a divine birth. For Israel, those who came to the throne were humans, and humans they remained, both during and after the coronation. Nevertheless, their relationship, and thus their responsibility to Yahweh, the true king, was intimate and intense, for they knew they were the means by which the Lord related to his people as a nation.

In addition to this notion of adoption, the coronation rite described in Psalm 2 includes God's promise of universal domain and victory as well as a warning to those unruly kings who conspire against the Lord and his messiah at the outset.

So in the psalm the king is crowned, and receives his status as son of God. But another psalm, 110, may contain even earlier parts of the coronation ceremony.

Psalm 110

Psalm 110, a difficult one to read because of a problematic Hebrew text, contains in the RSV the Lord's command to take the throne:

> "Sit at my right hand,
> till I make your enemies your footstool."
>   (v. 1)

Like Psalm 2, it then goes on to describe the reign of this Jerusalem king (note the reference to Zion in both psalms) over his enemies (v. 2). There is a reference to the king's leading an army—undoubtedly to victory (v. 3a), and then a very strange sentence:

> From the womb of the morning
> like dew your youth will come to you.
> (v. 3b)

The Septuagint, the Greek translation of the Old Testament, has a reading which makes more sense out of the difficult Hebrew:

> From the womb of the Morning Star
> I begat you.

This translation, just as likely as the RSV, repeats the assertion of Psalm 2 that the king is God's son. In this case, however, the sonship is acquired not by adoption but by the highly mythological process of being begotten of God through the Morning Star. That the king of Babylon is so conceived is clear at Isaiah 14:12 where he is called "Day Star, son of Dawn" or Morning Star.

Psalm 110 also announces to the Davidic king:

> "You are a priest for ever
> after the order of Melchizedek."
> (v. 4)

Apart from this verse there is no clear indication that Israel's ruler was a priest as well as king. The only other time Melchizedek appears in the Old Testament he does play a dual role. At Genesis 14:17–24 Abraham meets Melchizedek who is king of Salem, that is, Jerusalem (see Psalm 76:2), and also priest of God Most High (the Canaanite god El Elyon). Apparently when David conquered and took Jerusalem from the Jebusites, their Canaanite ways and ideas stayed on to help shape the nature of his court and its accompanying images.

The coronation psalm goes on to restate the king's victory over his enemies (v. 5), his rule and judgment among the nations (v. 6), and then his drinking from a brook (v. 7). The item is usually understood as a ceremonial act of purification in which the prospective king indulged before he entered the Temple to be crowned. It could, however, have been a sacramental drink after the crowning has taken place. In any case, some type of drink by the brook was part of the coronation ritual.

THE ROYAL PSALMS AND JESUS

This somewhat detailed discussion of Psalms 2 and 110 reveals that these two psalms, so often quoted in reference to Jesus in the New Testament, had their own meaning and their own specific use in the Old Testament. They were parts of the liturgy used for crowning the Davidic kings who came to the throne of Jerusalem by the principle of dynastic succession. In all probability the Israelites heard them sung in that setting for hundreds of years.

At the same time, in that same setting the psalms also express a future hope. They recall the fact that the Davidic king will come to rule over a universal kingdom by glorious victory won with the Lord (at his left hand). That God "will make the nations your heritage, and the ends of the earth your possession" was a hope of which the people of Israel were very much aware. In the days of David and Solomon, such a hope was at least a wild possibility. It must have appeared that things were headed precisely in that direction. But as time went on, that glorious hope became less and less a reality. When the kingdom split and the two halves fell under foreign rule, that longing for "the day" took more and more the form of a distant future hope. It was precisely this longing for fulfillment which became the source of expectation for a messianic king of the last days who would come from the house and lineage of David.

. . . The New Testament witnesses used . . . quotations from the royal psalms in order to demonstrate that Jesus Christ was the messianic king of the last days.

The formula of sonship found at Psalm 2:7 was used repeatedly in reference to Jesus in the New Testament (see Matthew 3:17 and parallels; Acts 13:33; Hebrews 1:5; 5:5; and 2 Peter 1:17). Likewise, Jesus refers to himself as Lord by quoting Psalm 110:1. (See Matthew 22:44 and parallels.) The same verse is quoted at Hebrews 1:13 to show Jesus' superiority and authority over the angels. Moreover, the notion of the right hand of God as the place where the king sits occurs repeatedly in the New Testament in connection with references to the enthronement place of the resurrected Christ. Finally, the saying about Melchizedek at Psalm 110:4 is applied to Jesus in the Epistle to the Hebrews (5:6, 10; 6:20; 7:11, 15, 21).

It becomes quite clear that the New Testament witnesses used these quotations from the royal psalms in order to demonstrate that Jesus Christ was the messianic king of the last days. It now becomes our task to investigate the prophecies concerning a messiah to see how they related to Jesus.

References and More Information

Biblical references: Genesis 15:7–21; 2 Samuel 7:14, 23:1–7; Psalms 2, 18, 20, 21, 45, 72, 89, 110, and 132—especially 2 and 110; and Isaiah 7:10–17

McCurley, Foster R., Jr. *Proclaiming the Promise.* Philadelphia: Fortress Press,

1974. See pages 76–83, on Genesis 22:1–19; pages 156–160, a sermon on the same passage.

Metzger, Bruce M. and Isobel M., editors. *The Oxford Concise Concordance.* See the following entry: Bethlehem

Reumann, John. *Jesus in the Church's Gospels.* Philadelphia: Fortress Press, 1968. See pages 251–295, on the claims of Jesus Christ.

Richardson, Alan. *A Theological Word Book of the Bible.* New York: The Macmillan Company, 1962. See the following entries: fulfill, preach, Son of man

20. The Kingdom and Messianic Prophecies

The hope that the Davidic king on Jerusalem's throne would lead to Israel's worldwide dominion took form not only in the royal psalms sung in Israel's court but also in the prophetic preaching heard in Jerusalem's streets. It was the Jerusalem prophets who were intimately involved with the promise of an enduring dynasty; it was they who announced the ideal king to come and the nature of his rule. Isaiah, Micah, Jeremiah, and Zechariah are the major prophets. In their collections of sermons we find the so-called messianic prophecies. Before we examine several of their important texts, two general comments are in order.

First, the authorship of the passages we shall discuss is highly debatable. In some cases it is very difficult to determine whether it was Isaiah, Micah, Jeremiah, Zechariah or one of their followers, or even a much later preacher who composed these passages. To spend a great deal of time and space on the question of authorship, promises small reward except when a particular passage is obviously linked to a historical situation. Therefore, the question of authorship will not occupy a major portion of our discussion.

Second, the word *messiah* is not used in any of the "messianic" prophecies. In other words, unlike the royal psalms (particularly Psalm 2:2) where the "anointed one" clearly refers to the reigning Jerusalem king, the prophecies about the ideal king to come do not use that term. The most explicit title is the word *king,* but most often the allusion is made simply to the Davidic family. This fact suggests that the word *messiah* was not in use as a technical term when these Old Testament prophecies were framed. We know from the Dead Sea Scrolls that at the time of Jesus there was lively expectation for a Davidic messiah who would deliver the pious. (There was also hope for an Aaronic or priestly messiah.) Hence at that time *messiah* was a technical term. But in the Old Testament the term was used for "one who is anointed" or commissioned to a certain task. For this reason there were not only anointed kings of Israel (1 Samuel 24:6, 10; 26:9), but also kings of other nations such as Hazael of Syria (1 Kings 19:15), anointed at Yahweh's order. Other functionaries in Israel who were anointed were prophets (see 1 Kings 19:16) and the high priest (Leviticus 4:3, 5, 16; 6:14–15; Psalm 84:10). Most striking is the precise designation of Cyrus, King of Persia, as Yahweh's "anointed," that is, his messiah, at Isaiah 45:1. Such general usage of the term shows that the word *messiah* in the Old Testament is a functional term. People are anointed for some purpose, to do some work for the Lord.

Apart from the title itself, however, the notion of an ideal ruler was known in Israel from at least the time of Isaiah in the eighth century B.C. on into the New Testament era and beyond. In what follows in this chapter we shall examine the major prophecies concerning such a king and his relationship to the kingdom of God.

THREE TEXTS FROM ISAIAH

Because of its usage at Matthew 1:23, the prophecy at Isaiah 7:10–17 concerning the Immanuel child is usually listed among the messianic texts. Our study of that passage in the previous chapter indicates that the passage is indeed messianic. That is, it is messianic in the sense that the Lord promises the continuation of the Davidic dynasty in Jerusalem and ends the threat of the Syro-Ephraimite alliance, deposing the king in favor of its own puppet. The child to be born is already well grown in his mother's body, and so the immediate threat against the Davidic house will be removed immediately. The text is not so much a prediction of a distant future event as it is a pledge of God's faithfulness in the face of the impending crisis of 735–734 B.C.

Isaiah 9:1–7 offers a more interesting portrayal of the hoped-for kingship of a Davidic ruler. The lands of Zebulun and Naphtali (see *Oxford Bible Atlas,* p. 61) had been conquered and subjugated by the Assyrian Tiglath-pileser III in 734 and 732 B.C. This disaster brought gloom and anguish, distress and darkness for the people in those areas of Israel. Over against that dismal scene Isaiah proclaims a contrasting promise:

> The people who walked in darkness
> have seen a great light;
> > those who dwelt in a land of deep darkness
> > on them has light shined.
> > > (v. 2)

Although the plight of the people resembles a description of the mythological netherworld or "land of the dead," it will be turned into a scene of joy and life when the Lord comes to set them free:

> Thou has multiplied the nation,
> thou has increased its joy;
> > they rejoice before thee
> > as with joy at the harvest,
> > as men rejoice when they divide the spoil.

1. The King shall come when morn - ing dawns And light tri - um-phant breaks;

1. O come, O come, Em - man - u - el, And ran-som cap-tive Is - ra - el,

1. Lo, how a Rose e'er bloom - ing From ten - der stem hath sprung!

3 He comes, the broken heart to bind, The bleeding soul to cure,

> For the yoke of his burden,
> and the staff for his shoulder,
> the rod of his oppressor,
> thou hast broken as on the day of Midian.
> For every boot of the tramping warrior in battle tumult
> and every garment rolled in blood
> will be burned as fuel for the fire.
>
> (v. 3–5)

In powerful battle imagery God is addressed as the one who causes rejoicing by removing the burden of Assyria's control over his people. Insofar as victory will result for Naphtali and Zebulun, the battle will resemble that described in Judges 6:33—7:25. There we read how Gideon summoned Asher, Zebulun, and Naphtali to join him against the Midianites and Amalekites who were invading the land. In the ensuing battle, "the Lord set every man's sword against his fellow and against all the army" (Judges 7:22). In typical holy war fashion he caused the enemy to destroy itself in panic and then flee. Thus the reference to the battle recorded in Isaiah 9:4–5 is similar to the one "on the day of Midian," implying that the Lord will bring about his victory over Assyria by means of a holy war. By a holy war God will accomplish victory in the future, and thus the passage becomes a "day-of-Yahweh" prophecy for the time when he will establish his kingdom. In other words, it is God himself who will fight the battle, gain the victory, and set up his rule. How does the Davidic ruler to come fit into this picture?

> For to us a child is born,
> to us a son is given,
> and the government will be upon his shoulder,
> and his name will be called
> "Wonderful Counsellor, Mighty God,
> Everlasting Father, Prince of Peace."
> Of the increase of his government and of peace
> there will be no end,
> upon the throne of David, and over his kingdom,
> to establish it, and to uphold it
> with justice and with righteousness
> from this time forth and for evermore.
> The zeal of the Lord of hosts will do this.
>
> (v. 6–7)

This hymn, sung by the people after the victory has been accomplished, celebrates the accession of a Davidic king to the throne. The words "a child is born . . . a son is given" refer not to the birth of a baby but to the adoption of a king by the Lord on the day of his coronation. This announcement has the same meaning as the formula, "You are my son, today I have begotten you" at Psalm 2:7. The joy expressed, therefore, springs from the fact that there will come to power in God's kingdom a

34

Davidic ruler who will receive the kingly titles "Wonderful Counsellor" (he needs no advisors to carry out his plans); "Mighty God" (as in Psalm 45:6–7 he is the legitimate representative of God on earth); "Everlasting Father" (his rule will be enduring and fatherly—a king in Mesopotamia was called "Father of the land"); and "Prince of Peace" (one who will rule with such righteousness that all creatures will experience life to the fullest, that is, *shalom*).

Finally, we read that this king will rule with justice and righteousness (see royal psalms 45:6–7; 72:1–2) and that his rule on the Davidic throne will be eternal (see 2 Samuel 7:16). Such a rule and the time of peace accompanying it are not the work of the king but of "the zeal of the Lord of hosts." The king's function is to rule justly and righteously in the kingdom of God which God sets up for him by holy war. That rule will extend to the northern territories of the former Davidic-Solomonic Empire and will be a time of glory in contrast to the gloom currently enveloping Zebulun and Naphtali.

> There shall come forth a shoot
> from the stump of Jesse,
> and a branch shall grow out of his roots.
> (Isaiah 10:1)

It is immediately clear that the hope following destruction lies in the accession to the throne of a Davidic ruler, for Jesse was the father of David to whom God made the enduring promise. God will bestow his spirit on this future ruler just as he first gave it to David (1 Samuel 16:13) and through which he spoke (2 Samuel 23:2). This gift of the spirit will make wise the future ruler. We can see this clearly in the words used to describe it: "wisdom," "understanding," "counsel," "might," "knowledge," and "fear of the Lord." (See Proberbs 1:7: "The fear of the Lord is the beginning of knowledge. . . .") This Davidic descendant, so richly endowed, will ably exercise his appointed function, to execute justice.

> He shall not judge by what his eyes see,
> or decide by what his ears hear;
>   but with righteousness he shall judge the poor,
> and decide with equity for the meek of the earth;
>   and he shall smite the earth [read "ruthless"] with
> the rod of his mouth,
>   and with the breath of his lips he shall slay the wicked.
> Righteousness shall be the girdle of his waist
>   and faithfulness the girdle of his loins.
> (Isaiah 11:3b–5)

Once again, as in Isaiah 9:6–7, the duty of this king who is to come is to rule with justice and righteousness. In this case, he will act as judge in the land not by means of advisors or even by his own perceptions but by righteousness, that is, by faithfulness to the duties imposed on him in his

35

relationship to the Lord on the one hand and to the people on the other. It is his relationships which determine his judgments! Hence as God's representative he will protect the poor and the needy and so do the work of God himself (see Psalm 9:9; 68:5; Proverbs 22:22–23; 23:10–11). Such care for those unable to care for themselves was a primary function of Davidic kings (see Psalm 72:12–14) and even of kings elsewhere in the ancient world. The wicked and "ruthless" (the suggested reading in verse 5 requires changing only one Hebrew letter and is based on the poetic parallelism at Job 15:20; 27:13) will experience the king's judgment as anything but benign, for he will slay those who oppose the will of Yahweh.

Such a reign of righteousness and faithfulness would stand in sharp contrast to the situation in which someone like Ahaz or Manasseh was king in Jerusalem. Indeed, the effect of such a king's rule would embrace all of God's creation in a golden age.

> The wolf shall dwell with the lamb,
> and the leopard shall lie down with the kid,
>   and the calf and the lion *and the fatling* [read "shall feed"]
>   together,
> and a little child shall lead them.
>   The cow and the bear shall feed;
> their young shall lie down together;
> and the lion shall eat straw like the ox.
>   The sucking child shall play over the hole of the asp,
> and the weaned child shall put his hand on the adder's den.
>   They shall not hurt or destroy in all my holy mountain;
> for the earth shall be full of the knowledge of the Lord
> as the waters cover the sea.
>
> (Isaiah 11:6–9)

All creatures will be affected by the king's righteous rule in God's kingdom. Animals now hostile to one another shall dwell and feed together. (The suggested change above is based on the Dead Sea Scroll of Isaiah and is required by the poetry.) Children will play around the haunts of serpents without harm. The reason for all this harmony in creation is that the whole earth under the king's rule is "full of the knowledge of the Lord"—not intellectual knowledge, nor mental discipline, but a personal, even intimate, relationship like that which exists between a husband and wife. "Adam knew Eve his wife, and she conceived and bore Cain" (Genesis 4:1). It is that close relationship of personal knowledge that characterizes both king and kingdom to come. Such a king in such a future kingdom will judge with righteousness and thereby effect *shalom*.

MICAH

Isaiah's contemporary in Jerusalem was the prophet Micah. The two differed in their preaching in one significant respect. For Isaiah, Jerusalem and its institutions were invulnerable to the onslaught of outside invaders. For Micah, however, Jerusalem and everything in it would be leveled to the ground. Nevertheless, Micah, also, looked beyond the destruction of the Lord's judgment to a New Davidic king.

> But you, O Bethlehem Ephrathah,
> who are little to be among the clans of Judah,
>   from you shall come forth for me
> one who is to be ruler in Israel,
>   whose origin is from of old,
> from ancient days.
>   Therefore he shall give them up until the time
> when she who is in travail has brought forth;
>   then the rest of his brethren shall return
> to the people of Israel.
>   And he shall stand and feed his flock
>   in the strength of the Lord,
> in the majesty of the name of the Lord his God.
>   And they shall dwell secure, for now he shall be great
> to the ends of the earth.
>
> (Micah 5:2-4)

Out of the birthplace of David, that is, out of the Davidic line, will come a ruler who will represent the Lord. His origin goes back to the days when God promised to David an enduring dynasty (2 Samuel 7). Until this new Davidic ruler comes to the throne, however, God will judge the people in the form of exile to a foreign land. Like a woman in the pain of childbirth, Jerusalem will be carried away to Babylon (see 4:9-10). But even in the midst of such pain the king to come will arise, and the people will return home. This king is portrayed as a kindly shepherd, as were other kings in the ancient Near East as early as 2000 B.C. This king fits the description in Ezekiel's view of the restoration of the Davidic dynasty after return from exile (see Ezekiel 34:23-24). The king's function here is not to redeem Israel from exile; the Lord will accomplish that (see 4:10). Rather, it is to "feed" the people when they return by ruling with the strength and power of the Lord himself and by giving glory to that God who established his kingdom. By so doing, the people "shall dwell secure," that is, experience *shalom,* in a universal kingdom over which the king rules in compassion and renown.

JEREMIAH

Jeremiah, too, looked beyond the present to the new Davidic ruler to come. In a passage which is repeated in almost identical fashion at 34:14-16, the prophet of the early exilic period announces the king of the Day of Yahweh.

> Behold, the days are coming, says the Lord when I will raise up for David a righteous Branch, and he shall reign as king and deal wisely, and shall execute justice and righteousness in the land. In his days Judah will be saved, and Israel will dwell securely. And this is the name by which he will be called: "The Lord is our righteousness."
>
> (Jeremiah 23:5-6)

The portrayal of the king here does not differ from that in the other passages we have examined. Davidic descent, wisdom, justice, and righteousness are marks of his reign. *Shalom* comes to the people of the once-again united monarchy of Judah and Israel. This king's name will be *Yahweh Tsidqenu,* "the Lord (is) our righteousness." This may be a throne name with specific historical meaning.

. . . Jeremiah's message about the king to come was intended to announce that the hope for the future lay not in "my righteousness is Yahweh" but in a "branch" established by the Lord himself, who will be called "our righteousness is Yahweh." He will be raised up on the day of the Lord and will reign in God's kingdom.

In 598-597 B.C. when Nebuchadnezzar quelled the rebellion in Jerusalem and carried off the first exiles to Babylon, he took with him King Jehoiachin. For some reason the Babylonian ruler replaced Jehoiachin with his uncle, also of the Davidic family, Mattaniah (see 2 Kings 24:17). Uncle Mattaniah was given a new name when he took the throne: Zedekiah ("my righteousness is Yahweh"). On this occasion Zedekiah's followers attached all kinds of illusory hopes to the event. Thus it may be that Jeremiah's message about the king to come was intended to announce that the hopes for the future lay not in "*my* righteousness is Yahweh" but in a "branch" established by the Lord himself who will be called "*our* righteousness is Yahweh." He will be raised up on the day of the Lord and will reign in God's kingdom.

ZECHARIAH

Several hundred years later, probably in the fourth or third centuries B.C., this song of an anonymous prophet was recorded in the Book of Zechariah.

> Rejoice greatly, O daughter of Zion!
> Shout aloud, O daughter of Jerusalem!
>   Lo, your king comes to you;
>   triumphant and victorious is he,

> humble and riding on an ass,
> on a colt the foal of an ass.
> I will cut off the chariot from Ephraim
> and the war horse from Jerusalem;
> and the battle bow shall be cut off,
> and he shall command peace to the nations;
> his dominion shall be from sea to sea,
> and from the River to the ends of the earth.
> (Zechariah 9:9-10)

At first the song seems simply to announce the arrival of the Lord him-self into the midst of Jerusalem. A similar song at 2:10, in fact, proclaims, "For lo, I come and I will dwell in the midst of you, says the Lord."

Similarly, a hymn begins at Zephaniah 3:14 which announces the presence of "the King of Israel . . . the Lord" in her midst, and it goes on to tell of the Lord's victory and rescue of the people. Zechariah 9 affirms this image of Yahweh who once for all ends all war by wiping out of existence chariot, war horse, and sword. But the passage surprisingly refers to a Davidic king's coming, as seen clearly in verses 9 and 10. The reference to the king's universal domain is a direct quotation from Psalm 72:8, a royal psalm which begs that the Davidic ruler on Jerusalem's throne have precisely that vast range of governance. Moreover, the use of the ass in his triumphal and victorious entrance into the city recalls the coronation of Solomon, David's first successor. As part of the coronation itself, it seems, "Zadok the priest, Nathan the prophet, and Benaiah . . . went down and caused Solomon to ride on King David's mule, and brought him to Gihon. There Zadok the priest took the horn of oil from the tent, and anointed Solomon. Then they blew the trumpet; and all the people said, 'Long live King Solomon!'" (1 Kings 1:38-39).

These are not the only songs of this kind that we find among the writings of the prophets, however.

In this way the passage looks forward to the imminent arrival of the long-expected Davidic king who will rule universally after God himself has established a condition of peace.

This text is important for us, of course, because in the New Testament the writer Matthew uses it (21:1-9) to describe the entry of Jesus into Jerusalem on Palm Sunday. Matthew gets two animals into the picture instead of the one in Zechariah. He also omits the reference "triumphant and victorious is he" in order to emphasize the humble entry of Jesus. But the point the author wants to make comes to focus in the question of verse 10, "Who is this?" Matthew's purpose is to explain who Jesus was, and one of the key elements in that regard is to show that Jesus was Messiah. Matthew accomplished this by quoting Old Testament texts about the future messiah. Here, as elsewhere in his Gospel, Matthew looks back to the Old Testament witnesses in order to proclaim to his community the identity and the work of Jesus.

PROPHETIC CONSENSUS

All of these so-called messianic prophecies are in essential agreement. Yahweh himself was to deliver the people and establish his kingdom. When he had set it up "on his day," the Lord would then raise up the new Davidic king to rule over his universal domain with justice and righteousness and wisdom. It is somewhat striking that this hope for an ideal Davidic messiah, though appearing now and again over the centuries, was of rather limited concern in the Old Testament. Beyond the five texts examined here, one must strain to find many others that clearly look forward to the future king.

In his Son, Jesus Christ, God fulfilled this hope of Israel—not in the way expected, to be sure. But in his own way God's surprise shows that he is not bound even to the testimony of his inspired witness.

It is also startling to realize that if one were to extract an image from these Old Testament messianic prophecies, one would never envision a man born in an animal's stable, working in a carpenter's shop with sawdust on his clothes and calluses on his hands, crucified like a common thief on two pieces of wood, and buried in someone else's tomb. These passages do not predict the life and times of Jesus of Nazareth. Rather, they testify to Israel's hope that one will come to rule in God's kingdom with justice and righteousness. In his Son, Jesus Christ, God fulfilled this hope of Israel—not in the way expected, to be sure. But in his own way God's surprise shows that he is not bound even to the testimony of his inspired witnesses.

References and More Information

Biblical references: Isaiah 9:1-7, 11:1-9; Micah 5:2-4; Jeremiah 23:5-6; Zechariah 9:9-10

McCurley, Foster R., Jr. *Proclaiming the Promise.* Philadelphia: Fortress Press, 1974. See pages 76-83 on Genesis 22:1-19; pages 156-160, a sermon on the same passage.

Metzger, Bruce M. and Isobel M., editors. *The Oxford Concise Concordance.* See the following entry: Bethlehem

Richardson, Alan. *A Theological Word Book of the Bible.* New York: The Macmillan Company, 1962. See the following entry: virgin (birth)

21. Jesus the Kingdom Preacher as Messiah

The combination Jesus Christ comes so naturally that we are apt to miss the depth of meaning it contains. The origins, richness, and complexity of this phrase require careful scrutiny.

JESUS CHRIST, NAME AND TITLE

Jesus, of course, is a Hebrew name. It goes back to a Hebrew form *Yehoshuah,* meaning "Yahweh is salvation" or "Yahweh saves" or "will save." The name is reflected in Matthew 1:21: ". . . For he [that is, either Jesus or God] will save his people from their sins." Probably many Jews (beginning with Joshua, of Old Testament fame) had borne this given name, but only one such Jew stands out today. He is Jesus of Nazareth who appeared in Galilee in the days of the emperor Tiberius and proclaimed the good news of the coming rule or kingship or kingdom of God (*UB I,* Chapters 1—2).

Christ is derived from an adjective, *anointed,* which in the Hebrew is *messiah.* This term was used in the variety of ways in Israel, especially from the time of King David and his successors. It referred to the Davidic king who was seen as "the Lord's anointed" (see *UB II,* Chapters 19—20).

By the time Jesus of Nazareth lived, the term *messiah* had taken on a bewildering array of meanings in the light of expectations about God's future reign. This was especially so in the apocalyptic expressions of the good news which developed in Israel's periods of despair and hopelessness. The phrase "the day of the Lord (Yahweh)" had become an important part of that apocalyptic language, as noted in Chapters 17—18.

But how does Jesus of Nazareth fit into and fulfill all of these Old Testament longings? How did he react to the age-old notions of an anointed ruler with a universal kingdom? In what ways does he bring to fruition what pious Jews were waiting for, and in what ways does he contradict their hopes by representing a new turn in God's revelation of God's own kingly rule?

We have already seen (see *UB I,* Chapters 1—2) that Jesus preached, taught, and introduced the kingdom of God by his own mighty works. Jesus' message was about God and not about himself. But Jesus' followers began to hail him as Lord. It was a very suggestive title which had a striking ambiguity. During Jesus' own public ministry the term might suggest nothing more than "sir" or "master." But after Easter the title conferred upon Jesus a name "above every name" (Philippians 2:9). Thus Jesus received lordship under the kingship of God (*UB I,* Chapter 12).

This lordship had reference to past, present, and future. Christians proclaimed Jesus' lordship in regard to the coming time when he would be Lord of all. They also proclaimed it to say, "Jesus is Lord" now, and God's agent at creation in the past, as well as the one who is "upholding the universe" today (Hebrews 1:2–3; *UB I,* Chapter 16).

Something of the same course of development holds true with the term *Christ (messiah, anointed one).* The early church clearly employed it as a title for Jesus. That "Jesus is the Christ" became a test for true belief and even for being recognized as a child of God (1 John 2:22; 5:1). Most likely this confession about Jesus made most sense in an Aramaic-speaking church or in a Christian community steeped in knowledge of the Old Testament and Jewish messianic expectations. The title was characteristic enough that followers of Jesus were nicknamed "Christ-ians," initially at Antioch (Acts 11:26).

But it is hard to guess what "Christ" and "Christian" meant to pagans who did not know much about either the Old Testament or the ancient Near Eastern practice of "anointing." Indeed, the Greek term *christos* could literally mean "smeared" or "rubbed." It would appear that a Hebrew adjective (*messiah*) came to have a remarkable history. It became first a technical term for Jewish expectations. Then it became a title for Jesus of Nazareth. As a title it came to be used so often that it merged with his name to become part of it. At least to many people since the second half of the first century "Christ" has become Jesus' last name and no longer a title.

Compare, for example, the phrase "Jesus Christ is Lord" (Philippians 2:11) from about A.D. 55–60 or even earlier. Here "Christ" has become part of the name itself. The honorific title for Jesus Christ, which is not part of the name, is "Lord."

A STRATEGY FOR OUR STUDY

But amid all these unfoldings how did Jesus look on the term? Three factors make it difficult to answer that question.

First, we must be careful to distinguish the viewpoint of Jesus during his lifetime from later acclamations of him by his disciples after Easter. How he is spoken of at Philippians 2:11 or 1 John 5:1 should not be identified with titles Jesus seemed to accept in his lifetime.

Second, one must also reckon with the variety of views about "messiah" abounding in Jesus' day. A Jew could say, "We have found the Messiah (which means Christ)," as Andrew did (John 1:41) and mean Jesus of Nazareth. But so could Rabbi Akiba in the early second century with regard to the leader of a Jewish revolt against the Romans, Simon bar Koseba, and mean a nationalist and revolutionist. A Samaritan woman could declare, "I know that Messiah is coming (he who is called Christ)" (John 4:25), but have in mind not an anointed king from the house of David or a military leader but "Taheb, the one who returns." Presumably Taheb was a "prophet like Moses" (based on the statement in Deuteronomy 18:15). We must always ask what was meant when someone used the term "messiah" in Jesus' day.

Third, we must look at what the Gospel texts actually say and not just how tradition has harmonized them. People often think there was a single clear view of messiah in the Old Testament and that Jesus took it over lock, stock, and barrel. *UB II*, Chapters 19—20 reveal how complex the Old Testament story is at this point viewed against the future hopes of Israel. In our study we must look at the Gospel passages which view Jesus as messiah, the bearer of the gospel of "God's victory" and "the day of the Lord," and scrutinize them in just as much detail.

One additional comment is needed. It pertains to the word *fulfill*, which has been used several times with regard to Jesus and the Old Testament. Matthew especially emphasizes how Jesus fulfills the Scriptures with his use of Old Testament quotations introduced by the formula, "This happened in order that it might fulfill what was spoken by the prophet, saying, . . ." The term *fulfill* can mean not merely "accomplish," "bring to pass," or "comply with that which was promised or predicted before." It may also have the sense of "fill full of new meaning" or "make complete by bringing to an end." Thus, it may even "annul" or "destroy"! All sorts of twists and turns can take place as part of God's surprises in the course of "fulfillment."

FULFILLMENT IN MATTHEW

We have ~~the first~~ *first the* series of formula ~~questions~~ *quotations* in Matthew, where Jesus "fulfills" what a prophet spoke (Matthew 1:23; 2:6, 15, 18, 23; 4:15 ff.; 8:17; 12:18–21; 13:35; 21:5; and 27:9 ff.)

We have already seen that the use of Isaiah 53:4 at Matthew 8:17 is, to say the least, an application we would not expect (see *UB I*, p. 26). The day-of-Yahweh passage at Isaiah 9:1–2, with its related verses about a Davidic king, 9:6–7 (see *UB II*, Chapter 20) is associated by Matthew with Jesus' relocation in Capernaum in a way that gives the passage a Christological sense it never had before. The text at Isaiah 7:14 about a young woman conceiving during the Syro-Ephraimite crises of 735–734 B.C. is

Matthew 4 14-17

given new meaning through the Greek rendering of the Hebrew word for "young woman" by the more specific term *virgin*. This Greek rendering in the first translation of the Hebrew scriptures into another language is picked up at Matthew 1:23 and applied specifically to the virgin Mary's conception of Jesus through the Holy Spirit. And when Matthew 2:15 says the return of Jesus from Egypt "fulfills" Hosea 11:1, we have a case where what the prophet spoke originally was not prediction of a future event, but rather a simple description of the Exodus. That is, it referred to Yahweh's action in calling his son Israel out of slavery in Egypt. Fulfillment here makes sense only if we see Jesus as a figure parallel to the people of God or Israel in the Old Testament. Surely this is to fill the Hebrew scriptures with new meaning.

We have, second, an important insight gained by looking at Jesus' teachings in Matthew. This shows even more clearly what the New Testament means by "fulfillment." Jesus warns those who might think his purpose is to set aside all prior expressions of God's will, "Think not that I have come to abolish the law and the prophets; I have not come to abolish them but to fulfil them" (Matthew 5:17). But how does Jesus in his teachings "fulfill" them? In some cases it is by heightening and radicalizing what the Old Testament had said.

> "You have heard that it was said to the men of old, 'You shall not kill [Exodus 20:13]; and whoever kills shall be liable to judgment.' But I say to you that every one who is angry with his brother shall be liable to judgment. . . ."
>
> (Matthew 5:21–22)
>
> "You have heard that it was said, 'You shall not commit adultery [Exodus 20:14]. But I say to you that every one who looks at a woman lustfully has already committed adultery with her in his heart."
>
> (Matthew 5:27)
>
> "Again you have heard that it was said to the men of old, 'You shall not swear falsely, but shall perform to the Lord what you have sworn' [Leviticus 19:12]. But I say to you, Do not swear at all. . . ."
>
> (Matthew 5:33–34)

These are three of the six antitheses of the Sermon on the Mount. That passage contains six very sharp contrasts between the old and the new, of which the above are the first, second, and fourth. Here Jesus sets his own word over against that of the Old Testament. In the cases cited he takes the old scriptural principle and fills it with a further meaning, extending its applications to thoughts as well as to overt acts. Or, in the case of 5:33–34, he carries the concern of the Old Testament for truthfulness to an undreamed of degree. Jesus looks for personal relationships where no oaths are needed to affirm one's honesty.

When, however, we look at the other antitheses in this same chapter, the pattern changes. How is the law being "fulfilled" here?

The traditional site of the Beatitudes and Sermon on the Mount is this low mountain on the west side of the Sea of Galilee, looking out over the sea and the surrounding hills.

"It was also said, 'Whoever divorces his wife, let him give her a certificate of divorce' [Deuteronomy 24:1–4]. But I say to you that everyone who divorces his wife . . . makes her an adulteress. . . ."

(Matthew 5:31–32)

"You have heard that it was said, 'An eye for an eye and a tooth for a tooth' [Exodus 21:23–24]. But I say to you, Do not resist one who is evil. . . ."

(Matthew 5:38–39)

"You have heard that it was said, 'You shall love your neighbor [Leviticus 19:18] and hate your enemy' [an admonition not found in the Old Testament or given by the Jewish rabbis but reflected in the Dead Sea Scrolls]. But I say to you, Love your enemies. . . ."

(Matthew 5:43–44)

In each of the above cases, the old command is not radicalized or heightened, as was the case with the first three cited, but abolished! No divorce, no vengeful "eye-for-eye" reaction, no hatred of enemies. Here the law is "fulfilled" by being set aside. The effect is to put an end to these particular laws. Jesus, of course, did the same thing with Old Testament food regulations (Mark 7:15) and in effect with all the cultic regulations about the Temple and its priestly life. The result is well summed up in Romans 10:4, "Christ is the end of the law." Here, *end* must be taken to mean not "goal of the law" but its "termination." Christ is the one who puts an end to the law as a way of salvation and life (NEB has "Christ ends the law"). *Fulfillment* in this sense means putting an end to something.

JESUS AND THE OLD TESTAMENT HOPE

Having seen that fulfillment comes in many ways, we may now ask how Jesus of Nazareth fulfilled the Old Testament hope of God's future reign. How did Jesus fulfill those messianic dreams, those expectations about a Davidic ruler to come, those feelings for a coming "day of Yahweh" when God would fulfill his promises and come and reign as king, intervening in some dramatic way and defeating the forces of evil?

It may be said that Jesus proclaimed and inaugurated the eschatological kingdom of God; he announced its dawning and drew out its implications for daily life. "The kingdom is at hand; repent! Believe!"

If one asks, "How near is the kingdom?" the answer is, "Near as never before." The first rays of the new day's dawn are to be seen in Jesus' activities, fulfilling the promises of the prophets:

The blind receive their sight and the lame walk, lepers are cleansed and the deaf hear, and the dead are raised up, and the poor have good news preached to them.

(Matthew 11:5; see also Isaiah 35:5–6 and 61:1–2)

His wondrous deeds were part of God's "holy war" now waged against Beelzebul and his demons (Matthew 12:27 and Luke 11:19). God's kingship is drawing nigh through and in Jesus. What prophets and kings in ages past longed to see and hear but did not is now taking place. Blessed are those who do see and hear! (See Matthew 13:16–17; parallel at Luke 10:23–24.)

Yet, for all this evidence about the kingdom here and now, Jesus also speaks of a future aspect of the kingdom! On the one hand, the kingdom is here, growing, at work like leaven (Matthew 13:33; Luke 13:20–21). Or it is growing like a mustard seed into a shrub and tree in which "the birds of the air will nest" (Mark 4:30–32; Matthew 13:31–32; see also Daniel 4:20–21). On the other hand, the kingdom is future. To pray, "Thy kingdom come," means it is not yet here for me. Jesus' solemn pledge in the Upper Room, "I shall not drink again of the fruit of the vine until that day when I drink it new in the kingdom of God" (Mark 14:25), implies that even on the eve of his death he does not regard it as present yet. Jesus even warns against people who make the claim, "Lo, the kingdom is here," or, "Lo, there." Rather, he says, "on that day" when the Son of man comes, there will be lightning flashes lighting up the sky and the normal routines of life will end (see Luke 17:22–37, especially verses 23–24, 26, 30–31).

If you have been alert for Old Testament phrases, you noted in the last two passages echoes of the day-of-Yahweh theme "that day" (Mark 14:25) and "on that day" (Luke 17:31; see also Luke 17:24, 30, and 34). An apocalyptic outlook sounds clearly in the sayings of Jesus and includes the note of impending judgment found in Old Testament day-of-Yahweh passages. True, Jesus does not refer to the "day of Yahweh" as Paul does, for example in 1 Thessalonians 5:2, "The day of the Lord will come like a thief in the night." But Jesus does speak of "the day of judgment" (Matthew 10:15; 11:22; 12:36), and he uses the same figure of speech which Paul employed:

> Watch, therefore, for you do not know on what day your Lord is coming. But know this, that if the householder had known in what part of the night the thief was coming, he would have watched. . . .
> (Matthew 24:42–43)

Perhaps Paul used the phrase with the words of Jesus in mind.

Jesus' words, "the days are coming," is a formula to introduce an apocalyptic warning, just as in the Old Testament (Luke 17:22, 21:6; 23:29). So is the phrase "in those days," referring to the dark, foreboding "last times" ahead (Mark 13:17, 19, 24). Just as in the Hebrew prophets and apocalyptists, there are also examples of Jesus' use of "on that day," referring to a time of judgment by God.

> "On that day many will say to me, 'Lord, Lord, did we not prophesy in your name, and cast out demons in your name, and do many mighty works in

47

your name?' And then will I declare to them, 'I never knew you; depart from me, you evildoers.' "

(Matthew 7:22–23)

See also Luke 17:31; Mark 13:32; Matthew 24:50.

Some of these New Testament references to the day of the Lord have, in effect, reinterpreted the Old Testament. They state that it is the Lord Jesus who now will serve as judge (as in Matthew 7 above). As a transition to this usage, see also references to the coming of the "Son of man" (such as Matthew 24:37 and 39; note also 24:42). A phrase uniquely Lukan refers to "the days [plural] of the Son of man" (Luke 17:22 and 26; see also v. 24).

"Son of man" was an Old Testament term denoting a man or mankind (see Psalm 8:4, and Ezekiel 2:1, 3, 6, 8, and many more in that book). The phrase came to be used in apocalyptic as a corporate representation of the people of Israel and also to refer to a supernatural figure who comes from heaven to earth. For the former usage, see Daniel 7:13 in the context of 7:9–22. For the latter, we must go outside the Old Testament canon to writings like 2 Esdras (Apocrypha) and Enoch (in Pseudepigrapha).

Whatever the background, "Son of man" was a term frequently found in the sayings of Jesus. Jesus is himself identified in those cited above as one coming in the future to deliver and to judge. Luke's verses seem to think of a series of such "days of the Son of man."

The most succinct section in Jesus' teachings dealing with the future aspect of God's reign is his major apocalyptic discourse. This is preserved for us in Mark 13, with parallels in Matthew 24—25 and Luke 21: 5–36 and 17:22–37. These three or four versions are called the "little apocalypse" to distinguish their content from that of the Book of Revelation, which is the "big" apocalypse. The several versions of the little apocalypse differ so much from each other that it would seem each evangelist has edited the genuine sayings from Jesus in a particular way. But all the passages have in common a future reference to impending troubles for Jerusalem, persecution for Jesus' followers, the need for watchfulness, and the "second coming" of the Son of man at the close of the age.

(Actually, no Gospel passage uses the phrase "second coming," but like the Greek word *parousia,* meaning "arrival" or "coming," the term is a convenient one to designate this promise of a divine event bringing normal history to an end with judgment, rewards and punishments, and fulfillment of promises. The only New Testament passage to come close to the phrase occurs in Hebrews 9:28, "appear a second time.")

It is, of course, possible that Jesus did not speak every last statement about the future attributed to him. Bible students wrestle with a saying like Mark 9:1 and its parallel in Matthew 16:28 and Luke 9:27 to try to ascertain which form of it, if any, goes back to Jesus' own ministry. But putting such niceties of interpretation aside, enough solid evidence remains to make it quite clear that Jesus taught that the kingdom is both present now and will be fulfilled in the future. But just what does that mean?

The answer is not to claim that Jesus' views about the kingdom developed over the years, that at first he believed the kingdom was immediately present but later changed his mind and saw it as belonging to the future, or vice versa. The Gospel verses fit no such unfolding pattern. Nor will it do to hold that Jesus vacillated, believing one thing one day and the opposite the next. The Gospels do not yield a "psychological profile" of Jesus. Nor can either element reflected in the data be thrown out as not stemming from Jesus.

We must recognize that Jesus, who pronounced the kingdom as imminent, breaking in and present, also assigned to it a future aspect. People do not have it at their beck and call or under their control. We are dealing with God's kingship, and although God may be wondrously present among us now, he is also always above, beyond, and ahead of us, his kingly reign not yet at the full. All this is true to the Old Testament experience where God's past victory and present activity begot further promises and hopes about the future.

Jesus' appearance, actions, and message pointed beyond themselves. They could not be confined to any one moment of time or unit of space. Great as was the gospel they brought for Jesus' own day, they stretch beyond that day to our own.

God's surprises

To put it simply, Jesus' appearance, actions, and message pointed beyond themselves. They could not be confined to any one moment of time or unit of space. Great as was the gospel they brought for Jesus' own time, they stretch beyond that day. God's revelation in Jesus generated further promises to be fulfilled after Jesus' earthly ministry. God had surprises for his world even after Jesus' day!

Another way of grasping this surprise element in the future orientation of the kingdom is to look at the story of the Gentiles. The Gentiles, or pagans, are the non-Jews. Jewish scripture had a number of interesting things to say about them. Old Testament prophetic teaching about the day of Yahweh anticipated a universal pilgrimage to Mt. Zion (Jerusalem). There all the nations would learn Yahweh's will and ways (see Chapter 17). In his own ministry, Jesus dealt by and large with Jews only (Matthew 15:24). Experiences with Samaritans (John 4:7 ff.), Canaanites (Matthew 15:22-28), and Roman army officers (Matthew 8:5-13; Luke 7:1-10) were rare. Jesus seems to have spread his good news before an audience of Jews in Galilee and Jerusalem. He trusted that any further spreading of the message would come in God's own time and way.

49

It may well be that, like the Old Testament prophets, Jesus looked for a day of Yahweh when God would manifest himself, call the Gentiles, and lead them to the "holy mount" where there would be a great banquet. (See Isaiah 25:6–9 and 56:6–8.) But God did not work it out that way. The hope that "many will come from east and west and sit at table with Abraham, Isaac, and Jacob in the kingdom of heaven" (Matthew 8:11) did not materialize in the first century with any divinely led pilgrimage to Mt. Zion as the world came to an end. Rather, the hope took the form of missionary endeavor moving out from Jerusalem (as in the Book of Acts) to the ends of the earth (Matthew 28:19–20). Jesus fulfilled the Old Testament hope by bringing near the good news of God's reign in a way that had never happened before. But this gospel created in turn its own future of further promises.

Jesus and the messianic hopes in his day

But now, what has all this to do with Messiah?

Chapters 19—20 have already traced the usage of *messiah* in the Old Testament. In the centuries between the closing of the Old Testament period and Jesus' own time, speculations about Messiah multiplied. Some still looked for a descendant of the old royal house of David. Some put their hope in an "anointed priest." The Qumran community looked for a combination of the two. Still others awaited a heavenly deliverer, one who existed in heaven from all eternity—like the Son of man. Of course there were those who looked for a militant revolutionist. And still others, in the circles of the pious, looked not for God's agent but for God himself to come.

Such was the gallery of messianic figures in Jesus' day. The pages of the first-century Jewish historian Josephus are dotted with men who claimed to be "anointed" or "chosen" by God to bring in the kingdom.

Jesus responded to this welter of messianic claims warily and with reticence. The Gospel accounts show Jesus acting cautiously on those occasions when the term *messiah* was introduced. Even if he was himself fully convinced that he was the Lord's anointed, apparently the situation suggested that he go easy until the term could be redefined in the way he wished.

Two passages in particular show how Jesus dealt with the messianic hope as applied to him. One concerns his trial, the other Peter's confession.

At the trial, the Jewish high priest asked bluntly, "Are you the Christ [Messiah], the Son of the Blessed?" (Mark 14:61). Matthew 26:63 and Luke 22:67 offer variant forms of the same question. Jesus replies in Mark "I am; and you will see the Son of man sitting at the right hand of Power, and coming with the clouds of heaven" (14:62).

50

But the reply in Matthew and in Luke is not quite as clear. In Matthew 26:64 we read, "You have said so. But I tell you, hereafter you will see the Son of man seated at the right hand of Power, and coming on the clouds of heaven." In Luke 22:67-68, Jesus answers, "If I tell you, you will not believe; and if I ask you, you will not answer. But from now on the Son of man shall be seated at the right hand of the power of God." Matthew's version can be interpreted to mean, "That's correct." Or it can be taken to imply, "You said that, I didn't!"

At any rate, all three Gospels agree that Jesus then went on to speak about not the Christ but the Son of man! He spoke of the Son of man to be seated at God's right hand, to come with or on the clouds of heaven. At the very least one must say that Jesus did not emphasize the title "Christ" when asked about it at his trial.

The other occasion of importance for grasping Jesus' reaction to the title "Messiah" is Peter's confession at Caesarea Philippi. It is the climax of Jesus' ministry in Galilee. In light of all the widespread rumors that Jesus is some sort of a prophet (Matthew 16:14), Simon Peter answers Jesus' question "Who do you say I am?" with the words, "You are the Christ, the Son of the living God" (Matthew 16:16). Jesus then goes on to praise Peter for this truth which has come to him not by human insight but by divine revelation: "You are Peter [*Petros*], and on this rock [*petra* in Greek; referring either to Peter's confession or Peter himself] I will build my church" (Matthew 16:17). (Traditionally Protestants take *petra* to refer to the confession, Catholics take it to refer to Peter himself.) In any event, in Matthew's account Peter is a great hero of faith because he sees who Jesus really is.

Attractive as that interpretation has often been, one must reckon with the fact that Matthew's account goes on to describe how Peter immediately misunderstands Jesus' goal in life, to go to Jerusalem and die. Hence, Jesus must reprimand Peter by saying, "You are a hindrance [literally, 'stumbling block'] to me" (Matthew 16:23). So Peter ends up on the side of men, not of God!

All this suggests a portrait of Peter as a typical disciple, one minute capable of great insight, the next of satanic misunderstanding. Like ourselves! Jesus' church can be built upon such a person when that person confesses Christ, but that same building stone becomes a stumbling block when he or she misrepresents the Lord. There is even a suggestion that the title "Christ" must be understood in light of going to Jerusalem and the cross.

But it is the parallel account in Mark which really raises question about the traditional understanding of Peter's confession in Matthew. In Mark, after Peter's statement, "You are the Christ" (8:29), there is no commendation of Peter. On the contrary, Jesus enjoins silence on the disciples, and he begins instead to talk about "the Son of man" being rejected, killed, "and after three days rise again" (8:31). (Recall that this pattern

51

appeared again at Jesus' trial: there is use of the term *Christ*, and Jesus goes on to talk about the "Son of man.")

In Mark, Jesus rebukes Peter as a Satan, opposed to "the side [or program] of God." For Peter had apparently had in mind by the term *Christ* a glorious, national, perhaps militaristic hero, a new Davidic claimant to the throne. Mark 8:27–33, as it stands without Matthew's additions, has been called "Peter's satanic misunderstanding of Jesus," not a heroic confession of Jesus, simply because Peter misused the term "Christ." (Here we remind ourselves that Mark's version is generally regarded as the first to be written down and that Matthew's version is based upon it. But Luke's terse report (9:18–22) is closer to Mark's than to Matthew's.)

What does all this add up to? Our accounts of Jesus' trial and of the Caesarea Philippi experience clearly suggest that Jesus did not uncritically accept the title "Messiah"! He was reserved about it because of the danger of its being misunderstood. It is even likely that he was positively opposed to using it!

To say that may be disturbing, even offensive to many. For our own piety has been shaped almost entirely by the post-Easter developments when the church quickly attached the title "Christ" to the name Jesus. But here we are trying to probe a little into the pre-Easter situation. And we find a Jesus who must combat the kind of mentality described in John 6:14–15 where the crowd, after the feeding of the five thousand, wanted "to come and take him by force to make him king." That is, they wanted to make him an anointed ruler and pit him against the Romans. That mentality was so deeply ingrained in the disciples that even after Easter they could ask Jesus, "Lord, will you at this time restore the kingdom to Israel?" (Acts 1:6).

The kingdom implied an anointed ruler. Jesus proclaimed God's kingship. But because Jesus made no pretense of becoming an earthly ruler himself, he had to be very chary about accepting the title "Messiah" during his earthly ministry. It remained for the cross and resurrection to show who Jesus really was. Then men and women could confess, "Jesus is the Christ," giving the Old Testament concept new meaning in light of the life he actually lived, the death he died, and the new dignity God had conferred upon him at the Resurrection.

In summary, Jesus did not adopt any predetermined notion of messiahship and conform to it. Because of the misuse of the term *messiah* in his own day, Jesus found it about as unusable as the term *covenant* (see *UB I*, Chapters 9—10). Jesus chose to speak of God's kingdom frequently and of covenant only rarely. He favored other terms over Christ, like "Son of man" or "Son" (of God) or aspects of the "servant of Yahweh" concept. In so doing, after his earthly work he provided the new contours for the usage of the term *messiah*.

Son of David

Every title used to refer to Jesus in the New Testament deserves to be explored in something of the way we have examined "Lord" and "Christ." However, space does not permit it. But one other term, "Son of David," merits treatment because it is closely related to "Messiah."

In Chapter 19 we learned how God covenanted with David to the effect that David's throne would be "established for ever," with Davidic offspring upon "the throne of his kingdom for ever" (2 Samuel 7:12-16). Historically, the Davidic line on the throne ended with Zerubbabel shortly after 520 B.C. But hope sprang eternal that a new descendant of David would arise as anointed king. The "Psalms of Solomon," a Pharisaic composition from the first century B.C., recall how God had chosen David king and then recount the calamities which had befallen Israel. This includes the conquest of Jerusalem by the Roman general Pompey in 63 B.C. Then comes a devout prayer for Israel: "Behold, O Lord, and raise up to them their king, the son of David" (Psalm of Solomon 17:23). The same book, however, also prays for God himself to become king.

Other Jewish devotional writings also pray for mercy "on the kingdom of the house of David."

The New Testament confesses Jesus the Christ as son of David, most notably at Romans 1:3-4 and 2 Timothy 2:8. In each instance Jesus' Davidic descent refers to his ministry and time on earth in contrast to his post-resurrection life. During that earthly ministry Jesus was occasionally addressed as "Son of David," that is, as a person descended from Israel's greatest anointed king. Bartimaeus, for example, cried out, "Jesus, Son of David, have mercy on me" (Mark 10:47). The title is especially common in Matthew (see Matthew 9:27; 15:22; 12:23).

The Davidic theme also comes to the fore in the stories about the birth and infancy of Jesus. In what we call the *Benedictus*, Zechariah, father of John the Baptist, prophesies redemption by a Savior in the house of David (Luke 1:68-69).

The angel Gabriel tells Mary that her son Jesus "will be great . . . and the Lord God will give to him the throne of his father David . . . and of his kingdom there will be no end" (Luke 1:32-33). Luke stresses that Joseph was "of the house of David" (1:27) and for that reason he went to "the city of David," Bethlehem, to be enrolled at the census (2:4). (Actually, Luke redefines the "city of David" here. In the Old Testament the phrase referred to Jerusalem, the city David took for his capital. Here it refers to the city of David's birth.)

Matthew also stresses Joseph's Davidic descent (1:20), and Revelation refers to Jesus' Davidic connections (3:7 and 5:5).

No doubt the *tour de force* linking Jesus to David comes in the genealogies of Matthew 1 and Luke 3. Modern readers often regard these lists of "who begot whom" as pretty dull and obscure and full of irreconcilable details. Yet Matthew and Luke each assigned a fair amount of precious space to these tables and Matthew chose to place them at the very beginning of his book. Matthew 1:1–17 includes forty-one or forty-two names (three groups of fourteen names). Luke 3:23–34 reverses the order, with seventy-seven names in groups of seven.

MATTHEW	LUKE
	1. Adam, the son of God (See 1 Chronicles 1:1–27 for a genealogy of Adam through Abraham.)
	2. Seth, the son of Adam
	3. Enos
	4. Cainan
	5. Mahalaleel
	6. Jared
	7. Enoch
	8. Methuselah
	9. Lamech
	10. Noah (See Genesis 5:3–32 for a genealogy of Adam through Noah.)
	11. Shem (See Genesis 11:10–26 for a genealogy of Shem through Abraham.)
	12. Arphaxad
	13. Cainan
	14. Shelah
	15. Eber
	16. Peleg
	17. Reu
	18. Serug
	19. Nahor
1. Abraham	20. Terah
	21. Abraham (Adam to Abraham, three groups of seven)
2. Isaac	22. Isaac (See 1 Chronicles 1:28–34 for a genealogy of the sons of Abraham and Isaac.)
3. Jacob (See 1 Chronicles 2:1–15 for a genealogy of Jacob through David.)	23. Jacob
4. Judah and Tamar	
5. Perez (See Ruth 4:18–22 for a genealogy of Perez through David.)	24. Judah
	25. Perez
6. Hezron	26. Hezron
	27. Arni
	28. Admin
7. Ram	
8. Amminadab	29. Amminadab
9. Nahshon	30. Nahshon
10. Salmon and Rahab	31. Sala
11. Boaz and Ruth	32. Boaz
12. Obed	33. Obed
13. Jesse	34. Jesse

MATTHEW	LUKE
14. King David and "the wife of Uriah" (Bathsheba)	35. David (Isaac to David, two groups of seven)
15. Solomon	36. Nathan (Nathan to Shealtiel, two groups of seven)
16. Rehoboam	37. Mattatha
17. Abijah	38. Menna
18. Asa	39. Melea
19. Jehoshaphat	40. Eliakim
20. Joram	41. Jonam
21. Uzziah	42. Joseph
22. Jotham	43. Judas
23. Ahaz	44. Simeon
24. Hezekiah	45. Levi
25. Manasseh	46. Matthat
26. Amos	47. Jorim
27. Josiah	48. Eliezer
28. Jechoniah (deportation to Babylon, 586 B.C.)	49. Joshua
	50. Er
	51. Elmadam
	52. Cosam
	53. Addi
	54. Melchi
	55. Neri
29. Shealtiel (end of Babylonian exile)	56. Shealtiel (end of Babylonian exile; see 1 Chronicles 3:17)
30. Zerubbabel	57. Zerubbabel (Zerubbabel to Jesus, three groups of seven)
31. Abiud	58. Thesa
32. Eliakim	59. Joanan
33. Azor	60. Joda
34. Zadok	61. Josech
35. Achim	62. Semein
36. Eliud	63. Mattathias
37. Eleazar	64. Maath
	65. Naggai
	66. Esli
	67. Nahum
	68. Amos
	69. Mattathias
	70. Joseph
	71. Jannai
	72. Melchi
	73. Levi
38. Matthan	74. Matthat
39. Jacob	75. Heli
40. Joseph and Mary	76. Joseph
41. Jesus, who is called (42) Christ	77. Jesus

Many features and difficulties in these genealogies will be apparent from even a few moments of study. Matthew traces Jesus back to David and Abraham, as is emphasized in 1:1, through three periods of fourteen names each (1:17). The third section is one short, unless we count "Jesus" as a name for his earthly life and "Christ" as separate, a title given later. Luke, with a more universal interest, traces the genealogy all the way back to Adam, son of God. (Luke also sees Jesus as "Son of God," 1:35.) Luke's seventy-seven names can be arranged in multiples of seven, although Luke's mathematical pattern is not as obvious as the one in Matthew.

Some of the difficulties stem from the Old Testament genealogies with which the evangelists worked. Others came from translation variants

from Hebrew to Greek. Some differences are accounted for by different lines of family descent. After David, for example, Matthew follows the line through Solomon, David's successor to the throne. Luke, on the other hand, traces the line through Nathan, David's third son born in Jerusalem (2 Samuel 5:14), a branch of the family which never came to the throne (Zechariah 12:12). Both evangelists agree on tracing Jesus' line through Joseph, even though they assume the virgin birth (Matthew 1:20–25; Luke 1:26–38). Luke even covers this by stating Jesus to be "the son (as was supposed) of Joseph" (3:23). Their genealogies seek to trace Jesus' legal parentage back to David. They are not concerned with physical paternity.

Matthew, oddly, mentions four women in his genealogy (see numbers 4, 10, 11, and 14, on the preceding chart), in addition to Mary (1:16). Each woman can be said to have been either a non-Jew, according to Jewish tradition, or to have had some irregularity which marked her marriage or her motherhood. Tamar was accused of harlotry when impregnated by her father-in-law Judah, though she was more righteous than he (Genesis 38); Rahab was a harlot (Joshua 2); Ruth turned up "at the feet" of Boaz and got him to marry her (Ruth 3); David's sin with the wife of his brave Hittite army officer, Uriah, is well known (2 Samuel 11). Why include the names of these women, and how do they relate to Mary (1:16)? Some have suggested Matthew is responding to Jewish charges that Jesus was illegitimate, just as in 28:11–15 he responds to Jewish charges or "explanations" that the empty tomb was a case of body snatching. In this case Matthew would be replying, "There was plenty of irregularity in King David's ancestry!" Others think Matthew is stressing human sinfulness and that Jesus, whose very name means "he saves," will deliver all such sinners (1:21). Still others stress the pagan background of these women and suggest that Matthew's aim is to show the universal nature of Christ's work (see also 28:18–20). Yet another theory is that Matthew reflects inner Jewish debate on the ancestry of the promised Davidic messiah and emphasized Jesus as the true anointed one.

One thing looms clearly: Matthew and Luke see Jesus as a descendant of David. And it is quite likely that Jesus, at least on Joseph's side, was of

---

. . . **The Christian faith down through the ages has let all these bewildering details fall into the background. In the foreground is the simple, powerful phrase, *Jesus Christ!***

---

the house of Israel's greatest king. Genealogical lines were taken very seriously in the Jewish world. It was necessary to keep careful records, especially for the priestly families. For lay folk like Joseph and Mary there was perhaps an oral tradition in family circles. Of course, the two varying lists we have may reflect differing family oral accounts, plus different readings of the fragmentary Old Testament records (as in Chronicles), plus varying concerns of the evangelists in putting together Matthew 1 and Luke 3. But in these several forms there existed what later was called a "Jesse tree," a family tree tracing Jesus' ancestry back to David and his father Jesse and beyond. ("Jesse windows" depicting the genealogy are found in cathedrals like Wells and Chartres and Dorchester Abbey near Oxford.)

JESUS AS MESSIAH—
IN GOD'S GOOD TIME

The likelihood that Jesus really was a "son of David" makes his handling of the messiah question even more intriguing. Of course he was "God's anointed." For there was anointment with the Spirit at Baptism, by his birth (conception), and through Joseph's Davidic descent. But "Messiah" had so many misleading connotations that Jesus was cool to the title, until he, by his death, and God, by raising him from the dead, could show what it really means to be the Lord's Messiah. He fulfilled prophecies by repudiating some current ideas and filling older ones with new meanings. There were surprises here because of the great surprise which reversed so many human expectations on Easter Day.

As a result, the Christian faith down through the centuries has let all these bewildering details fall into the background. In the foreground is the simple, powerful phrase, *Jesus Christ!*

References and More Information

Biblical references: Matthew 5:21-48; Luke 17:22-37. The "little apocalyses," Matthew 24-25; Mark 13; Luke 21:5-36. Peter's confession: Matthew 16:13-23; Mark 8:27-33; Luke 9:18-22. Jesus on trial: Matthew 26: 57-75; Mark 14:53-72; Luke 22:54-71.

Metzger, Bruce M. and Isobel M., editors. *The Oxford Concise Concordance.* See the following entires: fulfill, preach, promise

Reumann, John. *Jesus in the Church's Gospels.* Philadelphia: Fortress Press, 1968. See pages 251-295, on the claims of Jesus Christ.

Richardson, Alan. *Theological Word Book of the Bible.* New York: The Macmillan Company, 1962. See the following entries: fulfill, preach, Son of man

PART VI The Gospel in the Early Church

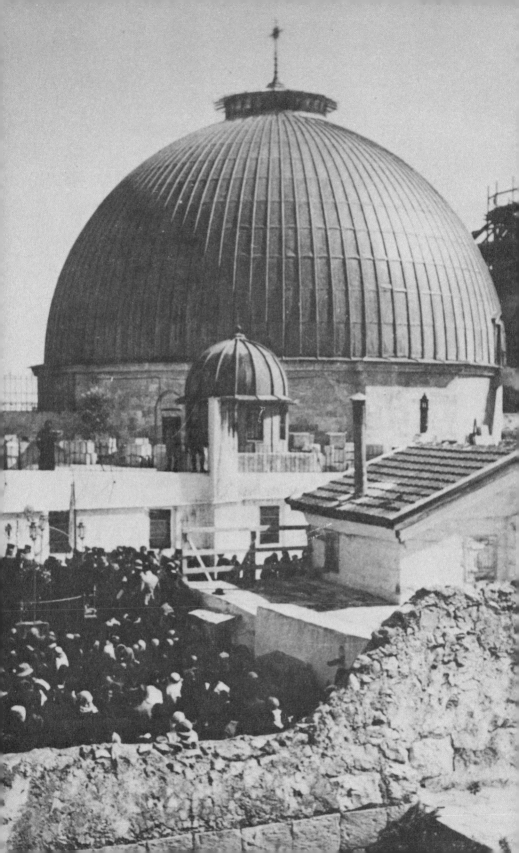

The Church of the Holy Sepulchre has been a chief shrine for Christian pilgrims for sixteen hundred years. Little wonder as we unravel the story of the development and proclamation of the Easter gospel, first in Jerusalem by the aroused disciples, then by Paul and later missionaries to the ends of the earth.

JESUS CHRIST, THE KINGDOM, AND MORE GOOD NEWS

We need to capture the dramatic change in the setting for this part of our study.

Jesus of Nazareth, who had preached the coming of the kingdom of God as good news, had come—and gone. In the spring of A.D. 30 he was gone not only from his familiar haunts in Galilee but also from the places where he had taught and preached in Jerusalem at Passover time. His life had come to an end in a shameful way upon a Roman cross.

After the events of that black Friday, his followers were in deep gloom. Disheartened, they scattered, some to Galilee, others into local hiding places. Only a few faithful women went about the necessary tasks of preparing to embalm the hurriedly buried remains.

Then in the midst of this sadness, began to come reports that someone had seen him—alive! Peter gave such a report. So did other disciples, a pair on Emmaus Road, eventually all eleven as a group. (Judas, ruing what he had set in motion, had committed suicide.) Stories were passed about how some of the women had found the tomb of Joseph from Arimathea, where Jesus had been buried, empty. What had been dismissed as female fantasy (they'd gone to the wrong place, or these women were making up "idle tales" [Luke 24:11] with their claims they had seen him alive) now began to make sense.

Thus began "the Easter gospel," the good news that Jesus lives. It was proclaimed not only that he was now alive but that he was exalted by God to life and lordship as a result of the triumph over death. Assertion of the lordship of Jesus was, in the light of Old Testament precedent, a result of this newest victory of God. (See *UB I*, Chapters 7—12, especially Chapter 12, "Jesus is Lord! Death and Resurrection as Victory.")

· Inevitably this acknowledgement of Jesus as Lord led those who hailed this latest and supreme manifestation of God's kingly power to bestow new titles upon Jesus. He was never declared king in place of God, though the idea that he reigns as king-regent within God's whole dominion occasionally does appear (Matthew 25:34, 40). But he was designated "Messiah" (*Christ; see UB II*, Chapter 21), and a host of other titles followed. Indeed, in time, as the magnitude of what God had done in and through Jesus dawned on people, new understandings of his functions and role in the plan of God emerged. They were tied both to creation (see *UB I*, Chapter 16) and to the future, especially eschatology (see *UB II*, Chapter 19).

Jesus as the Christ, Lord of the church, who played a role in creation and who would reign even more fully at the end as judge (2 Corinthians 5:10), loomed larger and larger as being himself the good news. Who he really was, now known in the light of Easter dawn, was reflected in confessions and accounts of his life and ministry and origin.

A good illustration is the way an Old Testament verse, Psalm 2:7, was applied to Jesus. In what may be the starting point, reflecting the Easter gospel, Paul in a sermon at Pisidian Antioch applies this verse to the fact God raised Jesus from the dead. Said Paul:

> "We bring you the good news that what God promised to the fathers, this he has fulfilled to us their children by raising Jesus; as also it is written in the second psalm,
>> 'Thou are my son,
>> Today I have begotten thee.'"
> (Acts 13:32-33)

Quoting an old Psalm verse originally used when an Israelite king was enthroned, Paul insists that Jesus was enthroned as Son of God at the resurrection on Easter Day. The same view is again reflected in Acts where Peter declares the resurrection to mean that God has designated Jesus "Lord" and "Christ" (2:32-36).

But this note of fulfillment in the Old Testament passage where "today" denotes the day of Resurrection need not be confined to Easter. We have already (in *UB I*, Chapter 1) examined the scene in the synagogue at Nazareth where "today" is equated with the beginning of Jesus' ministry and the fulfillment of Scripture. Hence it is not surprising that we should hear this same psalm verse quoted in some accounts of Jesus' baptism. In Luke 3:22, according to some manuscripts (RSV footnote), the heavenly voice says,

> "Thou art my beloved Son,
> today I have begotten thee,"

as if the point at which Jesus was elevated to sonship was his baptism.

The very phrase "I have begotten thee" points us to an even prior incident in the earthly life of Jesus when God designated him as "Son" at his birth. This is what eventually became "the Christmas gospel." Luke 1:31-35 reflects the idea that Jesus was begotten by the Holy Spirit. He will be called "Son of the Most High [God]" and is depicted as reigning "on the throne of his father David . . . and of his kingdom there will be no end."

The word *Today* in Luke 3:22 refers to Jesus' birth, or his conception, celebrated on church calendars as the Annunication of our Lord, March 25.

Of course, it remained for the Fourth Gospel to project back to the ultimate degree "the day" from which Jesus is God's Son. John 1:1-14 sets the time in eternity (also Colossians 1:15). Christian faith eventually came to say, "There never was a time when the Son was not."

After Easter, the New Testament witness quickly moved toward asserting Jesus' lordship in the nth degree, and this was regarded as good news or gospel in itself:

> "I bring you good news of a great joy . . . a Savior, who is Christ the Lord."
> (Luke 2:10-11)

> Now I would remind you . . . in what terms I preached to you the gospel . . . Christ died for our sins . . . he was raised on the third day . . . .
> (1 Corinthians 15:1, 3, 4)

> . . . the sufferings of Christ and the subsequent glory. . . . the things which have now been announced to you by those who preached the good news to you . . .
> (1 Peter 1:11-12)

The gospel or good news was thus destined to take new shapes after Easter in light of what Jesus had said and done and reflecting what the Old Testament had said. We will have more ways of stating the good news. But even as we explore them, we must also ask what became of Jesus' own gospel emphasis, the kingdom of God.

22. The Easter Gospel

THE GOOD NEWS
THE APOSTLES PREACHED

The news that Jesus was alive and regnant was enough to send anyone forth rejoicing—and preaching. His followers wanted to share the latest and most momentous story of all that God had done. This was especially true of Jesus' closest friends who had been with him during the Galilean ministry and followed him to Jerusalem, to death, and to unexpected victory. Furthermore, the Resurrection appearances recounted in the four Gospels regularly include a command from the risen Lord to go and share the news: "Go, tell his disciples and Peter . . ." (Mark 16:7). "Go . . . make disciples. . . ." (Matthew 28:19). "As the Father has sent me, even so I send you" (John 20:21).

The most succinct forms of this "new news" were no doubt the brief slogans, like auto bumper stickers, which summed up in a nutshell what had occurred. These very early statements, which are almost little creeds, are embedded in our New Testament Epistles. Paul and others liked to quote them as reminders of the essence of the faith which had been preached from the outset, or in the course of an argument to direct hearers to the "first things" and bedrock priorities. In many cases, if one simply puts the words "I believe that" in front of the statement, one has a short creed.

Typical is the statement, "God raised him from the dead" (Romans 10:9). Sometimes the emphasis is not simply on the past event but the present implication as well: "In fact Christ has been raised from the dead [by God]" and therefore "in Christ shall all be made alive (1 Corinthians 15:20, 22). In New Testament thought the emphasis is on God as the one who raised Jesus. When 1 Thessalonians 4:14 says "Jesus died and rose," (the phrase "rose again," which is the rendering in most translations, does not mean Jesus rose twice but is an attempt to do justice to a Greek verb which means literally "rose up" or "came back to life after death"), it is still understood that God raised him (1 Thessalonians 1:10). The same is true of slogans like 2 Timothy 2:8, "Remember Jesus Christ, risen from the dead. . . ." God is the one with the power and ability to raise the dead

(Hebrews 11:19; 1 Peter 1:21). This is the reason Christians believe (Romans 4:23-24). They also believe that God who raised Jesus will raise them up, too (1 Corinthians 6:14; 2 Corinthians 4:14). The Easter gospel is the work of God.

It has become apparent that the news of Jesus' resurrection is sometimes coupled with some other event in his career, such as his death (1 Thessalonians 4:14). Note also 1 Corinthians 15:3-4:

> That Christ died for our sins in accordance with the scriptures. . . . he was raised on the third day in accordance with the scriptures. . . .

2 Timothy 2:8 couples it with his descent from David. (This is not so much a reference to his nativity as to his messianic lineage.) Note also Romans 1:3-4 that the gospel concerns God's Son,

> Who was descended from David according to the flesh and designated Son of God in power according to the Spirit . . . by his resurrection.

Here, too, the "resurrection from the dead" is connected with the Holy Spirit, which is also suggested at Romans 8:11. On occasion Jesus' resurrection is linked with his future return, as at 1 Thessalonians 1:10. The Thessalonians are to henceforth serve God and

> Wait for his Son from heaven, whom he [God] raised from the dead, Jesus who delivers us from the wrath to come.

Even more elaborate is a passage like 1 Peter 3:18-22:

> Christ also died for sins once for all, the Righteous one for unrighteous people, that he might bring us to God, being put to death in the flesh but made alive in the spirit; in which he went and preached to the spirits in prison, . . . Who has gone into heaven and is at the right hand of God, with angels, authorities, and powers subject to him.

This is surely the language of the victory of God!

FIRST THINGS FIRST

Take note that while resurrection is coupled with Jesus' death, messianic descent, and future return, as well as with his present exaltation, there are no such passages which couple resurrection with parables or even miracles. These confessions of the Easter gospel linked God's victory over death with the person of Jesus (he is "Messiah" or "Lord") or his work (he "died for our sins"). What was important was the work of salvation as gospel, not moral instruction. The implications of the Easter victory for the ethical life follow, but they are not at the heart of the Easter gospel. First, what God has done; then (in this case even separately) what we do in response.

Much the same thing is true of the sermons we read in the Book of Acts. There in the fullest reflection of early Christian preaching to be found in the New Testament the accent is on how God has raised Jesus from death. That death is described in some detail. Sermons are longer and more detailed than the little creedal slogans; they are in narrative form rather than given as abstract statements that develop only one or two facets of Jesus' work. Hence, those in Acts often tell us more about the ministry of Jesus, that he taught or that he worked miracles. But even here there is rarely any content from his teaching. We look in vain for any reference to Jesus' theme, the kingdom of God, even when these sermons summarize his career. Contrary to the creedal slogans, the sermons in Acts do incorporate a note of response. They usually conclude with an admonition to repent and believe (as did Jesus' kerygma summarized in Mark 1:15) and be baptized. But of ethical imperatives—to do this or that in daily life—there is nothing. That comes later.

Most of the typical points can be seen if we look at Peter's sermon in Jerusalem, fifty days after Easter at Pentecost. The apostle catches his audience's attention with a reference to what has just happened, the amazing fact that Jesus' Galilean followers were able to speak about "the mighty works of God" in such a way that people of a dozen or more different nationalities and languages could understand their speech (Acts 2:1–13). This, Peter says, is not due to too much alcohol (certainly not at 9 a.m.!) but represents fulfillment of a prophecy by Joel (2:28–32) about the "last days" (Acts 2:15–21). Then comes the real message, the Easter gospel: "Jesus of Nazareth . . . crucified and killed . . . God raised him up" (vv. 22–24). There is a brief description of his ministry. He was "a man attested to you by God with mighty works and wonders and signs which God did through him in your midst" (v. 22). For a Jerusalem audience Peter emphasizes how God's "having loosed the pangs of death" (v. 24) and not abandoning Jesus to Hades (vv. 27, 31) fulfills the Old Testament. These may seem to us unusual expressions. Actually they come directly out of Psalms as passages which Peter sees fulfilled in Jesus, a descendent of David (his hearers believed that David wrote the psalms). Acts 2:25–28 quotes Psalm 16:8–10 (in a Greek version). Verses 29–31 explain how the words could not apply to David but must refer to the Messiah (Christ, whom Peter identifies as Jesus). The phrase in v. 24 about "the pangs of death" also reflects the language of the Psalms (see Psalm 116:3).

Here, for the first time in such clear fashion, we meet the important New Testament idea of "the definite plan and foreknowledge of God" (Acts 2:23). The sermons in Acts claim that even Jesus' death was no mere human contrivance. For all its tragedy it was part of God's overall design to save his human creatures, something he had thought out in advance. Hence the word foreknowledge is employed (v. 23). Note 4:28 or 13:36 and 20:27 where the RSV translates "the counsel of God." The sermon in Acts 2 also speaks of Jesus' exaltation (v. 33), in accord with the Old

Testament (v. 34), and the titles of honor which have now been given him (v. 36, "Lord" and "Christ").

When the crowd is moved to ask, "What shall we do?" Peter concludes with what is a standard answer in these sermons: "Repent, and be baptized . . . for the forgiveness of sins," and inherit the promise of God (2:37-39).

The outline uncovered in Peter's Pentecost sermon is rather typical of several other sermons in Acts which proclaim the Easter gospel. These include Peter's sermon to Cornelius, the Roman army officer, at Caesarea (Acts 10, in what is sometimes called "Pentecost for Gentiles"); Paul's long sermon at Antioch in Pisidia (Acts 13); and the briefer declarations involving Peter in Jerusalem (3:12-26; 4:8-12; 5:27-32). One could outline these sermons in the Book of Acts according to the chart which appears on page 68.

Clearly, these sermons in Acts share a common outline. Indeed, their very sameness is not without its difficulties, since Peter and Paul are made to sound almost exactly alike. One would expect to hear in Paul's addresses in Antioch, Athens, and Ephesus (Acts 13:16-41; 17:22-31; 20:17-35) many of the ideas and terms found in his Epistles. Characteristic Pauline terms do not occur in Acts. In any case, with these structural similarities Luke shows us what evangelistic preaching in the early church was like. We meet here the apostolic *kerygma* or proclamation by those "sent forth" to confront Jews and Gentiles with the Easter gospel. At its heart was Jesus, crucified and risen.

JESUS AND GOD'S KINGSHIP

We have seen how, after Easter, Jesus has changed from the one who proclaimed good news about the kingdom of God to the one who is now proclaimed. Jesus risen and exalted is the good news which brings forgiveness of sins and freedom (Acts 13:38-39). The gospel message has taken a new shape, an inevitability after the Easter victory of God.

But whatever became of Jesus' own emphasis on God and his kingship? The supremacy and power of God, of course, remains. We have seen that it is God who raised Jesus. Jesus was exalted, true, but to God's right hand (to a place of honor in relation to God the Father). The very term *kingdom* continues to be heard but with diminished frequency. Although the Gospel of Luke employed it forty-six times, *kingdom* occurs in Acts on just eight occasions. Those eight examples are enough, however, to show that Jesus' theme of the kingdom was continued after Easter in the early church, although with inevitable changes.

Jesus himself is depicted by Luke as continuing to speak of "the kingdom of God" to his eleven disciples throughout the forty days between

	Peter in Jerusalem	Peter to Cornelius	Paul in Antioch
1. *The Situation.* Sermons in Acts may have an Old Testament text near the beginning, but usually begin with the immediate local situation.	2:14–21; 3:12; 4:8–9	10:25–35	
2. *Fulfillment.* What was prophesied has come to pass. The "last times" are here.	2:16–21	10:36–43	13:27–29, 33
3. *Jesus.* This has come to pass in the ministry, death, and resurrection of Jesus who *a)* was born of the seed of David. *b)* went about doing good (ministry reference). *c)* died on the "tree" (cross). (See Deuteronomy 21:22.) *d)* was raised up and set before witnesses by God.	2:29 2:22 2:23 2:24–32	10:38 10:39 10:40	13:22-23 13:28–29 13:30–31
4. *Exaltation.* Jesus is elevated to God's right hand. (See Psalm 110:1.)	2:33–36	10:36	13:30, 34
5. *Holy Spirit.* A sign of the messianic dignity and power bestowed on Jesus is the presence of the Holy Spirit, now poured out.	2:33; 5:32	10:38; 44	13:52
6. *Further fulfillment.* This will come through Jesus at the last judgment and the "establishing of all that God spoke" when Christ comes again.	3:21	10:42	
7. *Witnesses.* Of all this we are witnesses.	2:32	10:41	13:31
8. *Our response.* Therefore one should repent, be baptized, receive the forgiveness of sins and the gift of the Holy Spirit.	2:38–39	10:47	13:38–39

The bare rock in the center of the photograph is Areopagus or "Mars Hill" where Paul's reference to the resurrection met with mixed reactions (see Acts 17:32).

Easter and his ascension (Acts 1:3). The disciples continued to misunderstand it and to regard it in the old nationalistic sense of the restoration of Israel to its ancient kingdom glory (1:6). Just as during Jesus' lifetime, some of them had hoped for positions of honor in an earthly kingdom (Mark 10:35-45; Luke 22:24-27), so, in the flush of Easter enthusiasm they looked for a return of Israel's old prerogatives. Jesus directed them instead to missionary witnessing under the Spirit (Acts 1:7-8).

Nevertheless "the kingdom of God," understood as Jesus had taught it, could still provide the theme of Christian missionary preaching. In Acts, Luke uses it as a kind of shorthand expression for what was preached by such evangelists as Philip and Paul.

In Samaria, Philip "preached good news about the kingdom of God and the name of Jesus Christ" (Acts 8:12).

In what is today southern Turkey, Paul and Barnabas exhorted the disciples in Lystra, Iconium, and Antioch of Pisidia "to continue in the faith, and saying that through many tribulations we must enter the kingdom of God" (14:22).

In a synagogue at Ephesus, Paul "spoke boldly, arguing and pleading about the kingdom of God" (19:8).

To the elders from Ephesus who came to meet with him at Miletus Paul described himself as one who went among them "preaching the kingdom" (20:25).

To Jews at Rome who visited his lodgings Paul expounded his position, "testifying to the kingdom of God and trying to convince them about Jesus both from the law of Moses and from the prophets" (28:23).

The closing words in Acts, as Paul resides in Rome for a two-year period, are that he "welcomed all who came to him, preaching the kingdom of God and teaching about the Lord Jesus Christ" (28:31).

It is also worth noting that often "the kingdom" is the theme when the audience is Jewish (19:8; 20:25; 28:23,31) or related to the Jews (8:12). "The kingdom" could still be *kerygma* or the topic of post-Easter preaching; at 20:25 and 28:31 the Greek verb is "preach kerygma." It could be "the good news" (8:12). And basically in these passages it is future (14:22). It is not here yet (1:6-8); first comes a missionary interim.

A final significant feature is the way the kingdom of God, as never in Jesus' lifetime, is now paralleled with Jesus himself, who is now crucified and risen (see 8:12 where "the name of Jesus" is equivalent to his person, 28:23, and especially 28:31). Jesus, the new form of the gospel, can stand in tandem with the kingdom or, as we shall see, supercede it, especially for preaching among non-Jews.

A vivid insight into what was happening in these exciting decades between A.D. 40 and 60 can be gained from a scene in Acts 17. At the Greek city of Thessalonica Paul and Silas have been making their gospel witness in the synagogue, no doubt testifying to Jesus Christ and the kingdom. They make converts, but there is also opposition, an uproar, and a mob which attacks the home of Jason, Paul's host. In the confused scene which follows, a serious charge is leveled against Paul and Silas: "These men who have turned the world upside down have come here also, and Jason has received them; and they are all acting against the decrees of Caesar, saying that there is another king, Jesus" (17:6-7). We can guess at the reason for the confusion. People heard the missionaries proclaim the kingdom of God and a new Lord, Jesus. The words must have conjured up the image of a king like Caesar, and they concluded that this Jesus was a revolutionist threat to the Roman government. Paul and Silas would then be seditionists, "acting against the decrees of Caesar."

The good news had to be presented in a new way for the non-Jewish audience who did not know the Old Testament background of the kingship of God which Jesus had preached.

At Thessalonica the charges did not stick, but Paul and Silas did have to leave town (17:9-10). A few experiences like this would have been enough to convince early Christians that they had to present their message with utmost clarity to avoid such misunderstanding. New ways had to be found to present the gospel to a non-Jewish audience who did not know the Old Testament background of the kingship of God which Jesus had preached. God's power, sovereignty, love, and rule could be expressed in ways other than "kingdom." Moreover, the Easter gospel which the Father had created in raising Jesus from the dead was now the new good news. But proof of the fidelity with which the early church preserved Jesus' message about the kingdom is clear. We see it in the way the Christian preachers in Acts preserved "the kingdom" as a theme and the way the evangelists preserved it as Jesus' theme in the Gospels, which were written even later than the incident in Thessalonica.

References and More Information

Biblical references: Acts 2, 10, 13

Metzger, Bruce M. and Isobel M., editors. *The Oxford Concise Concordance.* See the following entries: forgive, forgiveness, saint, Spirit

Reumann, John. *Jesus in the Church's Gospels.* Philadelphia: Fortress Press, 1968. See Chapter 2, pages 18-43.

Richardson, Alan. *A Theological Word Book of the Bible.* New York: The Macmillan Company, 1962. See the following entries: apostle, baptize, forgive, saint, Spirit

23. The Gospel Paul Received

The "Easter gospel" was the good news which Paul received from those who had been followers of Jesus Christ before him. He in turn passed it on to new converts, both Jew and Gentile, in the Mediterranean world.

So influential was this apostle to the Gentiles that it has often been assumed he was a kind of "second founder" of Christianity. Some have even argued that the man from Tarsus in Asia Minor perverted the simple religion *of* Jesus into a religion *about* Jesus, with church, sacraments, and all its trappings. True, he did find new and amazingly fruitful ways of restating the gospel (see the next chapter). But the fact is that many of the features credited to Paul were really the common property of apostolic Christianity as it developed in the thirties and forties. If Jesus died and rose in A.D. 30, and Paul was converted in A.D. 33 or 35, and if he did not begin his missionary career until the year 47 or so, we have almost two decades of development apart from Paul before his letters appeared in the fifties. The evidence for this development within the apostolic church of a common Christianity which Paul inherited can be read in the Book of Acts—written perhaps in the 90s—and ferreted out from pre-Pauline passages quoted in the Epistles by Paul and his circle of helpers. From such New Testament material we learn that Paul received much more than the message "Jesus lives" from the Christian church then taking shape.

Paul himself had been born "Saul," a name which stuck till it was changed during his first missionary journey in Cyprus (Acts 13:9; see also vv. 2 and 13). As a zealous Jew devoted to the law he had once persecuted the church (Galatians 1:13–14). To him, Jesus was an unrighteous rebel who deserved the cross, his followers heretics to be stamped out (Acts 9:1–2). As a Pharisee, Saul believed in a future resurrection, but that such a one as Jesus should be risen and exalted was unthinkable.

Nevertheless God was at work in Saul. Perhaps the change was wrought through conscience, or by reflection on the Hebrew scriptures, or by the impression Christian martyrs made on him (cf. Acts 7:59—8:1). Luke provides three separate accounts of how Saul was dramatically converted on the road to Damascus (9:3–18; 22:6–16; 26:12–18). As a result of the importance given to it in the Book of Acts, Paul's experience became the classic prototype of conversion. Rarely, however, is it pointed out that it was not conversion from worldliness and sin to faith but from one religion to another. While suffering the loss of much that had been important in his past (Philippians 3:8), Paul held on through this great experience to much from his Jewish heritage. That heritage included the Hebrew scriptures and rabbinic ways of interpreting them, high Jewish moral standards, and even practices learned in the synagogue. Paul himself explains his new experience with Christ as nothing short of a "revelation." God, who had set him apart by grace "from birth," was "pleased to reveal his Son" to him and through him to countless others. The experience parallels that of Jeremiah (cf. Galatians 1:15-16 NEB, and Jeremiah 1:5). Too many people have tried to imitate Paul's conversion experience, too few his Christian fervency and obedience.

PAUL'S GOSPEL INHERITANCE

The "little creeds"

What did Paul receive as gospel in the fellowship of Jesus Christ into which he entered? First, there were those small creeds summarizing the Easter gospel with its note of Old Testament fulfillment that we have already examined. They provided "building blocks" for further Christian thought; 1 Corinthians 15:3-5 (see Chapter 22) affords a good example. In their present setting these verses are part of a complex argument about the resurrection of Christians. The Corinthians had problems either with the Semitic idea that the resurrection involved bodies or with the promise that they would rise in the future. Perhaps they thought of the resurrection as involving only immortal souls or even that they were already raised. Whatever their problem, Paul sought to help them unravel it. First by patiently reiterating something they and he alike had accepted, a little four-line creed.

> Now I would remind you, brethren, in what terms I preached to you the gospel, which you received, in which you stand, by which you are saved, if you hold it fast—unless you believed in vain. For I delivered to you as of first importance what I also received,
>> that Christ died for our sins in accordance with the scriptures,
>> that he was buried,
>> that he was raised on the third day in accordance with the scriptures,
>> and that he appeared. . . .

Then follows a list (or lists) of Resurrection appearances, to which Paul adds his own revelatory experiences. Jesus appeared to Cephas, then to the Twelve, then to more than five hundred, to James, to all the apostles, and last of all, to Paul. It is even possible that verses 3 and 5 originally consisted of such separate little acclamations as, "Christ died for our sins" (cf. 1 Peter 3:18) and, "Jesus was raised" (cf. Romans 4:25), but here they have been put together in perfect balance. Both lines 1 and 3 of the little creed include the phrase "in accordance with the scriptures," perhaps a reference to Isaiah 53:5–12 and Hosea 6:2 or Psalm 16:10. Each has a prepositional phrase added. "For our sins" makes the death an atoning act. "On the third day" both fulfills scripture and provides chronology. And each has a supporting clause. The burial reinforces the reality of the death, and the appearances undergird the Resurrection.

This credo, Paul says, is what he inherited and faithfully preached when he came to Corinth. The Corinthians accepted it and lived by it.

The rest of the chapter draws out the implications of what they believed. If Christ has been raised, so too will they who are in Christ. There is a resurrection of the dead and it will be in bodily form, bearing the image of "the man of heaven," Jesus (1 Corinthians 15:49). And in good Old Testament fashion, Paul, draws ethical implications from all this. He describes how one is to live (15:58) and even give to a collection for relief of the needy in Jerusalem (16:1 ff.). The Easter gospel in creedal slogans thus helps build further good news and directions for the people of God.

The teachings of Jesus and the early church

A second element received by Paul was the teaching of Jesus and of the early church which guided the life of Christians in worship and daily life.

1 Corinthians again provides a good example at 11:23-25. The passage begins with the same formula found at 15:3. *Received* and *delivered* were technical terms from rabbinic use for passing on intact the teaching of some earlier authority. Hence Paul employs them here.

> For I received from the Lord what I also delivered to you, that the Lord Jesus on the night when he was betrayed took bread, and when he had given thanks, he broke it, and said, "This is my body which is for you. Do this in remembrance of me." In the same way also the cup, after supper, saying, "This cup is the new covenant in my blood. Do this, as often as you drink it, in remembrance of me."
>
> (1 Corinthians 11:23-25)

This time there is not the same precise parallelism as in 15:3-5, but the words of institution do balance each other: "This is . . . Do this . . . in remembrance of me." The reference to an actual happening is clear, the "Lord" is named as Jesus, his words are quoted, and a date and a setting are cited. The reference to a "supper" is to a meal at Passovertime. Some of the other terms, such as the reference to "new covenant," reflect Old Testament background (Jeremiah 31:31), as does the idea of "remembering" (see Exodus 12:14).

We are accustomed to reciting such words at celebrations of the Lord's Supper. That is likely how they were used in the thirties and forties by early Christians and why Paul passed them along to the Corinthians as part of his gospel teaching. They were words, Paul might have said to the Corinthians, "in which you stand" (15:1) every time there is participation in the cup and bread which actualizes the body and blood of Christ (1 Corinthians 10:16), that is, his presence. They announce his death and all its benefits, such as the forgiveness of our sins, as the verse added at 11:26 makes clear. The proclamation of the Lord's Supper concerns the cross and the subsequent victory of God at Easter, made real here and now, along with the promise that the Lord will come in the future and reign fully.

Paul has quoted all this in 1 Corinthians 11 again because of a problem in that troubled but gifted congregation. The communal meal was plagued with difficulties (11:17-22). When Christians assembled in what should have been a time of fellowship and unity, the existence of factions became apparent. The structure of the service in those days seems to have included an actual meal eaten *between* the sharing of the bread (body) and of the cup (blood). Note verse 25, "after supper." Later the practice changed to eating a meal first and *then* sharing bread and cup. This latter arrangement was apparently already in vogue in Corinth. The meal or "love feast" (Jude 12) was eventually discontinued precisely because of such abuses as Paul describes. For centuries Christians have been accustomed to sharing only the bread and wine in the sacrament, a development that had already occurred in New Testament times.

Apparently some Corinthians had gotten into the habit of greedily eating the food and getting drunk at the meal before the bread and cup were blessed. Paul seems particularly angered that there were members who got nothing and went hungry (11:21-22). Perhaps these were slaves or believers from the lower classes kept by work from getting to the service on time, and discriminated against by other Christians. (The situation at Corinth might have been even more scandalous. In 1 Corinthians 10:1-12 Paul had to warn Christians that sacraments were not magical rites which permitted them to do as they pleased.)

In dealing with the problems at Corinthian Communion services Paul cited the "words of institution" (11:23-25) which he had shared with the Corinthians from the beginning of their faith. It is the *Lord's* Supper that they eat (v. 20), not a private party of their own. The Lord is Jesus who died for them and who will come again, who is and will be their judge. Therefore, they are to "discern the body" (v. 29). By that Paul means not simply, "Be aware that you receive the true body and blood of the Lord" (see vv. 27-28, which Lutherans like to take as a reference to perceiving Christ in the elements). More important, they were to find the body of Christ in the Christian community (cf. 1 Corinthians 12:12, 27) even in those poor slaves who came late to Communion. Here, as in 1 Corinthians 15:3-5, a piece of traditional teaching that was part of the gospel Paul received (11:23-25) is used to provide further gospel and warning in a new situation and setting.

Other instruction and admonition

What Paul inherited included teachings about faith, worship, and daily life which could be used as the account of the Lord's Supper was used in 1 Corinthians 11. It also included a number of instructions quoted from Jesus and a common body of ethical admonitions which could be passed along to new Christians as a norm or guide. We cite here only a few examples. When Paul says, "The Lord commanded that those who proclaim the gospel should get their living by the gospel" (1 Corinthians 9:14), presumably he had in mind Jesus' words, "The laborer deserves his wage" (Matthew 10:10; Luke 10:7). When Paul writes, "I know and am persuaded in the Lord Jesus that there is nothing unclean in itself" (Romans 14:14), the pertinent teaching of Jesus is Mark 7:15 or Matthew 15:11. Paul seems to know something of what we call the Sermon on the Mount. Compare Romans 12:14, 17 with Matthew 5:39–42, 44. Paul's Greek still retains the Aramaic word for father, *Abba*, which Jesus no doubt used in the Lord's Prayer (cf. Galatians 4:6 and Romans 8:15 with Luke 11:2). In the first decades of Christianity there would even have been a collection of such teachings which Paul and others used.

As to common ethical admonitions, we know there were teachers in the early church who instructed converts in Christian doctrine and the ethical implications of their new commitment. Galatians 6:6 refers to "him who taught the word" and "him who teaches." The Greek expression used here is one from which we derive our terms "catechetical instruction" and "catechist." There are also New Testament references to the traditions Paul taught (1 Corinthians 11:2; 2 Thessalonians 2:15) and even to "the standard of teaching" to which his readers were committed (Romans 6:17). In reading the New Testament Epistles one cannot miss the common pattern of ethical admonition in letters by Paul and his aides as well as by Peter and James. These admonitions are often built up around some key verb as illustrated in the following chart.

"*Put off*" (bad habits)	Colossians 3:8	Ephesians 4:25	1 Peter 2:1–2
			James 1:21
"*Put on*" (good characteristics)	3:10, 12	4:24	Romans 13:12
"*Be watchful, pray*"	4:2	6:18–19	1 Peter 4:7, 11; 5:8
"*Stand*" or "*withstand*"	4:12	6:11	1 Peter 5:8–10
			James 4:7
"*Be subject to . . .*"			
husbands/wives	3:18–19	5:21–33	
fathers/children	3:20–21	6:1–4	1 Peter 3:1–7
masters/slaves	3:22—4:1	6:5–9	2:18–25

The imagery of "putting off" and "putting on" fits well with regard to ethical habits, but it also reflects the practice of Baptism. There the candidate would disrobe ("put off") outer garments and then, according to later practice, dress in white ("put on") after being baptized. The "subjection" theme came into Christianity from the Old Testament (1 Peter 3:6) and

77

the contemporary world. (In Chapter 27 we shall see how Christianity modified and reshaped some of its dangerous features.) The command to "be subject to" could also be applied to man's relation to God, the relations of the younger to their elders (1 Peter 5:5), and relations between citizen and state (1 Peter 2:13; Romans 13:1-7).

All of this points to a pattern of ethical instruction for people entering the Christian faith (particularly those entering from paganism), who needed rudimentary lessons in a type of life consistent with the gospel. Paul and other writers sometimes reflect this material.

Thus we begin to see a church which had, in connection with its good news, creedal announcements of the gospel, teachings from Jesus and those of a general ethical nature, and a sacramental life. For, in addition to the Lord's Supper, Baptism existed as the great rite of entrance, one's response to the good news, what one does upon hearing the kerygma (Acts 2:38). John the Baptist had practiced a water rite (Mark 1:4-5) and his disciples (Luke 11:1) no doubt continued the practice. Jesus could have baptized during his ministry, although one note says it was not he but his disciples who engaged in the practice (see John 3:22; 4:1-2). It was really after Easter, however, that the practice became the norm for entrance into the Christian community. Paul could even assume that Christians in Rome, a place he had never visited, knew all about Baptism. He argued *from* the practice and had no need to argue *for* it (Romans 6:3-11).

The songs of the early church

One other item deserves to be singled out of the rich heritage of the apostolic church in its first twenty or thirty years to which Paul was debtor. That is the hymnody of early Christians. Of course they had at hand the Psalms from the Old Testament Scriptures. Christians praised God in Aramaic and Greek. But since there are New Testament references to "psalms and hymns and spiritual songs" which they sang with thankfulness in their hearts (Colossians 3:16), we can safely suppose that there must have been an expanding collection of such hymnody. These songs were certainly sung at the time of celebration, particularly at Baptisms and Communion Services and at Sunday worship.

Already by the time Paul wrote 1 Corinthians in the mid-fifties, there seems to have been a shift in the time for worship from the Jewish Sabbath, the seventh day of the week, to Sunday the first day of the week (1 Corinthians 16:2; Revelation 1:10). The shift suited the celebration of the central fact of the kerygma, the Resurrection, which occurred on the first day of the week (Mark 16:1-2).

Perhaps 1 Peter 3:18-22 reflects such a hymn about Jesus' death, resurrection, and exaltation (see *UBI*, Chapter 22). Colossians 1:15-20 is commonly regarded as a hymn about Jesus' role in creation and redemption (see *UBI*, Chapter 16). Philippians 2:6–11 is an elaborate poetic composition concerning Jesus' descent to death and his exaltation as Lord (see *UBI*, Chapter 12). It surely was composed prior to Paul and may have roots in the Aramaic-speaking segment of the church. We may also cite here a snatch from a baptismal hymn in Ephesians 5:14.

> "Awake, O sleeper, and arise from the dead,
> and Christ shall give you light."

There is the longer composition about Christ quoted at 1 Timothy 3:16.

> He was manifested in the flesh,
> vindicated [or justified] in the Spirit,
> seen by angels,
> preached among the nations,
> believed on in the world,
> taken up in glory.

Here we seem to have references to Jesus' incarnation, resurrection, and ascension; the missionary advance of the *kerygma*; and Christ's glorious exaltation. There is a nice rhetorical pattern contrasting the two spheres of earth and heaven which many people of the day found natural in their thinking: flesh/Spirit; nations/angels; world/glory. Such passages are always hard to pin down as to precise meaning, largely because they are in the language of poetry.

KINGDOM LANGUAGE AGAIN

In such an emerging church, with its creeds, *kerygma,* teachings, ethical concerns, sacraments, and songs, what happened to Jesus' message about the "kingdom of God"? We have already suggested in Chapter 22 some good reasons why other ways had to be found to express God's sovereignty and Jesus' lordship in the Greco-Roman world. Nonetheless, in addition to the kingdom references in Acts already cited, a number of others appear in the Pauline Epistles written in the fifties and later. Some of them are part of the gospel material which Paul received; in other cases the writer chose to use kingdom terminology out of loyalty to Jesus and in fidelity to an Old Testament background.

A half dozen of these verses locate the kingdom in the future as the Old Testament and some of Jesus' teachings did. Some of these occur in what must have been part of the early church's body of ethical instructions. For example, Paul writes to the unruly Corinthians,

> "Do you not know that the unrighteous will not inherit the kingdom of God?
> Do not be deceived; neither the immoral, nor idolaters, nor adulterers, nor
> sexual perverts, nor thieves, nor the greedy, nor drunkards, nor revilers,
> nor robbers will inherit the kingdom of God. And such were some of you.

79

> But you were washed, you were sanctified, you were justified in the name of the Lord Jesus Christ and in the Spirit of our God" (1 Corinthians 6:9–11).

The types of sinners listed does not necessarily provide a profile of Corinthian converts; it may be simply a stock ethical list found in early Christian teachings. More important, Paul says these people, however bad they once were, are now baptized ("washed"), justified, and sanctified in Christ. Note also the verb *inherit* and its future tense; the kingdom is a gift yet to be received.

The same verb is used in a list of vices which Paul quotes at Galatians 5:19–21.

> The works of the flesh are plain: fornication, impurity, licentiousness, idolatry, sorcery, enmity, strife, jealousy, anger, selfishness, dissension, party spirit, envy, drunkenness, carousing, and the like. I warn you . . . that those who do such things shall not inherit the kingdom of God.

After the corresponding list of "virtues" or fruits of the Spirit in verses 22–23, one might expect to read, "Those who do these things will inherit the kingdom of God," but there is no such concession to salvation by good works. At 5:24 we have simply a reference to living a life in conformity with the cross of Jesus.

Thus, early Christianity certainly connected the kingdom with a morally responsive life, just as Jesus did in his words about fruit from a good tree (Matthew 7:16–20; 21:33–41). 1 Thessalonians makes the point well. The writer exhorts, encourages, and charges his readers "to lead a life worthy of God, who calls you into his own kingdom and glory" (2:12). This process may even involve suffering for the future kingdom of God (2 Thessalonians 1:5). It is clear that people as they are by nature ("flesh and blood" is the Semitic phrase) "cannot inherit the kingdom of God" (1 Corinthians 15:50). There must be change brought about by God at the second coming. Paul even preserves a highly apocalyptic little account of how at the end Christ will hand over the kingdom to God, who will then be all in all (1 Corinthains 15:22–28). This implies the possibility of a "kingdom of Christ" for a time, and occasionally we find a reference to just that, as in Ephesians 5:5; "any inheritance in the kingdom of Christ and of God".

All these allusions make the kingdom appear to be so much a future event, one is moved to ask if the early church lost all sight of the kingdom of God as a present reality breaking in on the world, as Jesus had proclaimed. While the future aspect was so very much preserved in the Epistles, the present side of the kingdom was not really lost. For example, Paul refers to it in a discussion about "strong" and "weak" Christians and their scruples over what a believer could or could not eat. At Romans 14:17 he writes, "The kingdom of God is not food and drink," and he then goes on to offer three equivalent terms which may reflect the mind of the early church. What the kingdom is can be summed up in the phrase "righteousness and peace and joy in the Holy Spirit." These are God's eschatological gifts, given now. Above them all rises God's gift of justifying righteousness. In such an accent Paul was to find yet another way to express the gospel and deepen its meaning, as we shall find in Chapter 24.

Shaped by the gospel which he received, Paul's own vocabulary clearly included "kingdom" as a theme. He used it to warn the Corinthians that "the kingdom of God does not consist in talk but in power"—present power—for the gospel is "the power of God" expressed as "righteousness" and "Christ crucified" (1 Corinthians 4:20; cf. Romans 1:16-17 and 1 Corinthians 1:23). As we read in 1 Corinthians 11:27-32, the presence of this Lord can mean judgment. There Paul was speaking to some who thought they were already in the kingdom and had "become kings" (1 Corinthians 4:8). They obviously overplayed the present aspect of the kingdom. Perhaps that is why Paul spoke so often of its future side (1 Corinthians 15:49-50).

Other Pauline writings pick up both aspects of the kingdom. Colossians 1:13 speaks of Christians as those "transferred . . . into the kingdom of his beloved Son." The imagery reflects the Old Testament Exodus from Egypt to the Promised Land. But Colossians reinterpreted these physical kingdoms as "the inheritance of the saints in light . . . the dominion of darkness" (1:12-13). Christians are delivered from the one into the other. Lest anyone misunderstand this metaphor, the kingdom of God's Son is further defined in terms of "redemption, the forgiveness of sins," which believers share now (1:14). This idea of the kingdom as present is also reflected in the description of several of Paul's Jewish-Christian companions as "my fellow workers for the kingdom of God" (Colossians 4:11). In 2 Timothy, on the other hand, the kingdom is seen in the future. It is coupled with the judgment and Christ's *parousia* or coming (4:1). It is God's "heavenly kingdom" for which Paul and others will be saved.

In their own writings and in their use of the heritage of the early church, Paul and other apostolic writers preserved the "kingdom" theme although they viewed it through the lens of the Easter gospel. Like Jesus, he and his fellows in the faith regarded it as both present reality and future event, as a gift, and as the basis for ethical demands (1 Corinthians 6:9-10; Ephesians 5:5; cf. Mark 1:14-15). As they gave new expression to the good news, they accented a joyous, liberating present reality, while still holding fast to future promises.

References and More Information

Biblical references: 1 Corinthians 11, 15; Colossians; Ephesians

Metzger, Bruce M. and Isobel M., editors. *The Oxford Concise Concordance.* See the following entries: atone, blood

Richardson, Alan. *A Theological Word Book of the Bible.* New York: The Macmillan Company, 1962. See the following entries: atone, satisfy

24. The Gospel Paul Advanced

The missionary career of Paul coincides with and, according to the New Testament, spearheads the greatest period of missionary advance in the first-century church. The Book of Acts begins in Jerusalem, the center of Israel's hopes, where Jesus had died and been raised. It ends with Paul preaching the gospel in the imperial capital, Rome. Paul's three journeys in Acts recount a campaign of incessant labors with long periods spent in key cities like Corinth and Ephesus. From these hubs the gospel spread to the surrounding countryside. His many epistles document the progress of the gospel from Palestine north and west into Asia Minor, Greece, and Italy. (Thirteen letters in the New Testament are attributed to Paul. Some of them have in them parts of more than one letter. Second Corinthians, for example, contains elements of three separate letters. Even the most radical critics give Paul credit for ten segments of this material.)

Of course, there must have been hundreds of other unnamed missionary witnesses plus dozens of Paul's friends and other apostles mentioned in the New Testament. These unheralded men and women, often in the course of their daily work, spread the gospel to Rome long before Paul got there and carried it east and south as well. But the New Testament in general and Acts 13–28 in particular single out Paul to symbolize this great advance. One gets the impression that after his death, somewhere between A.D. 60 and 67, the Christian movement had to devote more and more effort in the last thirty years of the century to coming to a new self-understanding before there could be much further advance. This was partly because of the upheaval caused by the fall of Jerusalem in A.D. 70, partly because of sporadic persecutions and internal problems.

As we have already seen, Paul inherited Jesus' message about the kingdom and the Easter gospel from the early church. He preached the same basic good news as the other apostles (1 Corinthians 15:11). His witness was even checked with Peter, James the brother of Jesus, and John in Jerusalem (Galatians 2:2, 7–10). They endorsed it and agreed that Paul should concentrate on Gentiles and the Jewish-Christian apostles on Jews ("the circumcised"). He was also to "remember the poor" at Jerusalem. Paul carried out that pledge, and a great deal of his energy in each congregation went into raising money for "the saints" at Jerusalem (1 Corinthians 16:1–4; 2 Corinthians 8–9; Romans 15:25–29).

82

Paul was a loyal churchman and he is portrayed as such in Acts. His sermons reported there sound much like those of Peter. Like other missionaries, he appears to have been subservient to "headquarters" in Jerusalem (Acts 9:26-30 [contrast Galatians 1:16-21]; Acts 11:27-30; 12:25 RSV note; Chapter 15; and 18:22, assuming "the church" means the one at Jerusalem). Because Luke limited the number of apostles to twelve he hesitated to call Paul an "apostle." Luke defined the conditions for apostleship in Acts 1:21-22. He reported the replacement of Judas in the "apostolic college" but no one thereafter. Paul is called "apostle" in only one story in Acts 14:4-14, but Paul himself defended vehemently his apostolic authority in his letters (1 Corinthians 9:1; 2 Corinthians 11:5; 12:11-12). Much of Galatians is a defense of Paul's apostolic office and apostolic gospel.

One gets the feeling that Luke's picture of Paul exaggerated certain features to fit his own theological view of history. Actually the "real Paul" revealed in his own writings was even more dynamic, almost volcanic. This is important to realize in order to understand what the gospel was for Paul. For while he received and transmitted the Easter message, he also developed, amplified, deepened, and extended this good news to make it speak to people who could not read a line of Hebrew or think in Semitic terms. Such folk had not been shaped from childhood by the high morality of Judaism. And they were likely to think the word Christ ("anointed") was a proper name meaning the "smeared" or "perfumed one" (which in Greek it could mean), and that kingdom was only synonymous with an earthly state.

Hence, Paul was almost forced to recast the gospel he received in order to make it comprehensible to his audiences and to fit the new situations which he faced. When he spoke about "my gospel" (Romans 2:16; 16:25), he did not mean one that he invented. It was the gospel he had received and developed along fuller and new lines. To be true to the gospel and to the Lord who was working in him through the Holy Spirit, Paul could not simply repeat; he had to proclaim anew. In Paul the gospel was given new shapes. Those shapes were true to the earlier traditions and not entirely unpredictable, if we keep in mind Paul's Old Testament roots and the world in which he labored. But they were destined to become the norms for subsequent centuries.

THE GOSPEL ACCORDING TO ST. PAUL

What is the gospel according to Paul? It is, of course, always the good news about Jesus Christ, crucified and risen (Romans 1:3-4, 9). It reveals God's power at work to save. But first and foremost it takes for Paul the form of "righteousness" or "justification." In the words of the Reformation leaders, the Pauline gospel is the message of "justification by grace alone,

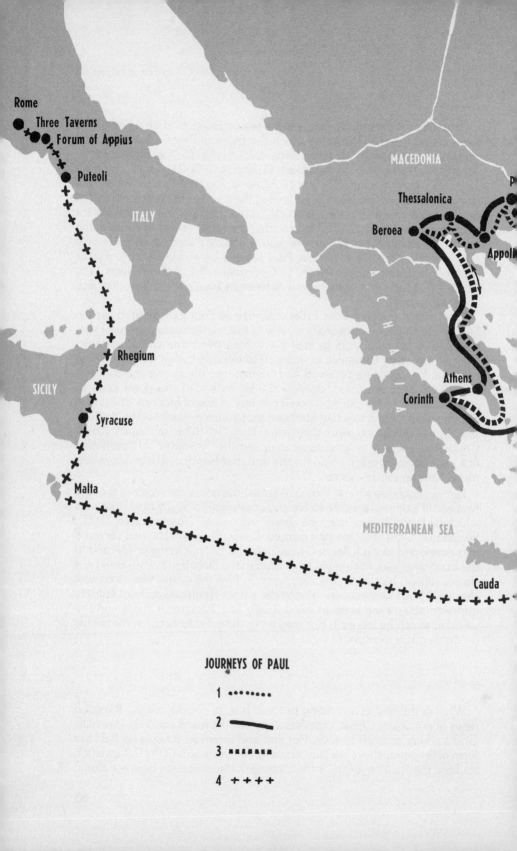

Rome
Three Taverns
Forum of Appius
Puteoli
ITALY

MACEDONIA
Thessalonica
Beroea
Appoll
P

A
C
H
A
I
A

Rhegium

SICILY

Syracuse

Athens
Corinth

Malta

MEDITERRANEAN SEA

Cauda

JOURNEYS OF PAUL

1 ·······
2 ━━━━
3 ▮▮▮▮▮▮
4 ++++

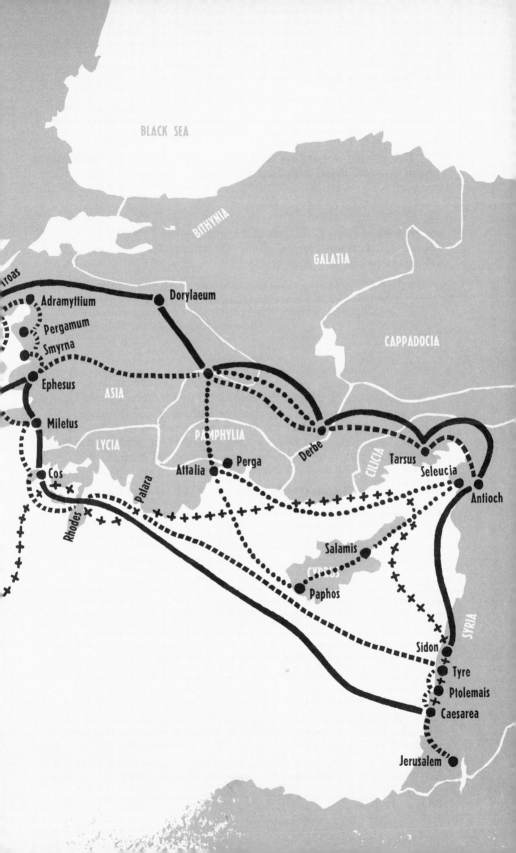

. . . The gospel according to Paul . . . is . . . always the good news about Jesus Christ, crucified and risen.

---

for the sake of Jesus Christ, received through faith." Paul himself makes it the subject of his most formal epistle, the letter to the Christians at Rome. Of the gospel, he wrote,

> It is the power of God for salvation to everyone who has faith, to the Jew first and also to the Greek. For in it the righteousness of God is revealed through faith for faith; as it is written, "He who through faith is righteous shall live." (Romans 1:16–17, quoting Habakkuk 2:4)

The gospel of justification

The gospel has to do with the twin facts "that he [God] himself is righteous and that he justifies him who has faith in Jesus" (Romans 3:26).

It is not easy to translate the Greek words behind "is righteous" and "justifies" and reflect the Hebrew ideas behind them. We have the choice of an Old English root "rightwise" and a Latin root, justitia:

	From Old English	**From Latin**
noun	righteousness	justice
adjective	righteous	just
verb	declare or render righteous	justify
noun	_____	justification

Each set of terms has its connotations and limitations, and translators shift from one to another. Note Romans 3:26 above, where the RSV shifts from "is righteous" to "justifies." *The Living Bible* paraphrases very freely: ". . . makes us ready for heaven—makes us right in God's sight" (1:17); "a different way to heaven" (3:21), and at 3:26 seemingly gives up the terms entirely! We must let the Bible fix the meaning for us. Basically the sense is "a relationship to what is right or just," but accurate English renderings are difficult.

This difficulty comes in part because the relationship is with God. It is "the righteousness *of* God." He sets what is right and just. But "God's righteousness" can mean a quality or attribute which belongs to God, rendered as "justice" at Romans 3:5. Or it can mean the righteousness which is valid before God, that is, the quality in a person which enables him to stand in the judgment by God—as at 2 Corinthians 5:21, perhaps.

Or the same phrase can suggest a righteousness which comes from God and saves or judges or helps the believer to stand in the judgment (see Philippians 3:9).

The matter in Paul's writings is clarified only when we consider the Old Testament background on which he drew. There are many references in the Hebrew scriptures to justice and righteousness as a demand from God for human conduct which conforms to the divine standards (Micah 6:8; Jeremiah 22:3; Psalms 11:7), for "righteousness and justice are the foundation of his [God's] throne" (Psalm 97:2). Yet Israel also knew that it was not the righteousness of the nation nor the just behavior of the people which brought God's blessings on them (Deuteronomy 9:4-6). And so at times we read that God's righteousness means his redemptive activity, his actions which bring righteousness and salvation. This emphasis came to the fore especially during the Exile in the writing of Second Isaiah (see UB I, Chapter 11, p. 137). "Righteousness" became synonymous with God's saving work. Note the parallelism at Isaiah 46:13 when God says:

I bring near my *righteousness*, it shall
   not be far off,
and my *salvation* shall not tarry.

Many modern versions, including RSV, translate what is literally *righteousness* here as *deliverance* (cf. also Isaiah 46:12; 51:6; 59:17; 61:10).

Thus Jewish and early Christian thought knew of "righteousness" or "justification" as an action of God that brought "salvation" (cf. Isaiah 45:8), and "salvation" can be equated with the good news that "your God reigns" (52:7). The links were there for the following equation.

Good tidings = salvation = kingdom = justification

Note also the Old Testament references often have one of two settings. One is a scene in a court of law where God enters into a lawsuit with his people and any hope for vindication rests solely with God (cf. Isaiah 41:1, 21; 43:9; 50:8-9). The other is the judgment of the "Last Day." There is also the hope that "the servant of the Lord" will bring justice/righteousness on that day (Isaiah 42:1-4).

It is likely that long before Paul wrote a line Christians had already begun to speak of God's victory at Easter in terms of the long-expected establishment of God's righteousness. The second line of the little creed or hymn at 1 Timothy 3:16 speaks of Christ as "vindicated in the Spirit." It literally means "justified in the Spirit" so that the Resurrection was a kind of "justification of Jesus" (see KJV and RSV notes). Jesus is therefore "the Righteous One" who was God's servant (Acts 3:14, 26) and who is "our righteousness" (1 Corinthians 1:30). His death and resurrection mean atonement for sins and therefore salvation. So we read in an early Christian slogan quoted by Paul:

87

[We believe in God who] raised from the dead Jesus
our Lord,
who was put to death for our trespasses
and raised for our justification.
(Romans 4:24–25).

People are set right with God not by anything they do but solely through what God has done in Jesus' cross and resurrection.

Perhaps the most elaborate of these early Christian statements about righteousness or justification which Paul inherited is embedded in Romans 3:24–26. It deals with how we are "justified . . . through the redemption which is in Christ Jesus." This was achieved when God sent him and he died on the cross as an "expiation" or bloody offering for sin, as on the Day of Atonement (Leviticus 16:11–16). In the complicated language of Romans 3:24–26, this death showed that although God seemingly passed over sins in former times, he still is righteous: Jesus' blood makes atonement for sins. Paul declares that the cross shows God *is just* and *justifies* those who believe in Jesus.

Here we have the nucleus of Paul's justification-by-grace theme. People are set right with God not by anything they do but solely through what God has done in Jesus' cross and resurrection. Salvation comes when one receives this in faith (Romans 10:9–10). Paul's shorthand expression for this is "the righteousness of God" (Romans 1:17; 3:22).

Three key ideas

It would be hard to overstress three key points as Paul uses them in this version of the gospel, especially in writing Galatians and Romans.

First, in Paul's day Judaism stressed an eventual judgment to be based on the good works people had done in life. Their deeds, particularly praying, fasting, and giving alms in accordance with the law would deliver them. Paul, on the other hand, denied that a person can ever get right with God by what he does (Galatians 2:15–16; Romans 3:20). At this point he is in tune with Jesus' demand for a righteousness beyond man's ability to achieve or the letter of the law to determine (Matthew 5:21–48). What Paul said is that with God's judgment salvation can come only by "grace as a gift" from God (Romans 3:24). Justification is thus by grace.

Second, Judaism saw God's judgment as belonging to the future. It was an experience to come on the day of Yahweh. But for Christians the last times had already begun. Jesus was risen from the dead, the first fruits of what was to come. Therefore Paul moved up the judgment for the

Christian to the present. He declared that the verdict of "justified" at the "last day" has already been pronounced for those who believe. *"Now* the righteousness of God has been manifested" (Romans 3:21, italics added). "Since we are justified by faith, we *have* peace with God" (5:1, italics added). Paul could even speak of the Christian's present situation as "a new creation" and "the day of salvation" (2 Corinthians 5:17—6:2). In this too he was true to Jesus who announced a kingdom breaking in with meaning for here and now.

Third, in conformity with Old Testament usage and Jesus' own demands, Paul also called on justified Christians to live righteously. The "fruits of righteousness" (Philippians 1:11) are part of Christian growth. In the terse slogan at Romans 14:17, the definition of the kingdom as "righteousness and peace and joy" could even mean "righteous actions" by Christians. More likely the reference is to righteousness in the sense of God's saving gift of redemption to us, but we must not lose sight of the ethical aspect which righteousness always includes. Christians are in every way "slaves of righteousness" (Romans 6:18), made what they are by God's righteousness and dedicated to the service of justice.

The gospel as reconciliation

Almost in the same breath that he said the gospel is righteousness, Paul could also say the gospel is reconciliation. This second way of describing

Ancient Philippi where Paul preached his first sermon to the Gentiles.

the good news occurs infrequently. Romans 5 and 2 Corinthians 5 are the chief examples. Both, however, are magnificent examples of presenting the message of God's grace in a gripping way.

During the Reformation, *justification* became the primary term for expressing the gospel; in a similar way, *reconciliation* has commended itself to many as the best way of telling people of our day what God has done.

During the Reformation, *justification* became the primary term for expressing the gospel; in a similar way, *reconciliation* has commended itself to many as the best way of telling people of our day what God has done. So the Presbyterian Confession of 1967 gave it a central place.

Reasons for such a choice are not hard to find. *Justification* is a figure drawn from the court of law and judgment, while *reconciliation* is a term related to "making up" within personal relationships. Justification requires a certain understanding of Old Testament thought, but reconciliation is understood by anyone who has ever suffered even a lover's quarrel. Unlike the words "righteousness" and "justification," the New Testament Greek presents no difficulties in translation. At Romans 5:11 where the KJV had translated, ". . . We have now received the atonement," the Greek phrase can be literally rendered in the RSV "received our reconciliation." The KJV phrase actually means "to be at one with God," to be reconciled. And in an age of anxiety and estrangement, "reconciliation" presents the gospel in meaningful terms. This is especially true when we think of its ethical implications for reconciling the fragments of a world which is divided socially, racially, and economically.

To grasp Paul's meaning, one should read and ponder Romans 5:9–11 and 2 Corinthians 5:17—6:1. The Romans passage paints a picture of a humanity alienated from God, God's "enemies." The great news is that we have been and shall be reconciled to God by the death of his Son, who now also lives to intercede for us (cf. Romans 8:34). That is how "atonement" or "reconciliation" has been achieved, and we can rejoice in it. In 2 Corinthians we find that the whole new life we have as new creations of God is God's work through Christ who reconciles us to himself. Our task is to proclaim to a sinful world, "Be reconciled to God." Ours is a "ministry of reconciliation."

This same theme occurs briefly in two other epistles. Colossians 1:19–22 comments on the phrase in the early Christian hymn, "God was pleased . . . through him [Christ] to reconcile to himself all things" (1:20) by saying that through Jesus' death God has reconciled to himself those who were estranged and hostile. Ephesians 2:16 says the same thing. Jesus' blood reconciled Jews and Gentiles to God. But that epistle goes on to add that the reconciliation was also *between* Jew and Gentile. God's reconciling act created a new humanity or "one new man" on earth "in one body," the church (Ephesians 2:15-16).

Some of these phrases might have been used prior to Paul's day in the Greek-speaking church as ways of describing what the word *Christ* meant. *Reconciliation* is a rare term in the Old Testament. But Paul often gives it a cosmic or universal touch. (cf. Colossians 1:20; Romans 11:15). The fact that the Jews in Paul's day largely rejected the gospel turned him to the Gentiles, thus bringing about "the reconciliation of the world."

Finally, it is noteworthy that the passages which touch on reconciliation so closely link it to justification that the Lutheran Confessions rightly say "justification is reconciliation" (Romans 5:11-16). And when those confessions add that the two terms also imply "forgiveness of sins" (2 Corinthians 5:19), we are brought back to the world of the historical Jesus who said, "Your sins are forgiven." And to be forgiven is to be reconciled.

The gospel as being "in Christ"

In addition to justification and reconciliation, Paul had a third way to present the gospel. It also means to be "in Christ." The phrase "in Christ" or some form of it appears over 160 times in the Pauline writings. There is nothing quite like it in Old Testament religion or even the Gospels and Acts. The closest thing to it is the idea of "in the name [or person] of Jesus" (cf. Acts 2:38; 3:6; Matthew 18:20). Paul himself may have been the one who created this relational concept.

Some uses of the phrase are natural enough. "To be justified in Christ" (Galatians 2:17) can simply mean that we are justified by Christ. So too with Romans 6:3, 11. To have been "baptized into Jesus Christ" and so to be "alive to God in Christ Jesus" need mean nothing unusual. Paul may have used this wording because he did not yet have use of the term *Christian*. The first recorded use of the Greek word *Christian* is at Acts 11:26. Hence to speak of "a man in Christ" may simply denote "a Christian man," as NEB actually renders it at 2 Corinthians 12:2. Thus, "in the flesh and in the Lord" (Philemon 16) means "both as man and as Christian" (NEB).

But the meaning deepens when we begin to explore Paul's use of this and related prepositional phrases and recall that no one in Paul's day would ever think of talking about being "in Moses" or "in Socrates." Putting all these elements together we get the following picture.

At times reference is made to what happened "in Christ Jesus," the historical Jesus who died on the cross (see Romans 3:24; Philippians 2:5). But because he is a living figure, larger than history now, one can also speak of him in the present tense as a figure in whom we live (see Romans 6:11; 1 Corinthians 1:30). This Christ figure is therefore related to the

In this small Syrian town with its Muslim prayer towers, the followers of Jesus were first called Christians. Named Antioch-on-the-Orontes, it is not to be confused with Antioch in Pisidia.

church (1 Corinthians 1:2) with which he so identifies that his body of believers is "the body of Christ" (1 Corinthians 12:27). What is more, this Christ will come again, and so "in Christ shall all be made alive" (1 Corinthians 15:22).

In this way the "in-Christ" theme overarches all Christian existence. As it has been said, "We follow Christ 'in Christ.'" No Christian can afford to overlook this vital relationship with him and with other Christians in the church, his body. 1 Corinthians 12 and Ephesians 1—3 are the great biblical passages on this theme.

The gospel of salvation

Some would suggest a fourth term, *salvation* or *salvation history,* as a means to sum up all of Paul's gospel emphases. He certainly did write of the gospel as "the power of God for salvation" (Romans 1:16) and of "now" as the "day of salvation" (2 Corinthians 6:2). Jesus is the Savior (Philippians 3:20). Christians are those who can say, "We are now justified . . . we shall be saved" (Romans 5:9–10). Justification, reconciliation, life in Christ are stages then which make up "salvation."

Others go further and try to construct a "history of salvation" in Pauline thought. This can be built around certain key figures he mentioned.

Adam, whose trespass brought death to all (Romans 5:14, 18; 1 Corinthians 15:22).

Abraham, who "believed the Lord," and was "reckoned . . . to him as righteousness" (Genesis 15:6) so that Abraham becomes a prototype of justification by faith (Romans 4; Galatians 3).

Moses, who introduced God's Law, which served only to accentuate sin and failed to get humanity right with God (1 Corinthians 10; 2 Corinthians 3).

Christ, who ended the Law of Moses (Romans 10:4) and fulfilled the promise to Abraham (Galatians 3:16).

Christ, who is to come (Romans 5:14), the life-giving Second Adam (1 Corinthians 15:45–49).

Such patterns can be bound up with "covenants" (Romans 9:4; Ephesians 2:12), and Paul could think in terms of two covenants (Galatians 4:24). We can also spot passages where Paul reflected the age-old idea of a "victory of God." This time it was Christ who overwhelmed cosmic, demonic powers (1 Corinthians 2:6–8; Colossians 1:16; 2:15; Ephesians 1:21). But Paul's letters provide no sustained treatment of these themes. Hence, we can only guess whether or not he operated with the sort of sketch of the whole sweep of salvation history some scholars credit him. One such sketch can be seen in the diagram that follows.

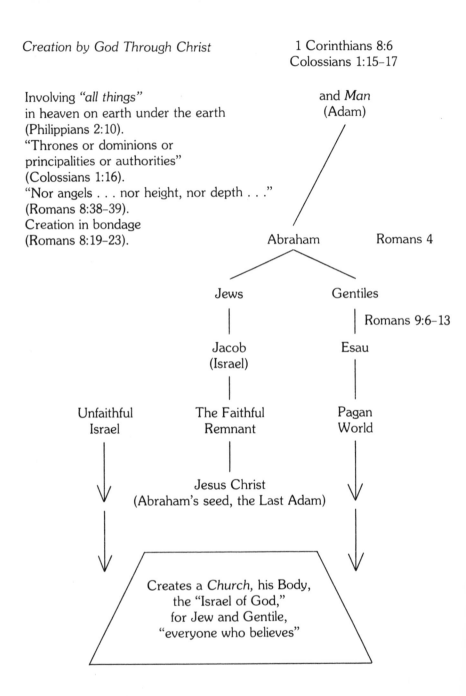

Creation by God Through Christ

1 Corinthians 8:6
Colossians 1:15–17

Involving *"all things"*
in heaven on earth under the earth
(Philippians 2:10).
"Thrones or dominions or
principalities or authorities"
(Colossians 1:16).
"Nor angels . . . nor height, nor depth . . ."
(Romans 8:38–39).
Creation in bondage
(Romans 8:19–23).

and *Man*
(Adam)

Abraham   Romans 4

Jews   Gentiles

Romans 9:6–13

Jacob   Esau
(Israel)

Unfaithful   The Faithful   Pagan
Israel   Remnant   World

Jesus Christ
(Abraham's seed, the Last Adam)

Creates a *Church,* his Body,
the "Israel of God,"
for Jew and Gentile,
"everyone who believes"

Paul's Larger Hope:

The cosmic powers will be
reconciled (Colossians 1:20),
the whole creation freed (Romans 8:21).

"All Israel" and "the full
number of the Gentiles"
will come in (Romans 11:25–32),
creating the "one man," reconciled
(Ephesians 2:14–18).

"all things . . . in heaven and . . . on earth
will be united in Christ (Ephesians 1:10).
"God will be all in all" (1 Corinthians 15:28).

Did Paul think like this? It is possible to spell out his gospel as a salvation history alongside justification, reconciliation, and life "in Christ." Little wonder that with so many ways of stating the gospel Ephesians refers to God's wisdom in all its varied forms. The gospel Paul developed is a many-splendored thing.

References and More Information

Biblical references: Romans 1—8

Metzger, Bruce M. and Isobel M., editors. *The Oxford Concise Concordance.* See the following entries: gift, grace, justify, reconcile, reconciliation, righteousness, santification, sanctify

Richardson, Alan. *A Theological Word Book of the Bible.* New York: The Macmillan Company, 1962. See the following entries: righteous, reconcile, remnant, sanctify

25. Apocalyptic Anew

We have studied apocalyptic writings in the Old Testament (Chapter 18). It may come as no surprise that apocalyptic appears also in the New Testament. However, the surprise may come when we discover that apocalyptic can be used to set forth "good news," and that apocalyptic has a place in the history of the gospel.

Not everyone has found it so. Many of us have struggled hard with apocalyptic literature, especially with that strange last book in the New Testament, the Revelation to John. It alone has given rise to countless aberrations and controversies. We shall note a few of these in Chapter 26, including the story of the ancient "chiliasts," believers in a literal fulfillment of the thousand-year reign cited in Revelation 20:1–6. One commentator on Revelation has said the book either found a man cracked when he began to study it or left him so afterwards! Martin Luther doubted whether the book even belonged in the Bible.

But apocalyptic does belong in the Scriptures, and it does have its place in the history of the good news. But it also can communicate bad news and judgment. As a result, the apocalyptic package should be labeled "Handle with Care."

We have already seen that apocalyptic is one of eight types of literature found in the Bible. The term itself applies to both the writings which unveil God's will and plans for the future and the mood or outlook which underlies such writings. Chapter 18 describes how apocalyptic arose in the days of Israel's exile and persisted during the even drearier times that followed exile. It viewed life in very negative terms and declared that only God's intervention could set life aright. This contrasted strongly with the prophetic view illustrated in Jeremiah's letter to the exiles. While Jeremiah told his hearers to live in the world and come to terms with it, apocalyptic said the world is very evil; look forward to its destruction. Wait passively for the "day of the Lord," fantasize about the day when evil will be wiped out and good rewarded. The key term here is *dualism*. As a description of apocalyptic, it picks up all the contrasts between good and evil, between this age and the age to come, between light and darkness, between God and Satan.

This dualism is to be resolved with ending "the present evil age" (a characteristic Jewish phrase found in Galatians 1:4), and by ushering in to re-

Albrecht Dürer

place it the promised "age to come." In dark times, apocalyptic thus kept alive the hope that God's kingdom would soon come in spite of all present evidence to the contrary.

We have seen that at times Jesus himself couched his message in apocalyptic terms. His words made people feel the inbreaking of God's kingdom, the presence and power of God's kingly rule (see *UB I*, Chapter 1). Yet he could also use apocalyptic imagery for its own sake, that is, for the power of its visionary elements apart from any immediately felt presence of God. He gave the kingdom a future dimension (*UB I*, Chapter 2) and told his hearers that they could look forward to "those days" when the sun would be darkened, the moon would not give its light, the stars would fall, and the "powers in the heavens will be shaken," when the Son of man shall come (Mark 13:24–27). The very fulfillment which Jesus himself brought about created new apocalyptic hopes.

Nowhere is this truer than with his resurrection and the Easter gospel which proclaimed him as living Lord. Any Jew of Jesus' day who heard that someone had been raised from the dead could interpret the event in only one way: the promised general resurrection was at hand and all other events of the "last days" would soon be realized. The Easter experience triggered the hopes that the end was at hand. As a result, the mood of the first Christians must have been one of *enthusiasm* in the technical sense of that word (in the Greek, the word means "to be inspired by God"). They were "full of God" and his Spirit; they expected great things; they boldly witnessed to their "new news"; they shouted the praises of Jesus Christ in cosmic terms. We see them caught up in an apocalyptic fervor which gave birth to new expressions of the gospel.

EARLY APOCALYPTIC EXPRESSIONS OF THE GOSPEL

Consider Peter and his first reported sermon. It is Pentecost. The Holy Spirit has come. Such happenings, he notes, fulfill "what was spoken by the prophet Joel":

> In the last days it shall be, God declares,
> that I will pour out my Spirit. . . .
> (Acts 2:16)

That apocalyptic fulfillment where sons and daughters prophesy and both the old and the young dream dreams (Joel 2:28–32) sets the mood for declaring Jesus "Lord and Christ" (Acts 2:36). Such enthusiasm born of the new faith led to hymning Jesus as Lord of the universe (Colossians 1:15–20 and Philippians 2:5–11). From Creation to expectations about the impending "last times" (see 2 Peter 3), everything could be caught up in a vision of life which owed much to the impact of apocalyptic. We still owe a great debt to this apocalyptic outlook. It mothered a great deal of Christian theology.

The apostle Paul illustrates the point. Before becoming a follower of Jesus, Paul already looked forward to a day of resurrection. He was a Pharisee and the Pharisees believed that God would raise the dead (Acts 23:6). They looked to the day when the good would rise and their evil oppressors would not (see Psalm 16:10; Isaiah 26:13–14, 19). In the Pseudepigrapha, the Apocalypse of 2 Baruch 30:2, 4 (a Jewish writing that dates back to the last part of the first century) declares:

> All who have fallen asleep in the hope of him [the Messiah] shall rise again . . .
> But the souls of the wicked . . . shall then waste away the more.

At times such texts refer only to the resurrection of Israelites, at times to the rising of all people in the world. Sometimes only the resurrection of the good is mentioned; at other times the resurrection of the evil is included. Daniel 12:2, for example, refers to the resurrection of the evil for punishment. The effects of such a series of expectations on such a one as Paul was inevitable. To accept the resurrection of Jesus meant just what was noted earlier. It was to believe that if one man has been raised, the resurrection of all persons must soon follow. This lies behind Paul's phrase about Christ being "the first fruits" of the dead (1 Corinthians 15:23) or "the first-born from the dead" (Colossians 1:18). Jesus is the harbinger of the future harvest. His resurrection guarantees a "good crop" to come. (See 1 Corinthians 15:35–42, where Paul even compares burial to planting a seed which will be raised in glory at God's own "harvest time.")

Apocalyptic, then, helped shape Paul's whole outlook. The basic shaping force was, of course, the gospel that "Christ died for our sins . . . that he was raised" (1 Corinthians 15:3–4) in fulfillment of past promises, that is, in accordance with the Scriptures. But the gospel Paul received also had a future side. It promised that the kingdom was an inheritance yet to be given (1 Corinthians 6:9–11; Galatians 5:19–21). This element of the good news certainly goes back to Jesus. Paul's use of it came to the fore in his encounter with such Christians as those at Corinth who thought the kingdom was already fully realized. For that matter, Paul always had some reservation about making Christianity here and now a finished product. He believed that God always has something yet to come, even though the decisive God-given event, the death and resurrection of Christ, has already taken place.

The New Testament stresses the good news of what has been done but never lets go of the good news for the future.

Thus, as Paul proclaimed the good news, the accent was on justification here and now, on reconciliation with God now, on life in Christ today. But his message had a future dimension. In the same way Paul's sketches of salvation history, the broad sweep of God's plans through past, present, and future, always stretch toward a larger hope in Christ (see Chapter 24 of this book).

In general, the New Testament stresses the good news of what has been done but never lets go of the good news for the future, whether in Jesus' teachings or in Paul's letters. There is always an openness toward what God will yet do. Both these sides of the gospel may employ apocalyptic categories. One side may deal with promises already fulfilled, the present emphasis; the other side promises yet to be fulfilled, the future emphasis. In this way, the line of development for apocalyptic runs from the Old Testament, through Jesus, to Paul and other New Testament writings and on into future centuries. We may diagram it like this:

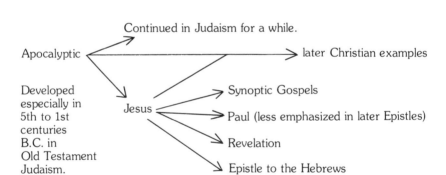

We have already examined Old Testament examples and Jesus' use of apocalyptic. Jewish examples continued to appear at least into the second century A.D., along with many Christian apocalyptic writings. The latter include the Apocalypse of Peter (in the New Testament Apocrypha), the Shepherd of Hermas (in the Apostolic Fathers), and the Apocryphon of John (from among recent finds of Gnostic literature). These do not concern us here.

Apocalyptic material, however, is also in each of the first three Gospels in their so-called little apocalypse sections (see Chapter 21). Hebrews 12:22–29 can be cited as an example from a different sort of book. Note the gift of the kingdom at verse 28 and of a new covenant mediated through Jesus at verse 24, along with the warning that God will shake the heaven and earth "yet once more" in verse 27 (see Haggai 2:6). Christian writers frequently picked up Old Testament passages about apocalyptic signs in the heavens, as at Mark 13:24-25, but they did not always make much of conventional details of apocalyptic writing. For example, Joel 2:28-31 with its portents in the heavens and on earth involving blood and fire and columns of smoke is quoted in Acts 2:17-21. But nowhere in the rest of Acts 2 is there any emphasis upon such details. We have already learned that only once does the New Testament come close to the phrase "second coming" at Hebrews 9:27-28.

In this chapter we shall focus on a few examples of apocalyptic from Paul and from the Book of Revelation.

PAUL'S LETTERS TO
THE THESSALONIANS

When Paul arrived in Thessalonica, just before A.D. 50, he was proclaiming his missionary gospel with its witness to "a true and living God" and his Son, Jesus, risen from the dead, whom we await from heaven, who will deliver us from the wrath or judgment to come (1 Thessalonians 1:9-10). It was an apocalyptic style of preaching. Paul taught a gospel with a future orientation and the Thessalonians came to expect that Christ would come soon and that they themselves would be raised to the full life of the promised kingdom (2:12). But in the few months between the time Paul left the city and his writing the letter we now call 1 Thessalonians, a couple of members of the little congregation must have died. Their deaths raised questions which Paul sought to answer by invoking apocalyptic and citing other materials from the great stores of Scripture and faith.

First Thessalonians 4:13-18 attacks the problem from the point of view of Christian hope (see v. 13). The discussion begins with the basic proclamation (or *kerygma,* to give it the technical Greek term used by theologians), that "Jesus died and rose" (v. 14). Then comes its corollary that believers who died will be brought to life by God through Jesus (v. 14). But when? And how? Paul assures the anxious Thessalonians, that, as a "word of the Lord," the Christians who are alive at Christ's coming will not have any advantage over believers who have died in the interim (v. 15). Or, to put it the other way, the dead will have no advantage over those then alive. Neither group, the living or the dead, will have any head start on the other in getting into the kingdom of God. Then Paul uses vividly apocalyptic terms (verses 16-17). The Lord will descend, the dead in Christ will be raised up, and Christians who are living at the time shall be "caught up together with them in the clouds to meet the Lord in the air."

Here Paul leaves his scenario literally hanging in midair, concluding simply with the comment, "So we shall always be with the Lord," and the admonition to "comfort one another with these words" (vv. 17-18). Note that Paul's use of apocalyptic stops short of any speculation about what things will be like after we are "with the Lord." Our goal is simply to be with him. Paul's purpose was to comfort Christians concerned about who gets into the kingdom first, the living or the dead.

(From this passage in 1 Thessalonians 4 has come the idea of the "rapture" of the saints, also called the "rapture" of the church. "Rapture" is not a biblical term and can not be found in Bible dictionaries. It is used by sectarian groups to refer to the sudden rendezvous of all Christians, dead and living, with the returning Christ. First Thessalonians 4 is the only passage of its kind in the Bible. It has been linked with other passages in order to arrange a series of dramatic events for the end time.)

But some people in Thessalonica did worry about "the times and the seasons" even though Paul had earlier taught them as much as they needed to know. In 1 Thessalonians 5:1-11 he again goes over what he had formerly explained. The tone is markedly catechetical. The entire passage should be read with the background of each unit kept in mind.

5:1 The topic "times and seasons" has already been the subject of instruction.

5:2 "The day of the Lord will come like a thief in the night." See also Jesus' saying at Matthew 24:43-44, with parallels at Luke 12:39-40 and Revelation 3:3.

5:3 Its suddenness and inevitability are like the birth of a child. The analogy to a woman's labor pains is common in the Bible. See Psalm 48:6; Isaiah 13:6-8; John 16:21.

5:4-5 The moral implication is that we ought not be "of the night or darkness" (when thieves operate) but "children of the light and of the day." The comparison between night and light is found both in Scripture and in the Dead Sea Scrolls. See Romans 13:11; Ephesians 5:8-14.

5:6-7 Hence the exhortation to keep watch and be sober. See Romans 13:11-13.

5:8 As "daylight people," arm yourselves with faith, love, and hope. Here Paul employs the imagery of armor. This is taken from Isaiah 59:17, but Paul works in the Christian trilogy of the three leading features of the believer's life; see also 1 Thessalonians 1:3 and 1 Corinthians 13:13.

5:9-10 The grounding and goal for this eschatological admonition lies in God and the salvation he grants through Jesus. Note the use of the little creedal phrase, "Christ, who died for us." See also 1 Thessalonians 4:14 and 1 Corinthians 15:3.

5:10-11 Awake or asleep (referring to the problem of 4:13-18), we belong to the Lord Jesus and our aim is to "live with him." See also 4:17 and Romans 14:8-9 where the argument is similar.

Therefore, not only "comfort one another" (4:18) but "encourage one another" (5:11, the Greek verb is the same in each instance), and "build one another up."

Many modern sectarians must be disappointed to get eleven verses on the "times and seasons" for the rapture and second coming, only to discover that Paul avoids all timetables and speculations. Paul simply says that there is a day of the Lord that will come, but don't try to guess God's plans. Instead, give yourself all the more to living the life of faith, love, and hope. Affirm and help others. Christian existence *now* is what matters, based on the cross and resurrection of Christ in the past and a hope which shapes life in the future for the better. But no speculations, please, about the rapture or the date. Paul is a pastoral theologian, not an apocalyptic alarmist.

There is a day of the Lord to come, but don't try to guess God's plans. Instead, give yourself . . . to living the life of faith, love, and hope.

There is evidence, however, that some in the congregation at Thessalonica wrongly applied Paul's teaching on apocalyptic eschatology. Second Thessalonians 3:6–13 refers to some Christians who were living undisciplined lives of idleness. They were "busybodies instead of busy" (3:11, Moffatt's translation; see also v. 6). Perhaps they had quit their usual jobs and had given up on charitable works in a world they thought was soon to end (see v. 13). Paul's advice was to keep on with the daily round. If such advice went unheeded the "no work, no food" principle was to be invoked (vv. 10, 12). Paul underscores this point in 2 Thessalonians 1. Using a host of apocalyptic details about the judgment to come (vv. 6–10), Paul encouraged the Thessalonians to "fulfill every good resolve and work of faith by his [God's] power." In this way they would be worthy of his calling and kingdom (vv. 5, 11). For the apostle, eschatalogy serves ethical exhortation.

Second Thessalonians 2:1–12 picks up a quite different problem. Here we read of those who were claiming that "the day of the Lord has come" already (2:2; but see also 2 Timothy 2:18, where heretics are teaching the same sort of overly realized eschatology); the kingdom had already arrived in its fullness. Apparently a letter purported to be from Paul had been circulating to this effect. It had been shaking up the Thessalonians about "the coming of our Lord Jesus Christ and our assembling to meet him" (2 Thessalonians 2:1–2). The reference was to the *parousia* (coming) and the gathering of Christians to Christ, though there was nothing about meeting him in midair, as at the "rapture." Here Paul stayed close to the future side of Christianity. He insisted that the day of the Lord will come, but that it hadn't come yet, as anyone could see. And it wouldn't come before certain "signs" were seen. Paul followed this assertion with an elaborate compendium of apocalyptic materials in verses 3-4 and 6-12.

The gist of these materials is that "the rebellion" (cosmic?) and the appearance of a mysterious figure opposed to God variously called "the man of lawlessness" or "son of perdition" (vv. 2:3-4) must come before the day of the Lord. Since these things had not yet occurred, the day of the Lord had not yet come!

The imagery has been interpreted in many ways through the centuries. Each time looks to its own needs. In Paul's day the phrases "he who restrains the mystery of it [lawlessness]" (2:7) and "that which restrains the man of lawlessness" may have referred to the Roman emperor and empire or Paul himself. The former did restrain lawlessness and Paul and his gospel preaching had certain goals to attain before the end could come (compare Mark 13:10). We can choose neither with confidence. Indeed, the writer may have intended to use the phrases without precision. The important thing is that the apostle used extremely apocalyptic language to cool off some extremist eschatological speculations about whether the end had already come. Paul used apocalyptic to accent the primacy of the gospel.

Some supporting evidence

Two illustrations support the argument. One comes from 1 Corinthians 15, the other from Romans 8:19-22.

In discussing the resurrection of the dead at 1 Corinthians 15, Paul began with the article of faith about Jesus' resurrection (vv. 3-5) as the heart of the gospel he received (vv. 1-11). Then he went on to apply it to our own resurrection, which had been in dispute among the Corinthians. First, Paul asserted that the dead do rise (15:12-34). Second, he told how they will rise (15:35-58).

Verses 20-28 provide a rather apocalyptic picture of the "last things" in salvation history. The resurrection of Jesus is the starting point. He is the "first fruits" from the dead. At his *parousia* or second coming, those who belong to Christ will rise. After "the end" (v. 24), following Christ's victory over all cosmic powers and enemies of God (including death), the kingdom will be turned over to God.

Jesus was raised and those in Christ will be raised also . . . Christ's resurrection victory . . . (is) the basis of the hope for our own future life in the kingdom.

Occasionally, commentators have wanted to interpret verse 24 to mean "the end" of the resurrection in the sense of its completion through a raising up of all dead persons, Christians and non-Christians alike. In that case, the order of events in regard to the raising would be

1. Christ (already occurred)
2. "Those who belong to Christ" (at the *parousia*)
3. "The rest" of humankind

Other commentators seek to read into the sequence a period supposed to fit between Christ's "coming" and "the end." This would be a sort of "millennium" or "interim kingdom of Christ" of the kind found in Revelation 20:4-6. The evidence for such a view is flimsy, and the sense of the text is against it. The large majority of scholars see here Paul's usual teaching, that Jesus was raised and those in Christ will be raised also, and say the passage is intended to stress Christ's resurrection victory as the basis of the hope for our own future life in the kingdom. And that is good news, indeed!

Paul's most grand and inclusive passage dealing with such hope is Romans 8:19-22. It describes the whole cosmos groaning in bondage and waiting for a deliverance when we, the children of God, will come into our heritage. It is a glorious expression of concern and hope for the nonhuman and inanimate world. Luther must have had 8:21 in mind when, we are told, he said to his dog, "In heaven you too shall have a golden tail!"

But the climactic words of Paul's paragraph say nothing about our pets or animals or trees or any part of creation except the human part. The ultimate benefit is expressly limited to those "who have the first fruits of the Spirit," that is, to Christians. Paul's interest in citing this immense apocalyptic hope was to encourage Christian people in their present sufferings to live in hope, to meet every day expectantly (vv. 18, 23-25).

Here we have a very important clue for the interpretation of Revelation. Paul used apocalyptic to proclaim the future aspect of the gospel. This future side is expressed as hope and exhortation to persevere in the world with hope and faith and love. This is the clue we can use to test the most apocalyptic of all New Testament books, the Revelation to John.

THE REVELATION TO JOHN

The Book of Revelation has had a checkered history. In the ancient church it suffered from both friends and enemies. Enthusiastic friends were often heretics, like the Montanists, a group who believed that the promised gifts of the Holy Spirit had come in the person of one Montanus, who lived around A.D. 150. Enemies, because they were often in powerful positions, included bishops who vigorously opposed such disruptive forces as those precipitated by believers in the thousand-year reign promised in Revelation 20:4–6. (Such believers are often called "chiliasts," after the Greek word for "thousand." *Millennium* means the same thing and comes from the Latin root.)

Moreover, the contents of Revelation seemed to contradict other parts of the New Testament. The detailed signs of the end, cited, for example, in 8:7–11, seemed to be inconsistent with the teaching that the day of the Lord would come suddenly, "like a thief in the night" (1 Thessalonians 5:2). The book did not win its place in the New Testament canon easily. Luther had great difficulty with it, finding it neither prophetic nor apostolic.

One result of this is the poor transmission of the text. Revelation was less frequently copied by scribes. Hence, its text has been more poorly preserved in comparison with the other books of the New Testament.

It is possible, however, to strip away some of the mystery of the book. A first step is to put the book squarely in its apparent historical setting. The time is about A.D. 95. The Roman emperor Domitian is laying claim to be Lord and God and so bringing himself conflict with the Christian movement. Persecution is inevitable. The writer is one of the persecuted, an exile driven from his homeland for his witness to the kingdom not of Caesar but of God (1:9). His name is John (1:1) and he is living on an island called Patmos off the coast of Turkey. His audience consists of seven representative churches on the mainland (1:11). Although later tradition has identified him with the son of Zebedee, who has also traditionally received credit for the Fourth Gospel, such a conclusion is questionable. For one thing the style of Revelation is entirely different from that of the Fourth Gospel.

A second step is to remind ourselves that Revelation is an apocalypse with all the features of such literature cited at the beginning of this chapter. The faithful are being persecuted by immoral powers and their eyes are turned to God looking for his soon-to-come redemptive intervention. He will bring them life in the new heaven and the new earth. Other features of apocalyptic literature are also abundant: colors (especially gold, red, and white), sounds, dramatic actions, and even numbers. Note the number 666 for the beast at 13:18. This is the mark of all that is sinister, as the number 7 denotes perfection.

A third step is to get an overview of the book's contents. Opinions differ somewhat, but there is general agreement on the basic outline of the book. It has eight large sections:

I.   Prologue (ch. 1)

II. Letters to the Seven Churches in Asia Minor (chs. 2—3)

III. The Vision of Heaven (chs. 4—5)

IV. The Three Series of Judgments (chs. 6—16)

V. The Destruction of Babylon (Rome), Oppressor of God's People (chs. 17:1—19:10)

VI. The Victory of the Word of God, Including Christ's Thousand-Year Reign and Satan's Final Defeat (chs. 19:11—20:10)

VII. The New Heaven and Earth, a New Jerusalem, the City of the Lord God and the Lamb, the Place of Life after the Last Judgment (chs. 20:11—22:5)

VIII. Epilogue, Closing Warnings, Beatitudes, and Exhortations (chs. 22:6—21)

Sections I—IV may need a little more detail.

I. Prologue

A. Title and Introduction (1:1-3)
B. Salutation and praise to the risen Christ (1:4-8)
C. John's vision of the risen Christ (1:9-20)

II. Letters to the Seven Churches

(Two are praised unreservedly, Smyrna and Philadelphia. Three are approved but criticized—Ephesus, Pergamum, and Thyatira. One, at Sardis, is severely rebuked; and the church at Laodicea is utterly condemned.)

III. The Vision of Heaven

A. Vision of God in majesty (4:1-11)
B. Vision of the Lamb and the scroll with seven seals, (5:1-14) (The Lamb, Christ, who was slain to ransom people from every tribe and tongue to make them a kingdom, is the one who opens God's plan for the world and who has carried it out.)

IV. The Three Series of Judgments

7 Seals (Chapter 6)	7 Trumpets (Chapters 8—9)	7 Bowls (plagues) (Chapters 15—16)

1. Conquest (vv. 1-2)
2. War (vv. 3-4)
3. Famine (vv. 5-6)
4. Death (vv. 7-8)
5. Souls crying for judgment (vv. 9-11)
6. Earthquake, with signs in the heavens, the great day of wrath (vv. 12-17)

7 Seals (Chapter 6)	7 Trumpets (Chapters 8—9)	7 Bowls (plagues) (Chapters 15—16)
7. Silence, 8:1	1. Hail, fire on *earth* (8:7)	1. On *earth*, sores on men (16:2)
	2. Fire on the *sea* (8:8)	2. *Sea* becomes like blood (16:4)
	3. *Rivers* poisoned (8:10-11)	3. *Rivers* becomes like blood (16:4)
	4. *Sun,* moon, and stars darkened (8:12)	4. *Sun* scorches men (16:8-9)
	5. Invasion by locusts from the underworld (9:1-12) This is the first woe.	5. Pain, sores, and darkness on the throne of the beast (16:10-11)
	6. Slaughter by four angels from the *Euphrates* and calvary (9:13-19)	6. *Euphrates* River dried up; three demonic spirits (16:12-14)
	7. "The kingdom of the world has become the kingdom of our Lord and of his Christ" (11:15)	7. "It is done"; earthquake, Babylon destroyed (16:17-21; see also chs. 17—18)

As the three series of judgment stand, they give the impression of one disaster following another, with twenty-one steps in all. But note that there is a certain parallelism in parts of the sequences marked by the words in italics. Note, too, that the repetition has the effect of heightening the sense of judgment.

Subthemes and patterns

The total picture is not quite so simple, however. Subthemes are interwoven among the main ones. This is apparent from the fact that only a portion of Chapters 6—16 is used to list the twenty-one judgments.

One subtheme is that of the three "woes" announced by the fifth and (apparently) sixth trumpets. Another has to do with related catastrophes described in Chapters 9:20—11:13. Also in the judgment and terror-bringing category are the dragon and the beast from the sea of Chapter 13.

In all this we face sharply negative imagery. But complicating this structure is the occasional relief afforded by more positive imagery. The author inserts four parenthetical interludes as if to say, "Here's hope amid all the suffering and gore":

1. The marking of the saints with God's seal and their ultimate triumph, Chapter 7.
2. The angel and his scroll (Chapter 10) and the resurrection and exaltation of two martyred witnesses as harbingers of victory (11:1-13).
3. The woman, the child, and the dragon—a way of describing in code Christ's victory for the church (Chapter 12).
4. The Lamb and his redeemed on Mt. Zion (Chapter 14).

Our hope kept alive by those interspersed scenes, we move on to the final outcome set forth in the remainder of Revelation.

The details of this masterful construction never cease to amaze us, even if some, like the "three woes," were not finally worked out. There are many subtle interrelationships. The "mark of the beast" on his followers (13:16-17) is a devilish parody of the seal God places on the forehead of his chosen ones (7:3-4). The "supper of God" in 19:17-21 is a grim counterpart to the Lord's Supper (3:20; 22:17). The bride of the Lamb (21:9) is in contrast to the great harlot (17:1).

Throughout the book there is a general movement from things as they are, such as persecution, apathy, apostasy within the churches, as well as some bright spots of faithful witnessing (Chapters 1—3), to things as they will be in the apocalyptic plan for the future (Chapters 6—12). The link between the present and the future is God and his Son, the Lamb, whose blood redeemed those to be saved. This is depicted in the magnificent visions of Chapters 4—5. God and Christ will bring about the promised victory. Meanwhile his people must stand firm in the faith.

As we have noted, *apocalypse* means "revelation" or "unveiling." The Book of Revelation is an apocalypse not "of John," as we conventionally call it, but "of Jesus Christ." (Note that Paul uses exactly the same phrase found at Revelation 1:1 in his letter at Galatians 1:12.) It is a revelation which God gave to Christ to show to his servants through John (Revelation 1:1-2). While the Book of Revelation conforms to many apocalyptic conventions, it has nonetheless some distinctive features, for it is a Christian apocalypse.

Three features

We note three distinctive features. First, the way the Old Testament is used; second, the emphasis upon Jesus Christ; and third, the inclusion of much liturgical material from the early church in the book.

Revelation is more saturated with Old Testament references than any other book of the New Testament. Of its 404 verses, some 278 have been read to refer in one way or another to the Old Testament. The references are not the formal citations found often in Matthew or in Paul. Rather they are Old Testament ideas and allusions frequently given a new twist that suggests a new meaning. For example, the calamities poured from the bowls of the angels in Chapter 16 remind us of the plagues of Moses' day in Egypt in Exodus 7—10. Boils on man and beast become sores on all men who have the mark of the beast! Locusts, frogs, and water which has been turned to blood are found in both lists.

Of course, the parellel is not exact; there were ten plagues and only seven bowls or vials of wrath. But the parallel is close enough. Decoded, and in terms of biblical theology, it says that as Yahweh defeated Pharaoh he will also through Christ overcome the dragon and his beast. (To let the secret out of the bag, the beast with the seven heads and ten horns in 17:7-14 represents Rome and its emperors, most likely from Augustus to Nero or Domitian.)

Another parallel is at the naming of the site for the last climactic battle, Armageddon (16:16). In Hebrew *Har Megiddon* is the Mount of Megiddo, the site of several decisive battles in Israel's history. These included Josiah's defeat by Pharaoh Neco of Egypt (2 Kings 23:29; see also 9:27; Judges 5:19).

A second feature of Revelation is the way it generally uses the Old Testament to describe Jesus Christ. One might *expect* that such a passage as Revelation 4 with its picture of God upon his throne would draw from the Old Testament, especially Ezekiel 1:26 and Isaiah 6. But we would *not* necessarily expect that the portrait of Jesus in Revelation 5 should also do this. There Jesus is described as "Lion of the tribe of Judah" (see Genesis 49:9), "Root of David" (Isaiah 11:1, 10), and a lamb with seven eyes (Revelation 5:6; Zechariah 4:10). Here is a whole chain of phrases from the Hebrew scriptures!

One also can not escape noticing the number of times Revelation applies to Jesus Christ certain Old Testament phrases formerly used for Yahweh alone. We have already noted the use of "first and last." We can add such things as the almost surrealistic description of Jesus Christ in Revelation 1:12-16. Here we have hair like wool, eyes that are fiery flames, and a voice like the sound of many waters. These were originally Old Testament phrases to describe God (see Daniel 7:9-10; Ezekiel 1:24; 43:2). By such use of Old Testament images, the author of Revelation is making the common confession of the New Testament, "Jesus Christ is Lord."

One final example. At Revelation 19:13 Jesus is described as coming "clad in a robe dipped in blood." This is a reference to Isaiah 63:1-2, where we see God coming from Edom in garments crimson with blood. But there is a new twist. In Isaiah it is the blood of enemies on God's vestments. In Revelation, since Jesus is the one who ransomed us by his blood (1:5 and 5:9), it is his own blood poured out for those who were once enemies that stains his robe. Here we see the Old Testament being used Christologically, that is, to interpret the nature and person of Christ.

The third distinctive feature of Revelation is that it embodies much liturgical material, such as its wealth of hymns. For example, there are songs of the Lamb's worthiness (4:11; 5:9–10). These inspired Horatius Bonar to write:

> Blessing and honor, and glory and power,
> Wisdom, and riches, and strength evermore,
> Give ye to Him who our battle hath won,
> Whose are the kingdom, the crown and the throne.
>   (*SBH* 166)

There are also 15:3–4, a new "Song of Moses" to celebrate God's mighty deeds; and 19:1–3, 6–8, a "Hallelujah Chorus." These hymns likely came out of early Christian worship and were inserted by the author to convey the mood of triumph amid despair—a further Christian touch which departs from the normal pattern of use in apocalyptic.

The seven letters

Beyond such distinctive features, we should also note the collection of letters in Chapters 2—3. Their content and structure owe more to the early Christian form of letters than to the apocalyptic heritage. They also depict the church and speak to it in a remarkably frank way. Each letter has the same structure:

- An address to the church's "angel"—either its pastor, or guardian spirit with God.
- An authoritative assertion—"These words of him who," followed by some appropriate description of Christ.
- The "body" of the letter—praise, exhortation, or reproof for the church in its situation.
- A conclusion—an admonition to give heed and the promise of reward.

In style these letters have nothing in common with the rest of Revelation, but in content they are the same. They address Christians in their current crisis where they are threatened with persecution so great that they may fall away. The letters warn of judgment and encourage hearers to stand firm. They reveal why some of the extreme forms of apocalyptic were needed later on in the book; the churches were in a bad situation; sin and indifference were increasing. Christians needed to hear the full measure of God's message for their day; they had to hear both judgment and grace.

Many think the phrase "Satan's throne" mentioned in Revelation 2:13 refers to the altar and temple of the emperor at Pergamom. The command to worship Emperor Domitian precipitated a crisis for Christians in Asia Minor which led to the writing of the Book of Revelation to encourage them.

Like the three distinctive features noted above, these letters constitute an important clue for assessing the whole Book of Revelation. They help answer the question, What was the author trying to do?

To what end?

In structuring and giving content to this work the writer of Revelation tried above all to preach God's message to a specific situation. The situation was the time and place in which John and the congregations he knew found themselves. Revelation is not a secret plan for shaping subsequent centuries of history. Attempts to apply it to predict current events have regularly failed. Nor is it just a literary garden to be interpreted figuratively to fit our own situations and needs. The book addressed its own day. It dealt with what "soon" must come to pass, the time that was near (1:1,3). Thus, in all probability, it refers to the impending crisis that broke around *A.D.* 95. For Christians in what is modern Turkey that crisis was caused by demands that they worship the Roman emperor Domitian instead of or alongside of Jesus Christ. The recognition of Jesus' absolute lordship was at stake.

In addressing the situation John used the variety of resources at hand. These included the letter form; beatitudes (see 1:3; 14:13; 16:15; 19:9; 20:6; 22:7; and 22:14—the seven promises in the book which begin with "blessed"); the Old Testament; hymnody; apocalyptic from the past; and visions related specifically to John's own situation. The writer wove these all together in artful form to speak to his day. "Stand fast," he was saying, "God will soon intervene."

He was wrong, of course, if one read into his words the prophecy of an immediate end to human history. He was right in saying that Rome would eventually fall, and that God's cause would triumph in the "present" crisis ("present" to his audience). In a crisis time of life, one sees the detail and meaning of current events more sharply, while the long-term perspective may be blurred. The lasting value of Revelation is that it proclaims God's victory in Christ in the face of an imminent and specific danger. "Hold on!" it cries. And time and again in subsequent crises Christians have found strength in both the book and its cryptic imagery.

"Hold on!" and "Stand fast!" may have been the most immediate and urgent messages of the Book of Revelation at its first appearance. Through the years, however, it has also kept its message of "an eternal gospel" (see the vivid summary in 14:6-7). At its heart is the crucified Christ, who is deliverer, judge, and Lord. The book never tires of saying that he has won the victory and will triumph again. The mysterious Chapter 12 describes Jesus' victory in the language of myth. First it is told in terms of a child (Christ), born of a woman (Israel as God's people, 12:1-6), then in terms of a "war in heaven" (12:7-12) where the dragon is bested. But in each case the real victory was won "by the blood of the Lamb" (12:11). That is, it was won at the cross. As for God's people, they will win out in the present struggle with Satan's forces on earth if only they hold true to Christ.

In this version of the gospel, is there any room for "the kingdom"? Decidedly. Good news is several times put in "kingdom" terms. For example, there is the assertion that Christ, by his blood shed on the cross, out of sheer love and to free us from our sins, has "made us a kingdom, priests to his God and Father" (1:6 and 5:10, echoing the hope of Exodus 19:6). John, the author, spoke of sharing with his audience "in Jesus the tribulation and the kingdom and the patient endurance" (1:9). Over against God's kingdom stands that parody of the kingdom with the beast and his earthly emperors. (This does not refer to all governments, but rather to Rome of A.D. 95, where the ruler sought to be worshiped in God's place—see 16:2; 17:12, 17–18.) Yet the apocalypse can triumphantly assert that "Now the kingdom of our God and the authority of his Christ have come, the accuser has been thrown down" (12:10). The message reverberates,

> The kingdom of the world has become the kingdom
>   of our Lord and of his Christ,
> and he shall reign for ever and ever.
> (Revelation 11:15)

He shall reign! That is good news; that is "kingdom" news. Revelation makes the tidings of the Old Testament new (21:5). God reigns, has reigned, and will reign in Christ.

References and More Information

Biblical references: 1 and 2 Thessalonians; Revelation

Metzger, Bruce M. and Isobel M., editors. *The Oxford Concise Concordance.* See the following entry: crown

Richardson, Alan. *A Theological Word Book of the Bible.* New York: The Macmillan Company, 1962. See the following entries: adversary, Antichrist, angel, hell

26. The Gospel as Life, the Writings of John

In the Gospel and Epistles of John we move into a world different from any experienced thus far in Scripture. In John's setting we hear the gospel being proclaimed as eternal life.

True, there are links and associations with other parts of the Bible, but the Johannine writings present us with "the word of life" (1 John 1:1) in a way no other portion of the Bible does. The First Epistle of John was written to "proclaim to you the eternal life which was with the Father and was made manifest to us" (1:2). The Fourth Gospel was written

> That you may believe that Jesus is the Christ, the Son of God, and that believing you may have life in his name.
>
> (John 20:31)

THE FOURTH GOSPEL AND OTHER PARTS OF THE NEW TESTAMENT

Traditionally the Fourth Gospel, the short book we call First John, and the two little notes (Second and Third John) which follow it in the canon have been associated with the Apocalypse of John. This notion rests on the theory that John, "the beloved disciple" and one of the Twelve, wrote them all. But the mood and content of the other Johannine writings are manifestly different from Revelation. John's Gospel and the Epistles nowhere reflect the idea of a series of impending catastrophes marking the imminent end of the world. Contrariwise, they reflect a mood of calm and a Christ who is *always* in command, not just at the *parousia*. The reader's attention is directed inward to the community of believers, rather than to the world raging outside.

We have already seen that the man who wrote Revelation was a Jewish-Christian prophet of considerable authority in the parts of Asia Minor

In telling of the ministry of Jesus on earth, John seems to impart to it something of the glory and power of the risen Lord.

around Ephesus. Later we shall see that identifying "the beloved disciple" with John (the son of Zebedee) as author of the Fourth Gospel poses difficult questions. While there are some themes common to Revelation and other Johannine writings, there are good reasons for emphasizing where and how the two differ in contents. As a result, it is suggested that the Johannine Gospel and Epistles were authored by someone other than John (the seer) who wrote the last book in our New Testament collection.

The Johannine Gospel and lessons also have affinities with Paul and Paul's Easter Gospel (chs. 23—24). All these writings emphasize the death of Jesus and his lordly status. Indeed, in telling of the ministry of Jesus on earth John seems to impart to it something of the glory and power of the risen Lord. John's Gospel could be called a meditation on Paul's words, "You know the grace of our Lord Jesus Christ, that though he was rich, yet for your sake he became poor, so that, by his poverty you might become rich" (2 Corinthians 8:9). Such an experience with Jesus Christ is mirrored in the words, "From his fulness have we all received, grace upon grace" (John 1:16). Yet Jesus strides through the pages of this Gospel as anything but "poor" and in "poverty." For while he can be weary and thirsty (John 4:6-7) and can even cry with people who are hurting from the tragedies of life (11:35), Jesus remains in command of every situation (cf. 4:10, 13-14, 16-19, 25-26). His own death is no tragedy, but life laid down according to God's will and plan (10:17-18). Jesus carries his own cross to the crucifixion; he does not need someone to help him (19:17; see Mark 15:21). His death marks a triumph because God's work for him on earth is successfully finished (19:30).

There are other features in John which have their counterparts in Paul besides this emphasis on the crucified and risen Lord. On the other hand, it is also true that in John certain key Pauline ideas are either totally absent or only weakly accented. *Justification* is an example; "righteousness" or "justification" occurs only in 16:8-11. "Grace" occurs only in the passage already noted above (1:14, 16-17). "Faith" is mentioned as a noun only at 1 John 5:4, although the verb "believe" is rather common. "Justification by grace through faith" is simply not a Johannine way of expressing the good news. One might counter by saying one of Paul's alternate expressions, to be "in Christ," is echoed in Jesus' words about the disciples as branches who must abide in Christ, the true vine (John 15). All in all, however, the Johannine writings betray no direct dependence upon Paul. They represent a different way of expressing the gospel.

Finally, there are also links between the Fourth Gospel and the first three. But once more in John, we are in a world which differs from that of Mark, Matthew, and Luke. All four of the first books in the New Testament are Gospels insofar as literary type is concerned, but John is a different sort of Gospel. It is separated from the first three in structure, style, and themes. This does not mean that John and the Synoptics do not often overlap; they do. They share an emphasis on the passion of Jesus, for example, and report some of the same miracle stories, such as the Feeding of the Five Thousand (John 6:1-15; see Mark 6:32-44, Matthew 14:13-21, Luke 9:10-17). This is, of course, the only miracle story in all four Gospels. Yet, even when relating the same event, John does it in his own way as a witness to Jesus for his own day.

A geographical outline of John

Nowhere can this difference from the Synoptics be seen more clearly than in the basic outline for the story of Jesus. The structure in Mark and Matthew is familiar to us: an introduction, with some nativity stories in Matthew; Jesus' ministry in Galilee; the journey to Jerusalem; and Jesus' passion, death, and resurrection. After an introduction and infancy material Luke's sequence is Galilee, the Samaritan or travel section, and Jerusalem. Thus, the Synoptic Gospels tell of Jesus going to Jerusalem only once during his ministry. That was to attend the festival of the Passover, at which time he was put to death. (Luke 2:41-51 adds Jesus' visit to Jerusalem as a twelve-year-old boy.)

John has a completely different outline. It places Jesus in Jerusalem four or five times in the course of his ministry, so that there is a shuttling back and forth between Judea and Galilee. What is more, all of these trips to Jerusalem seem times to coincide with a Jewish festival and what Jesus says or does at times even relates to that festival.

The following passages should be consulted to see John's geographical outline:

John 2:13, 23—*Passover.*

After an initial ministry in Galilee (1:43—2:12), Jesus cleanses the Temple in Jerusalem and engages in conversation with a member of the Sanhedrin named Nicodemus. This is followed by a period of baptizing in Judea (3:22; 4:1-2) and of witnessing in Samaria (4:3-45) before the return to Galilee (4:46-54).

John 5:1—*"A feast of the Jews," Passover, or Tabernacles, or New Year's in the fall.*

Jesus heals a lame man at the Pool of Bethzatha (or Bethesda, or Bethsaida—manuscripts have differing spellings) near the Sheep Gate in northeast Jerusalem. After a challenge to his authority to heal on the Sabbath, we find him at 6:1 again by the Sea of Galilee. The Feeding of the Five Thousand is now narrated. This, together with a discourse by Jesus on the bread of life, is dated with a reference indicating that "the Passover, the feast of the Jews was at hand" (6:4). This would be the second Passover during Jesus' public ministry.

John 7:2—*"Tabernacles," a feast in September or October.*

After first saying he will not go to Jerusalem for the feast, Jesus does go up in private (7:10) and on the last day of Tabernacles speaks publicly about

117

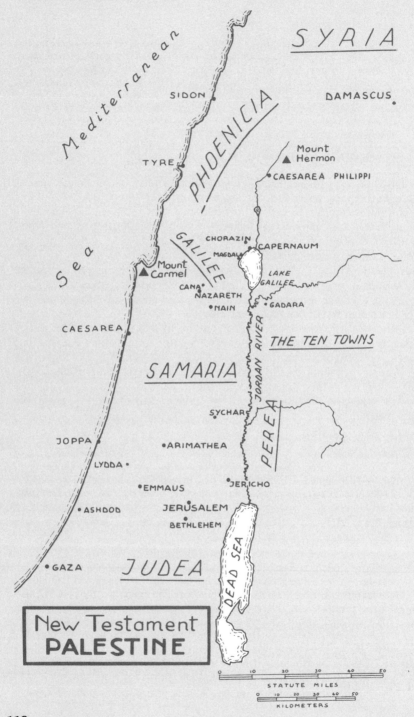

New Testament PALESTINE

"living water" (7:38). In spite of opposition from the chief priests and Pharisees (7:45–52), he speaks about himself as the light of the world (John 8:12). He heals a blind man while still in Jerusalem (John 9), as the reference to the Pool of Saloam (which is in the southeast section of the city) proves (9:7). The discourse about the Good Shepherd (John 10) also takes place in Jerusalem, since no change of scene is indicated. John 10:22 finds Jesus still in Jerusalem at the time of the December feast which commemorated the rededication of the Temple in 164 B.C. (That was the year Judas Maccabeus had recovered it from the Syrians. The feast is known today as Hanukkah.) Because the Jews sought to stone Jesus for his claims to be "one" with the Father (10:30), he withdrew "across the Jordan" to the other side of the river into Perea, near where John had baptized (10:40; see 3:23).

John 11:55; 12:1; 13:1; 18:28; 19:31—"the Passover of the Jews."

After a visit to Bethany, east of Jerusalem, where Jesus raised from the dead Lazarus, the brother of Mary and Martha (John 11), Jesus withdrew to a wilderness "town called Ephraim" (11:54). We do not know the location of Ephraim though the reference may be to a place some fifteen miles northeast of Jerusalem. Jesus returns to Bethany (John 12), makes his entry into Jerusalem hailed by festival crowds (12:12), but is crucified before the citizens of Jerusalem eat their Passover meal. According to John, Jesus died just as the Passover lambs were being slain at the Temple for the feast that night. He is thus, literally, "the Lamb of God" (1:29).

This analysis of John yields four festival trips to Jerusalem. If we count Tabernacles (7:2) and the Feast of the Dedication (10:22) separately, the number is five. We can add two more instances to this pattern of "Galilee

---

John gives us a witness to Jesus as the Christ in a way that is all-encompassing.

---

to Jerusalem." Jesus first appears on the scene in his ministry in Judea (1:19 refers to Jerusalem) and then moves to Galilee (1:43). The Resurrection takes place in Jerusalem, of course (John 20), but in John 21 we read about how Jesus also revealed himself in Galilee.

A theological outline

Overlaying this geographical outline we can place a "theological outline." Like the Synoptics and Paul, the Fourth Gospel is concerned with proclaiming who Jesus is. It does so within the following structure:

Prologue about the Word, Jesus Christ (1:1–18)
The Work of Jesus as he comes from the Father, into the world (1:19—12:50)

As John tells of it, the ministry of Jesus stresses his deeds or miracles as "signs," and his words in terms of long discourses.

The Return of Jesus to the Father (13:1—20:29)

The Passion-Resurrection account is expanded with discourses, especially about the Holy Spirit, "the Paraclete," who is to come when Jesus goes away.

Epilogue in Galilee (John 21)

A post-Resurrection appearance in Galilee after the three in Jerusalem.

This sequence witnesses to Jesus

- As one who was with God, who came.
- As a man of flesh (1:14) among us in Galilee and Jerusalem.
- As the Son of man who is lifted up (3:14) not only upon a cross but also in exaltation.
- As the lord who goes away but sends the Paraclete or Comforter in in his stead (16:7).

In all this, John's Gospel is often closer to the thought of the early church and Paul than to the picture of Jesus in the Synoptics.

This way of looking at Jesus within the broad spectrum of God's glory has over the centuries become a favorite of many Christians. John gives us a witness to Jesus as the Christ in a way that is all-encompassing. But alert readers frequently spot problems in relating John to the other Gospels. For example, was Jesus' public ministry a single year long or did it cover three Passovers or more (as in John)? When was the Temple cleansing? Was the raising of Lazarus (John 11) the event which sealed his fate, or was it Jesus' disputes with the scribes and Pharisees (Mark 2:1-3, 6; 11:27-12:40)? John and the Synoptics leave different impressions at these points.

Distinctive styles in John

John differs from the other Gospels in style, too. In the Synoptics Jesus speaks in parables or in short memorable saying. His words often reflect a parallelism typical of Hebrew poetry or the repetitiveness found in the Old Testament Wisdom literature, as, for example, the Antitheses of the Sermon on the Mount (Matthew 5:21-48). Only occasionally does Jesus give a lengthy speech (Mark 13; the five discourses in Matthew). But even these collections of teaching differ in tone from the discourses in John (see 3:5-21; 5:17-47; 6:22-59; 10; 15). In John, Jesus' tone seems more elevated, less earthy. His words soar majestically; they strike some as almost mystical. He is a revealer in the way the Jesus of the Synoptics never is.

The distinctive style of the Fourth Gospel can be illustrated in several ways. For example, in Mark, Matthew, and Luke, "parables" are Jesus' characteristic way of communication. In John's Gospel the term *parable* is never used. Not only is the word missing, but in John there are no examples of story-analogies which begin, "The kingdom of God is like. . . ."

Another unusual element in John is the use of the Hebrew word *amen*. In the Synoptics Jesus uses it as no one else of his day. He inserted it at the start of an important declaration: "Amen, I say to you . . .," usually rendered in English, "Verily" or "Truly I say to you . . ." (see Mark 10:15; Matthew 6:2). In John, however, the Hebrew word is regularly doubled, "Amen, amen, I say to you . . ." (see 1:51; 3:3: "Truly, truly . . ."). We can therefore recognize as characteristically "Johannine" in style the discourse in Chapter 10. It begins, "Truly, truly, I say to you . . ." and goes on to develop a "figure" about the sheepfold and the true or good shepherd.

(Read John 10:1-6, then 7-18. This passage is as close as John's Gospel comes to a parable. To many readers it seems to verge on being an allegory, a figure of speech in which details take on literal significance. Thus Jesus is the Good Shepherd; the sheepfold is the church, his flock; the thieves and robbers are false teachers which threaten it.

Jesus' discourses about himself

This last example introduces us to the fact that in the Fourth Gospel Jesus talks about himself and his work in a way never found in the Synoptics. In the other Gospels Jesus proclaims the kingship of God above all else. In John he speaks of himself and his mission in relation to the Father.

Nowhere in John is this emphasis on who Jesus is clearer than in the "I am" sayings. Seven times he speaks of himself in the first person singular.

"I am the bread of life" (6:35).
"I am the light of the world" (8:12).
"I am the door [of the sheep]" (10:7).
"I am the good shepherd" (10:11, 14).
"I am the resurrection and the life" (11:25).
"I am the way and the truth and the life" (14:6).
"I am the true vine" (15:1, 5).

To some extent these amazing statements are paralleled in the Synoptics by assertions beginning with "I came. . . ." See, for example, Mark 2:17, "I came not to call the righteous but sinners." Or Mark 10:45: "The Son of man [I] also came not to be served but to serve." But there is no parallel in the Synoptics to the seven claims Jesus makes for himself which appear in John.

There are also nine places where Jesus employs "I am" without any word following the verb. Sometimes this means nothing more than "It is I."

When walking on the water, Jesus approached the frightened disciples in their storm-tossed boat, saying "It is I [literally, 'I am']; do not be afraid" (John 6:20). Such usage can be found in the Synoptics (see Mark 6:50). But when Jesus says in John's Gospel, "Truly, truly I say to you, before Abraham was, I am" (John 8:58), we seem to hear him declare that he antedates Abraham and takes priority over him. But there is more.

In the Old Testament the "I-am" formula is used to identify Yahweh. In Exodus 3:14–15, for example, we are told that God told Moses to say to Israel, "I AM has sent me to you." The phrase is especially prominent in Deutero-Isaiah: "I, I am the Lord"; "I am He"; "I am God" (Isaiah 43:11; 41:4; 43:13). Against this background Jesus is claiming to be God when he says, "You will die in your sins unless you believe that I am he" (John 8:24). See also 8:28 and 13:19 with reference to his passion. A striking incident is found in 18:5–6. Here what seems to be a simple act of identifying himself to the soldiers who come to arrest him in the garden of Gethsemane by saying "I am he" has a deeper significance. It causes the soldiers to fall back in awe.

. . . In John . . . Jesus reveals that he is "the revealer of God."

Putting all these observations together we see in John a series of "revelation discourses" in which Jesus reveals that he is the revealer of God. The way this is done often follows a pattern. An "I am" saying is followed by a call and some promise or warning. Two passages illustrate this pattern.

Chapter 10	Chapter 15
"I am the door . . . the good shepherd" (10:7, 9, 11, 14) is followed by a warning against false shepherds (10:8, 10, 12–13) and then a promise, "I lay down my life for the sheep . . . there shall be one flock, one shepherd" (10:15–16).	"I am the true vine, and my Father is the vinedresser" (15:1) is followed by the warning, "If a man does not abide in me, he is cast forth as a branch and withers" (15:6).
	In a similar manner, 15:2 provides the warning, "Every branch of mine that bears no fruit, he takes away," and the promise at 15:7, "If you abide in me . . . ask whatever you will, and it shall be done for you."

These discourses in John emphasize the divine nature of Christ. (John may even call him "the only God." See the textual variant to 1:18 in the RSV footnote or in the NEB note, "himself God, the nearest to the

Father's heart." This reading is supported by the recently discovered earliest papyrus copies of John.) The climax of the Fourth Gospel comes when Thomas confesses Jesus as "My Lord and my God!" (20:28).

John's discourses also mix warning and promise in presenting the message of the Son who reveals the Father. These warnings and promises are quite different in style from the teachings of Jesus in the other Gospels.

Kingdom of God and life

John's themes also differ considerably from those of the Synoptics. John is the Gospel of life, proclaiming Jesus as the one who reveals the Father. This raises questions about the kingdom theme which was so prominent in the Synoptics as the central message of Jesus.

The kingdom theme does not disappear in John, but it is muted. Consider, for example, Jesus' nighttime conversation with Nicodemus in John 3. Nicodemus was a ruler of the Jews, a member of their Sanhedrin (or governing council). He eventually became enough of a disciple to support Jesus in council sessions (7:50–52), and he helped to bury him (19:39). In their conversation Jesus tells Nicodemus in one of his "amen sayings" that "unless one is born anew [the Greek can also mean "from above" or from God], he cannot see the kingdom of God" (3:3). Two verses later Jesus enlarges upon the thought:

> Truly, truly, I say to you, unless one is born of water and the Spirit [a reference to Baptism], he cannot enter the kingdom of God.
>
> (John 3:5)

These verses remind one of the Synoptic sayings about entering the kingdom (see Matthew 18:3). John 3:3 is a call for radical renewal. The call is expanded in 3:5 and tells how one is born "from above" or "anew" by water Baptism and the gift of the Spirit which accompanies it. That ties in with John's report that Jesus' disciples engaged in water Baptism (3:22, 4:2). But when we add the Johannine teaching that the Spirit would not be given until Jesus was "glorified" (i.e., on the cross; see 7:39), then 3:5 seems to refer to a baptism accompanied by the coming of the Holy Spirit to the early church after Easter. These verses show that the Johannine community or church viewed Baptism as grounds for perceiving and entering into God's kingdom. But they are the only two places in John where the phrase "kingdom of God" occurs.

The one other possible cluster of references to the kingdom can be found in Chapter 18, the report of Jesus' trial before Pilate. Jesus speaks of "my kingship" three times, meaning a "kingdom of Jesus Christ." There are several references to Jesus as a king. Pilate asks, "Are you the King of the Jews?" (18:33). Jesus eventually answers, "My kingship is not of this world; if my kingship were of this world, my servants would fight . . ., but my kingship is not from the world" (18:36). When Pilate muses, "So you are a king?" Jesus does not quite accept his use of the term. "You say that I am a king. For this was I born, and for this I have come into the world, to bear witness to the truth. Everyone who is of the truth hears my voice" (18:37). Pilate breaks off the dialogue with his famous retort, "What is truth?" and goes back to calling Jesus "the King of the Jews."

Scattered throughout the Fourth Gospel are other references to Jesus as a king (1:49; 12:13, 15; 19:3, 12, 14–15, 19, 21) and even to an attempt to make him an earthly king by force (6:15). Jesus rejects this effort.

Underlying these passages is a feeling that Jesus truly is a king, but not in a human, physical sense. Pilate misunderstands, as do all who want to make Jesus an earthly ruler. We find enough references in John to convince us that the writer knew the Synoptic theme of the kingdom of God and that he was also aware of the tendency after Easter to give Jesus a share in God's kingship. But ultimately John shied away from kingdom language just as Paul and the preachers did in the Book of Acts. "Kingdom of God" or the idea of "King Jesus" could be too easily misunderstood as a worldly, political rule like Caesar's (see Acts 17:7 and the material under "Jesus and God's Kingship," in Chapter 22 of this book).

John simply uses as a basic term to express the gospel "life" or "eternal life." Equating life with the kingdom as the center of the gospel is an accent we already found in the Synoptic Gospels. Note the parallelism in the following warning to disciples in Mark 9:43–47 (italics added).

> If your hand causes you to sin, cut it off; it is better for you to *enter life* maimed than with two hands to go to hell, to the unquenchable fire. And if your foot causes you to sin, cut it off; it is better for you to *enter life* lame than with two feet to be thrown into hell. And if your eye causes you to sin, pluck it out; it is better for you to enter the *kingdom of God* with one eye than with two eyes to be thrown into hell.

The kingdom of God means life. Martin Luther captured this connection in the *Small Catechism* when he wrote that the purpose of Christ's work is that we "may . . . live under him in his kingdom."[1]

Miracles and signs

What of the miracles in John? Though fewer in number than in the Synoptics, the Fourth Gospel does contain miracle stories. For one thing, the Johannine accounts often heighten the miraculous. Thus, when Lazarus is raised he has already been dead for four days and not just a few minutes, as in the case of Jairus' daughter. Structurally, John's miracles are often tied to discourses. For example, five thousand are fed, and Jesus says, "I am the bread of life" (John 6). A man born blind is healed, and we hear, "I am the light of the world" (John 8:12).

Rather interesting and even puzzling is the fact that the miracle stories seem to reflect a trace of yet a third outline in addition to the geographical and theological outlines already described. After the report of the wedding feast at Cana, where Jesus changed a hundred gallons of water into wine, it is said, "This, the first of his signs, Jesus did at Cana in Galilee, and manifested his glory" (2:11). Then after the healing of an official's son, it is stated at 4:54, "This was now the second sign that Jesus did. . . ." Yet, in between these two signs are references to other "signs" or miracles (see 2:23; 3:2).

Many students of John think there was once a source which presented seven miracles done by Jesus as "signs." The word *sign* is, of course, an Old Testament term for the wonders wrought during the Exodus and Israel's pilgrimage in the wilderness (see Deuteronomy 7:19; 34:11). "The Book of Signs" is a title suggested for this supposed collection, the contents of which are now incorporated into John's Gospel. A possible list of these miracle/signs would include:

1. The transformation of the water at the wedding feast at Cana (2:1-11);

2. The healing of the official's son (4:46-54);

3. The healing of the lame man at the Pool of Bethzatha (5:1-9);

4. The Feeding of the Five Thousand (6:1-13);

5. Jesus walking on the waters of the Sea of Galilee (6:16-21);

6. The restoration of sight to the man born blind (9:1-34);

7. The raising of Lazarus (11:1-44).

Stories 2, 4, and 5 have counterparts in the Synoptics. Matthew 8:5-13 and Luke 7:1-10 are analogous to healing the official's son; and Mark 6:32-44 and 6:45-52 are parallel passages for the Feeding of the Five Thousand and Jesus' walking on water. Therefore, these stories need not have come from a "signs" source. Some would suggest that the miraculous draught of fishes also belongs on the list (21:2-14; see also Luke 5:1-11).

Regardless of where these stories came from or their exact number, the important issue is the concept of "signs." It is obviously a significant term in John (see 6:2; 7:3; 11:47; and, above all, 20:30, which is part of the concluding paragraph, assuming John 21 is an epilogue added later). John 20:30 sums up the purpose:

> . . . Jesus did many other signs . . . which are not written in this book; but these are written [the seven, or however many John includes] that you may believe. . . .

The purpose of the signs was to promote faith. That is the very thing said about the first sign at Cana: "This, the first of his signs, Jesus did . . ., and his disciples believed in him." There are occasions when miracles pro-

Siloam is the pool to which Jesus sent the blind man for healing (John 9:7). It was a large reserv[
that drew its water through a subterranean canal. Hence the Hebrew name *Sender* originally giv[
to the canal. The evangelist seems to find in it a cryptic allusion to Jesus, often referred to as "the c[
sent."

mote faith, and through the ages many Christians have respected them because they thought a miracle would produce faith.

It is therefore all the more surprising that with all this emphasis on signs as promoting faith, we find in the story of the official's son the statement by Jesus, "Unless you see signs and wonders you will not believe" (4:48). The important thing in this story is that the father believed Jesus' promise before the healing happened. He first believed, then went on his way (4:49–53). Here is not only an implied criticism of faith based on miracles, but the approval of faith based on nothing but promise. The Gospel of John is indeed an unusual book.

WHEN, WHY, AND BY WHOM

The Fourth Gospel has long been an enigma to those who study it. Who could have written it? When? Why? Fifty years ago there was a tendency to date it well into the second century. In 1935, the publication of a tiny papyrus fragment from Egypt showing parts of five verses from John helped to push the time back considerably.

Beginning with the 1800s many Bible students tended to identify John with the world of the Greeks and Romans rather than of the Jews. The book contained metaphysical discourses and referred to Jesus as the Logos or Word (1:1–18). Such ideas belonged not to Judaism but to the kind of philosophy that was taught at Alexandria in Egypt. Still, there were those who continued to champion an Old Testament Jewish background for the writing. They said the Logos theme could have roots in Proverbs 8:22–31 where Wisdom is personified and assists in creation. Such a view found support in the Dead Sea Scrolls, and it became reasonable to think of the Fourth Gospel in a Palestinian background. Some even argued that John was the earliest of the four Gospels to be composed!

Present-day studies generally agree that John's Gospel appeared in the 90s somewhere in the eastern Mediterranean, perhaps Syria or Asia Minor, as the product of a long process of theological refinement of materials about Jesus. Very likely the situation in which the Gospel was put together included certain definite opponents or options to Christianity. One such opponent appears in John's references to "the Jews." Unlike the Synoptics, the Fourth Gospel does not pick out just the Pharisees or Sadducees as opponents of Jesus but lumps them together as "the Jews" (see 9:22; 19:7, 12, 14, 16–17). It is even said, "They will put you out of the synagogues and kill you in God's name" (16:2). Such statements no doubt reflect the split between the Jewish synagogue and the Christian community that occurred in John's own day.

Because John's statement about such divisions has all too frequently been used to fuel anti-Semitism among Christians, it is well to bear in mind the suggestion that John is using the term "the Jews" to refer to all representatives of unbelief. It embraces anyone who hesitates and doubts the claims of Jesus Christ. Thus, at 6:41 "the Jews" who murmur against Jesus as "the living bread which came down from heaven" (6:51) are to be equated with "the people" (6:24) or "multitude" (6:2) who misunderstand Jesus, and ultimately with "the world" which lies in darkness and unbelief (1:5, 10).

The Gospel of John may also have been directed against the Gnostics (from the Greek word for "knowing") who stressed knowledge, especially a particular breed of Gnostics called the Docetists. They taught that Jesus had merely seemed to be a man and that the Lord had not come in human form. That may be why the Fourth Gospel stresses the verb *to know* but never the noun *knowledge,* and why it insists Jesus came in the flesh (John 1:14; 1 John 4:2).

Similarly, at least elements in the book may have been directed against those who still thought John the Baptist was God's Promised One. In a way the Synoptics never do, John's Gospel makes the Baptist a witness to Jesus (1:19–27). But he is a witness who must diminish while Jesus increases in importance (3:22–30). Only Jesus the Christ matters; the forerunner pales to insignificance once he has played his appointed role.

Who was responsible for the Fourth Gospel? Clearly a community of Christian believers is involved: "We have beheld his glory," they testify (1:14; see 1:16 and also 19:35 as part of their certification of the truth). It would be a community such as speaks in First John, "That which we have seen and heard we proclaim also to you" (1:3). But there is also involved here an individual called "the disciple 'whom Jesus loved' " (13:23–25; 19:26–27; 20:2–8). He is also referred to as "another" or "the other disciple" (18:15–16) and "the other disciple, the one whom Jesus loved" (20:2; see also 20:3, 8). He is the only disciple who was an eyewitness at the cross. "He who saw it has borne witness—his testimony is true, and he [God? Christ? The evangelist? Or, most likely, the eyewitness?] knows that he tells the truth (19:35).

The first twenty chapters of John provide no further help in identifying this beloved disciple. Some have speculated that he represents an idealization of discipleship; he was one who was close to Jesus, who stayed with him at the cross, who was quick to believe the Resurrection (20:8). Others suggest that Lazarus was the man since he was the one person of whom it is said in this Gospel that Jesus loved him (11:3).

Chapter 21 offers a few additional clues. At 21:7 the beloved disciple is the first in Galilee to recognize the risen Jesus and call him Lord. Of the seven followers mentioned in the scene by the lake—Simon Peter, Thomas, Nathanael, "the sons of Zebedee [James and John], and two others of his disciples" (21:2)—he is not Simon Peter, for the beloved disciple is distinguished from him (21:15–20, 22). Apparently this disciple whom Jesus loved is now dead (21:23). But the community (21:24, "we know") certifies that he is the one who bore witness and wrote the things in the Fourth Gospel. Tradition has identified him with John the son of Zebedee.

Modern scholars have spent much time pulling together all this evidence. The final product of their work stands something like this. There was an eyewitness. He may have been one of the Twelve, perhaps even John the son of Zebedee. This person knew a great deal about Jesus and his teachings and passed on what he knew. Over the decades his message was cast and recast by him and his pupils in certain distinctive patterns. Under the Spirit of the living Lord, these traditions about Jesus took on even deeper significance. Those who preached them and meditated upon them finally put them in the form of a Gospel built around a series of signs. Later the evangelist or a final editor revised this story of Jesus to meet further needs of a new day. By the end of the first century a finished Gospel reflected the testimony of the community of Christians who treasured the Johannine witness (1:14; 19:35).

LIFE AND LOVE

However John's Gospel came about, its message is clear. It proclaims a new life from God given through Jesus Christ. When the Johannine writings call it "eternal life," they do not mean existence strung out everlastingly. It is rather a life marked by a God-endowed quality characteristic of the new age of which apocalyptists dreamed. It is life marked by God's promises fulfilled. According to John, the good news is that this life of the coming age is available not just at the resurrection of the dead in the future (John 5:28–29), but *now*. The implication is that one has already gone through the judgment and been accepted by God (5:24). This life means knowing God and Jesus Christ whom God sent here and now (17:3). It means to be born from above (3:3, 5) by Baptism and to abide in God and Christ. It assumes that what people call "life" in the world is merely existence, even a kind of death (5:24). Christians are people who know that they "have passed out of death into life" (1 John 3:14). The gift of God is eternal life in Jesus Christ. If we spell *life* with a capital *L*, that distinguishes it from all other forms of "mere living."

First John adds that "regeneration," to be "born anew" (John 3:7), lies at the start of this process. Note how often the verb *born (of God)* is used (1 John 4:7; 5:4, 18). Rebirth through Baptism makes one a child of God but never in isolation. The stress is on fellowship with other Christians as well as with God (1 John 1:4, 7). Indeed, family fellowship in God's community is essential. In this fellowship even "born-again believers" continue to sin (1 John 1:8–10). Perfection awaits the future fulfillment at the parousia: "We are God's children now; it does not yet appear what we shall be, but we know that when he [Christ] appears we shall be like him

(1 John 3:2). But the call is to live Christlike loving lives, to become what one already is, a child of God, to live without continuing to sin all the time. (This is what the Greek of 3:6-9 and 5:18 implies, and the way TEV translates: "Whoever is a child of God does not continue to sin," 3:9).

A changed person, though not yet perfect, a sinner who abides in Christ—such is the portrait of the Christian seen in the Johannine writings. So powerful is this concept that people sometimes have misread John as saying the very substance of one's being is changed by the new birth and that "in . . . regeneration God creates . . . a new man in such a way that the substance and essence of the Old Adam . . . are completely destroyed."[2] This is the view the Lutheran Confessions rejected in the Formula of Concord, Solid Declaration II, 81. John says that the tendency to be a murderer like Cain or to close one's heart to people in need (3:11-18) is always threatening to break out in us. So, even as they abide in Christ, God's people need the "new commandment" (John 13:34) to remind them to keep on loving one another; love must be in deed and truth (1 John 3:18). Regeneration and renewal are moral matters and the writer never tires of urging love in things great and small (1 John 3:16-17). One writer has even suggested that First John is constructed around three everyday tests for life—righteousness or doing right, loving, and believing.

THE HOLY SPIRIT

What emboldened the Johannine writer or writers to speak so confidently in Jesus' name? What helped them to take teachings that went back to Jesus' days on earth, to amplify them, and to preach them in new situations? The answer lies in a final theme in the Fourth Gospel, the Holy Spirit or, in John's terms, "the Paraclete."

. . . The Spirit became the power for Christian life and witness in the face of persecution . . . and for all our experiences of sorrow and joy and prayer.

For John, "God is spirit" (4:24). "Life" is a work of the Spirit (6:63). Rebirth comes through the Spirit (3:5-8). Here the Fourth Gospel reflects the experience of the early church as seen in Paul and Acts more than the historical Jesus in the first three Gospels. But the five "Paraclete sayings" in John 14—16 go beyond anything to be found in either Paul or the other Gospels.

The term *paraclete* literally means someone "called to the side of" a person to bring help. As a result, the term could be used to designate a lawyer in a court case. Hence the translation "advocate" in the NEB, at John 14:16. Less legalistic is the synonym "Counselor" (RSV, 14:26). More consoling is the old King James Version's "Comforter" (14:26). Others have used the translation "Helper" (TEV) or "the one who is coming to stand by you" (Phillips).

The First Epistle of John uses this almost untranslatable term in designating Jesus as our "advocate with the Father" (2:1), one pleading our case with God in heaven. The Fourth Gospel, however, employs this word to identify the Holy Spirit as God's advocate or spokesperson with us. Five short statements unparalleled in the other Gospels describe the Spirit's functions.

The father will give you the Spirit of truth to be with you (14:15-17).

He will "teach you all things and bring to your remembrance all that I have said to you" (14:25-26).

He will bear witness to Jesus with you who are witnesses (15:26-27).

Jesus must go away before the Spirit can come to carry out a mission of setting the world in order with respect to sin, righteousness, and judgment (16:5-11).

This Spirit will guide you into all truth, glorifying Jesus and taking what is from Jesus and declaring it to you (16:12-15).

This Spirit/Paraclete who takes the place of Jesus when he departs is also a personal indwelling presence. When first granted on Easter Day by the risen Christ (20:22), the Spirit became the power for Christian life and witness in the face of persecution (15:26—16:4) and for all our experiences of sorrow and joy and prayer (16:16-24).

This Spirit or Christ figure who lives within the Christian community has, among other things, three significant characteristics in Johannine thought.

First, the Paraclete takes Jesus' teaching and develops it to meet new needs (16:14). Not new revelations but that which was once revealed in Jesus of Nazareth is now carried to new heights. The best example is the Fourth Gospel itself; it is the Paraclete's taking, in Jesus' words, "what is mine and declaring it to you."

Second, the Spirit is John's answer to the question of a second coming of Jesus. The Johannine writings still include such future events as the parousia, resurrection of the dead, and judgment (1 John 3:2; John 5:28-29). But the stronger emphasis is that "another Paraclete" like Jesus has already come. With the Spirit present, one need not worry about a parousia as the apocalyptists did.

Third, at 14:15-21 where we read of the coming of a Paraclete whom the world cannot see or know, yet bringing life and love to disciples who keep the commandments, we are coming close to a Johannine version of the kingdom of God. Such a kingdom is realized here and now in the Spirit.

There is much to explore in John's lush, verdant world. Different, deep, endearing—the good news according to the Johannine Gospel and Epistles is like a river appropriate for a child to wade in and for an elephant to swim in. Yet at its heart it remains the truth we have long known and treasured.

> God loved the world so much he gave his only Son, so that everyone who believes in him may not die but have eternal life.
>
> (John 3:16, TEV)
>
> The testimony is this: God has given us eternal life.
>
> (1 John 5:11)
>
> We have seen and tell others. . . .
>
> (1 John 4:14)

Do you?

References and More Information

1. *The Small Catechism by Martin Luther, in Contemporary English,* p. 12.
2. Formula of Concord, Solid Declaration, Article II, 81, from *The Book of Concord,* trans. Theodore G. Tappert (Philadelphia: Muhlenberg Press, 1959), pp. 536–537.

Biblical references: John, 1 John

Metzger, Bruce M. and Isobel M., editors. *The Oxford Concise Concordance.* See the following entries: born, life

Richardson, Alan. *A Theological Word Book of the Bible.* New York: The Macmillan Company, 1962. See the following entries: light, birth

27. Living "in Christ": Family, Church, Society, World

The Johannine message impels us, in light of God's love for us in Christ, to a life of Christian living (John 3:16; 1 John 4:11). Christians are to "love not the world" (1 John 2:15) but one another, totally, sharing their goods and giving of themselves (1 John 3:16–17). Rooted in the true vine Jesus Christ, his disciples are to bear "much fruit" (John 15:1–9).

The gospel message of Paul also calls on all brothers and sisters in the faith to present themselves in living, sacrificial service to others in the world. This is their response to God's mercies shown above all in Jesus and his cross. They are not to be conformed to a world which is passing away (Romans 12:1–2; see also 1 Corinthians 7:31) but attuned to God's promised age to come (1 Corinthians 2:9–10), an age already upon believers where not death but life is at work (2 Corinthians 5:17; see also 4:10–12). Christians are therefore to love and "do good to all, especially to those who are of the household of faith" (Galatians 6:10). There is to be "fruit produced by the Holy Spirit," virtues in which their lives are to abound (Galatians 5:22–23); they are to express love in dozens of practical ways each day (Romans 12:9–21).

This emphasis on Christian living existed in the early church from the outset. It appeared among the churches addressed by Paul, in the Johannine community, among congregations facing persecution in Asia Minor and Italy, and within the groups of disciples in Jerusalem and Galilee. Almost every New Testament writing shows an ethical concern for personal conduct, family life, church fellowship, and actions in society and the world of the day. The followers of Jesus Christ—justified, forgiven, hoping in God's promises—had to work out what "life in Christ" meant as citizens or slaves in Caesar's empire, as a minority group in Palestine, or as tiny enclaves scattered among the cities of the Gentile world.

Those "in Christ" knew they possessed a living Lord whose word touched upon them every moment of life. But how were they to live and act in a hostile world? The world often had its own contrary styles of life that denied the Christians' faith and questioned their practices as folly or as fantasy inherited from a Jewish God called Yahweh. To carry out the will of Yahweh and express the lordship of Jesus Christ in daily life was one of the toughest assignments the early Christians had. Nor is the task any easier in our day.

SOME DIFFICULTIES

Bible study does not always include this area of New Testament morality or ethics. Indeed, there are reasons for avoi ing it. The relevant passages are often scattered. This leads to treating them in isolation apart from the context the New Testament writer has given them. More practically, one suspects people often react with less than burning interest here because they assume they already "know all about it." They may think what Scripture says about sexual morality or divorce is "old hat" or too old-fashioned. Or they say yawning, "Another lesson on love," assuming that they know everything the Bible has to say on the topic. Actually, to define *love* without an explanation of what the Bible means by it can become a matter of merely reinforcing our own human, secular impressions and experiences. A particular menace for Lutheran Evangelicals is the tendency to take the isolated Bible verses and make of them a new code of law. On the other hand, to say, "Love or perish," may be literally true in some cases and good psychological advice, but it threatens to turn the response of loving into a means for seeking to earn salvation.

A further difficulty in studying what the New Testament includes under "life in Christ" is the great variety of material and emphases. Some documents, like the Epistle of James, seem to make few references to Christ, while others abound in Christocentric passages. While James stands closer to wisdom tradition, Paul draws his inspiration more directly from the impact on life of Christ as crucified and risen Lord. Each document addresses a specific situation and tries to apply the gospel to it. But this very variety of settings makes it hard for us to systematize New Testament teaching about Christian living.

Of course, the same holds true for us today as we seek to be Christian in a wide range of situations.

A related problem is how to relate expectations about the end of the world to ethical actions. Paul's two letters to the Thessalonians were written with the expectation that Christ was coming soon. He could appeal to a very rigorous life. One could sustain it for the short time before "the end" arrived. Paul even has been interpreted at times as advising Christians to avoid marriage because "the appointed time has grown very short" (1 Corinthians 7:8, 29, 32–35). Yet the Pauline writings also provide wholesome advice on the relations between husbands and wives (Ephesians 5:21–33) and in Ephesians the *parousia* is barely mentioned at all.

Even the social-economic-political situation varies from book to book in the New Testament. The Book of Revelation confronts a scene of impending persecution. The world is a place of evil ruled by Satan and soon to pass away. The government is a menace to faith. On the other hand, Luke deliberately shows Roman governmental officials in the best light, especially in Acts. Or, again, James condemns the rich (see 5:1–6; 2:17), but Luke reflects a positive attitude toward the well-to-do. Patches of the New Testament sound downright revolutionist (see Luke 1:51–53; Acts 5:29); other sections can be read as an appeal to support the *status quo* (1 Peter 2:17). The writers of 1 and 2 Timothy and Titus took great pains to describe details about living in church and society and so may seem solidly middle class. Some might even say "bourgeois" or "square."

All this suggests that we must take seriously the variety of settings in which the New Testament deals with life in Christ. Life shaped by the Lord Jesus can take many forms. Christian life-styles in the early church varied. This was not only because of the situation in which the gospel was being applied and lived or the type of eschatology being taught, but also because of what each convert brought to his new existence. A bourgeois Christianity became inevitable as middle-class people embraced the faith. So it is in the Lutheran Church in America today. To be "middle class" is not salvation in itself or a barrier to being saved but a milieu in which one practices his faith within the structures of society. In the early church eschatologies which related to ethics were bound to wax and wane as conditions heightened expectation that Jesus would come soon or the hope for a fulfillment took new forms. Faith had to come to terms with the need for order for life and the world. Hence, such mundane things as how to care for "real widows" and regulate possible cases of fraud required a place on the church's agenda (see 1 Timothy 5:3–16). As Christian faith came to new self-understandings in the many worlds where Christians lived, it had to deal with such realities as government, family, church, and social life.

In discovering how our ancestors in the faith worked out their life and witness, we may find the gospel imperatives which still hold for us and the ways of working out our witness in life, different as our conditions may be.

We can uncover how Christian life and witness manifested themselves by looking at some resources available to the first Christians. These include theological emphases from the gospel. We can also examine a few specific passages to find out how their ethical patterns for "doing the truth" of the gospel work out in certain New Testament writings. In discovering how our ancestors in the faith worked out their life and witness, we may find the gospel imperatives which still hold for us the ways of working out our witness in life, different as our conditions may be.

135

DIVINE DIRECTIVES FROM THE GOSPEL

Jesus Christ

At the heart of any Christian endeavor to live in Christ is the vibrant, vital experience of a living Lord. Jesus of Nazareth, who ministered in Galilee and Judea before his death, was now alive and reigned as Lord. He was an influence, a presence, a means to life for all his followers.

We dare not underestimate the impact of this Resurrection faith upon Christian behavior. Sir Edwyn Hoskyns, famous teacher at Cambridge University, always began his lectures on New Testament ethics with the remark, "We shall begin, of course, with the passages about the Resurrection." That Jesus lives and rules as one's Lord is the starting point for working out one's manner of life. "It is no longer I who live, but Christ who lives in me," wrote Paul (Galatians 2:20).

Thus, Jesus is the agent of the new life; he mediates it. Paul rarely speaks of being "in God." Much more commonly he talks of being "in Christ." Seldom does he refer to "Christ in us." Much more often it is a matter of our being "in Christ." This is not to say that something of Christ is in each one of us but rather that by Baptism we individuals are united in him, in his body the church, and are caught up into his purposes. John's Gospel says it similarly. "Abide in me, and I in you" (plural), Jesus says (15:4). The Johannine writings continue in a way Paul does not, to tell of the mutual indwelling of the Father and the Son and of believers in both of them (see John 17:21). In describing the life imparted by the Word, the First Epistle of John goes even further with this emphasis that "he who abides in love abides in God" (4:16).

Yet this Jesus who relates people to God in an abiding way is not only the means "that we might live through him" (1 John 4:9); he is also a model for the life to which God would lead us. That Jesus Christ became such a pattern was almost inevitable. John pointed out that no one had ever seen God. But in that the Son had made him known, the Son became an expression of what God the Father is like (John 1:18; see also Hebrews 1:3). We know self-giving love as an expression of divine care because Christ laid down his life for us (1 John 3:16).

The imitation of Christ

A term Paul uses to indicate this role of Jesus as example of the heart of God is "imitation." Paul says, "Be imitators . . . of Christ" (1 Corinthians 11:1). It is a term which often worries Lutheran Christians, especially when it is linked with persons offered as models to be imitated, as when Paul says, "Imitate me" (1 Corinthians 4:16). Even more daring is the imitation of God (Ephesians 5:1). We sense the danger of thinking too highly of ourselves and making other humans into saviors and idols.

Yet Paul does address baptized, believing Christians with such expressions. If we are careful to hear what he really says, the dangers diminish, and "imitation" becomes an earthly way of spelling out the divine intent for human life. For one thing, when Paul speaks of Jesus Christ in this way he is not saying there are such things as mannerisms or pious practices that we should duplicate. Rather, he holds up as example the preexistent Christ, along with the way in the spirit of sacrifice Jesus gave himself to the cross. Read again Philippians 2:5–11, and note what is said about the "mind of Christ" which is to control our relations with each other. Humility and not conceit, a willingness to forego rank in order to serve, are characteristics of Christ's obedience commended to us. Recall also in 2 Corinthians 8:9 Paul's appeal for generosity in putting together a gift of grace through relief funds: "You know the grace of our Lord Jesus Christ, that though he was rich, yet for your sake he became poor, so that by his poverty you might become rich." Moreover, when the apostle urges others to imitate himself, it is always with reference to the way he seeks to imitate Christ, who in turn is a reflection of God. Note the progression.

1. Paul (1 Corinthians 11:1)
2. Christ (1 Corinthians 11:1; see also 1 Thessalonians 1:6–7)
3. God (Ephesians 5:1)

To reverse the sequence, where it is written, "Be imitators of God" (Ephesians 5:1), the context is ethical ("walk in love," 5:2), and the real example is Christ. If Paul is spoken of at all in an exemplary way, it is in connection with how he reflects and radiates his Lord (see especially 1 Thessalonians 1:6). When Paul says, "Become as I am" (Galatians 4:12), he refers to his freedom and humility in Christ, his freedom to be a servant for his Lord. When Paul dares to hold up as example for the Corinthians "my ways in Christ" (1 Corinthians 4:17), the reference may be to what he teaches but is more likely to his Christian "way of life." When we look up 1 Corinthians 4:9–13, this turns out to be the practice of returning blessing for insults and patience for hostility, a style of life scorned and labeled as weak in the world's eyes. What Paul captured here is the spirit of Jesus Christ. The apostle found it in what Jesus taught and in the way Jesus had conducted himself during his passion (see Matthew 5:39, 44).

Indeed, the whole idea of imitation, whether of Paul, Christ, God, or of other Christians and whole churches, is nothing more nor less than further development of Jesus' words about a heavenly Father whose sun and rain are gifts to all alike and whom we are to emulate. Can we really imitate his beneficence and love which we so lavishly receive? Such imitation is the ethical application of God's love. "Freely ye have received, freely give" (Matthew 10:8, KJV). Dare we today point to a God-like generosity in our lives as testimony to the divine love we know? The New

Testament suggests, as a test of Christianity, the degree to which our lives reflect the generosity we have experienced.

The will of God

In discussing the living Christ and imitation of God's love, we are faced with God and his will as a further factor in shaping Christian life. Just as the Father and his Son could not be separated in considering love, neither can one separate love and the will of God. For God's will is a loving force, and it is spoken of in the New Testament not only in connection with a plan to save humankind, but also with regard to believers' daily lives.

"Thy will be done," Jesus prayed (Matthew 6:10). In the Fourth Gospel he speaks again and again of doing "the will of him who sent me" (John 4:34; 5:30; 6:38–40). According to Paul, God's will is to save humankind through Christ (Galatians 1:4). God's "purpose," to use another word, was effected through the cross. It comes to us in a call for acceptance; behind it is an eternal purpose of love. Read Romans 8:28–39 in this light. God's will and purpose uphold us amid all changes and difficulties in this world and the judgment to come!

For Paul this meant in particular that his call to be an apostle and to witness for Christ was by the will of God (see 1 Corinthians 1:1 and the opening verses of 2 Corinthians and Ephesians). As a missionary, he learned to say, imitating Jesus, "The will of the Lord be done" (Acts 21:14; see Mark 14:36). He regularly qualified his plans with "by God's will" (Romans 1:10; 15:32; 1 Corinthians 4:19). The most famous example of so conditioning Christian conduct is in the Epistle of James. Read James 4:13–17 for a warning to affluent businessmen who plot out lives and forget God may have other plans. Here is Jesus' story about the foolish farmer who left God out of his plans (Luke 12:16–20) restated to include the advice to qualify future plans with the phrase that pious Christians for centuries have appended to their statements: D.V., *Deo volente*, "God being willing."

Curiously, in his personal plans, Paul sometimes speaks without any reference to divine guidance or God's will, even at points where some people might expect it. Note, for example, his hope to go to Spain to preach (Romans 15:24) and his travel plans from Corinth (1 Corinthians 16:1–9). Here he was quite flexible. He had plans and dreams, but God's program for him was not "cast in concrete," as if he had "telegrams from heaven" about every stop on the way. Nowhere is this openness more beautifully expressed than when Paul contemplates possible death while in prison.

> For me to live is Christ, and to die is gain. . . . My desire is to depart and to be with Christ, for that is far better. But to remain in the flesh is more necessary on your account.
>
> (Philippians 1:21, 23–24; read also vv. 19–26.)

Paul regarded his call and the overall work of salvation as God's will. That colored what he did day by day. But even this great apostle did not claim divine guidance for every little detail. Indeed, some of his big decisions seem to reflect common-sense planning, not revelations.

Paul recognized, however, an important area of human activity where God's will does dominate the ethical aspects of daily life. He never relaxed his emphasis on the growth of Christians toward what God wills. Some aspects of God's will and the application of it to daily life can be seen in the following verses:

"Let your minds be renewed, your whole self transformed, in order that you may discern God's will, that is, that you may know what is good and acceptable, and the perfect thing to do in life" (Romans 12:2, author's translation). This rich verse has been paraphrased here, on the basis of several English translations of the Greek, but keeping key RSV terms. *Good* means that which is morally good and beneficial to others (see 1 Thessalonians 5:15). *Acceptable* means "pleasing to the Lord" (see Ephesians 5:10). *Perfect* means "mature," as Phillips renders it (see Colossians 4:12), not just good intentions but carrying a thing through consistently. The sentiments of this verse are put into the form of a prayer for Christian growth at Colossians 1:9–10 which should be made the content of our prayers for others.

The will of God for us is to "rejoice always, pray constantly, give thanks in all circumstances" (1 Thessalonians 5:16–17).

"This is the will of God [for you], your sanctification" (1 Thessalonians 4:3).

The content of 1 Thessalonians 4:3–8 deals with sex life and is very much down-to-earth. The King James translation was sometimes subject to misinterpretation with regard to "each one" knowing "how to possess his vessel in sanctification and honour." Modern translators suggest it deals with taking a wife (RSV). The passage as a whole ties God's will to abstaining from immorality (v. 3) and acting in holiness in marriage (vv. 4–5) and, indeed, all of life, including business affairs (v. 6, RSV footnote). God's will is not only a commanding, but also an enabling force. God gives his Holy Spirit "to you" (v. 8) as power.

The Spirit who sanctified

That brings us to the role of the Holy Spirit in ethics as part of the early church's emerging Trinitarian faith. Christ the Lord is agent and model for the new life. God's will abides in and shapes that life. But the Spirit also plays a part. In the New Testament the Holy Spirit is regularly seen as the force and person linking the risen Christ to those in the world who believe.

139

Recall 1 Thessalonians 5:8 or the works of the Paraclete described in the Fourth Gospel (John 16:13; 14:26).

The particular function of the Spirit in connection with living ethically is sanctification; God's will is "your sanctification" (1 Thessalonians 4:3). Sanctification is something Christians pray God has done, is doing, and will continue to do with them. Paul must often have prayed for his people, "May the God of peace himself sanctify you wholly" (1 Thessalonians 5:23). Christians rejoice because God chose them "to be saved, through sanctification by the Spirit and belief in the truth" (2 Thessalonians 2:13).

Holiness

But what does "sanctification" mean? The root idea in the Old Testament implies both "holiness" and "separateness." What was sanctified to Yahweh was separated from ordinary usage and dedicated to God. It passed from the realm of the profane to that of the holy. Thus for Israel there were holy times like the Sabbath, holy places like the "Holy Land" of Palestine and the "Holy City" Jerusalem (see Exodus 15:13; Isaiah 11:9, 52:1), and holy persons. These last included the priests (Exodus 30:30-32) and all Israelites (Exodus 19:6; Leviticus 19:1-2). There were also holy objects like the Temple and its sanctuary and its offerings (Exodus 30:25-29; Leviticus 27:30-33). Behind it all stood, of course, a holy God Yahweh (Exodus 6:1-5), the "Holy One of Israel" (Isaiah 5:19). He demanded, "You shall be holy, for I the Lord your God am holy" (Leviticus 19:2). So Leviticus 19 provides a holiness code dealing with the various aspects of life among the people of God.

The New Testament does not drop this passion for sanctification or holiness as part of God's will for his people. Even after Christ's coming, God's will is still "your sanctification." The divine command still holds, "You shall be holy, for I am holy." 1 Peter 1:15-16 quotes the command and applies the consequences. Those in Christ are "a royal priesthood" just as Israel had been (1 Peter 2:9; see Exodus 19:6). So it is that all Christians addressed in an apostolic letter are called "saints," literally "holy ones" (Romans 1:7; 1 Corinthians 1:2). If we ask where this sainthood or holiness or sanctification comes from, the answer is Christ. He is "the source of our life, whom God made . . . our righteousness and sanctification . . ." (1 Corinthians 1:30). If we ask how this comes about, the answer is through Baptism which unites us to Christ. In 1 Corinthians 6:11, Paul simply reflects what was common belief by the year A.D. 50:

> You were washed,
> You were sanctified,
> You were justified
> in the name of the Lord Jesus Christ
> and in the Spirit of our God.

(The NEB translates here, "You have been through the purifying waters; you have been dedicated to God and justified . . ."). Here Baptism, as the point of entry into Christian life, is described as justification and sanctification, the possessions of every Christian.

If sanctification (holiness) is a gift every believer has been granted, it can also be the basis for an appeal to live in sanctified (holy, God-pleasing) ways. Romans 6:19-22, rings out the appeal for Christians to yield themselves "to righteousness for sanctification" ("a holy life," NEB; "for holy purposes," TEV). The imperative of sanctification follows hard upon the indicative of God's gift.

But the New Testament is realistically aware that although sanctification is God's gift and is something we are called to and toward, it is never fully accomplished in this life. One prays for it all through life, knows it comes from God, and learns to expect it fully at the future *parousia* (1 Thessalonians 5:23-24). "Perfection" comes only at the end. Part of the good news, however, is that "he who sanctifies" (Jesus Christ) and "those who are being sanctified" (we and all who believe in Christ) are one family and that by his suffering Christ has already "perfected for all times" and sanctified a people who strive for holiness (Hebrews 2:10-11; 10:10; 12:14; 13:12).

It should be added that in spite of all the parallel Old Testament passages found in the New, the two also differ considerably. In New Testament times, no longer are holy times like the Sabbath exalted over human needs (see Mark 2:27-28; Colossians 2:16). The concept of a "holy city" or Holy Land is replaced by the idea that the whole earth is the Lord's— indeed the Lord Jesus Christ's (1 Corinthians 10:26; Colossians 1:16). The Jerusalem Temple is of little consequence, for there is a universal church (Ephesians 2:19-22). The priesthood is universalized, too, to include all Christians in their ministry of service and witness (1 Peter 2:4-9). What really matters are the holy God, his holy servant Jesus (Acts 4:27), and Christ's people dedicated to sanctification.

To sum up we can chart the New Testament Trinitarian dynamics for ethical behavior.

The living Lord, Jesus Christ
    Agent and model for "imitation."
God the Father
    His "will" calls and guides.
The Holy Spirit
    For enabling and deepening a life of "sanctification."

But the New Testament provides even more resources which helped shape the ethics of the early church.

ADDITIONAL HELPS

The early Christians faced all sorts of daily dilemmas. What should be their responses to the state and society? Should they eat foods which bore the stamp of pagan gods? Did holiness demand that they should stay away from such social activities as banquets at a Corinthian temple (1 Corinthians 8; 10:14–30)? They needed more guidance than that provided by the dynamics of the gospel.

Very often they found such direction in the Hebrew scriptures, interpreted to fit new situations and in light of Christ. We have already seen how the New Testament could quote from the Old Testament with respect to the will of God and holiness. Thus Paul cites the four commandments dealing with relations to one's neighbor as incumbent upon Christians (Romans 13:9). The whole law of God is seen as summed up in the words of Leviticus 19:18, "You shall love your neighbor as yourself" (also Galatians 5:14). Even on matters of church discipline, the Old Testament can be quoted to undergird an argument (see 1 Corinthians 5:13, which cites Deuteronomy 17:7).

Of course the Old Testament scriptures came to the early church accompanied by centuries of Jewish interpretations, especially from the rabbis. The New Testament contains reflections of some of these Jewish insights. Jesus himself at times accepted them and at other times spurned them. At Mark 10:2–9, for example, we hear Jesus teach that a man should not divorce his wife. Here is expressed the viewpoint of Rabbi Shammai rather than that of the more liberal Rabbi Hillel in interpreting the law in Deuteronomy 24:1–4. When Paul said that the body is a temple of the Holy Spirit, which we receive from God (1 Corinthians 6:19) or that we are to bear God's "image" (1 Corinthians 15:49; Colossians 3:10), he echoed a thought found in Hillel: "See what care is bestowed on the statue of the emperor to keep it bright and clean; ought we not likewise keep God's image, our body, clean and free from every blemish?"[1]

Teachings developed to help converts to Judaism apply the Old Testament law to their situation as Gentiles now following the God of Israel also must have been helpful many times to Christians. *Halacha* (or how one "walks" before the Lord in life), the name used for such teachings, is even reflected in some places in the Epistles, such as Romans 6:4; 13:13. (Some modern translations may render it "conduct ourselves," however.)

A fourth source of help for first-century Christians lay in the ethical teachings of the Greco-Roman world. Each of the various philosophical movements of the day had its canons of morality. Sometimes the New Testament writers picked up this wisdom from the contemporary world and quoted it as an aid to Christians. For example, 1 Corinthians 15:33 endorses a line from the play *Thais* by the Attic Greek poet Menander, "Bad company destroys good morals." When Philippians 4:8 talks about "whatever is true, whatever is honorable, whatever is just, whatever is of good report . . ," as the object for Christian meditation, it is using stock phrases of Stoic philosophy. The occasional emphasis on "what nature teaches" (1 Corinthians 11:14; Romans 2:14-15) also reflects good Stoicism.

Particularly striking as examples of teachings about morality picked up from the world of the early Christians are the list of vices and virtues and tables of household duties. The latter are collections of instructions for household groups such as husbands and wives, parents and children, or masters and slaves. Appropriate admonitions are given for each group. (See, for example, Colossians 3:18—4:1; Ephesians 5:22—6:9; and 1 Peter 2:18—3:7). The virtues-and-vices lists consist of a string of good and bad practices about which Christians are encouraged or warned.

Such lists and tables often reflect contemporary morality which had been more or less Christianized and offered to guide believers in their walk in the world. We could call them sanctified common sense viewed from the perspective of the Christian dynamics.

Galatians 5:19-23 provides a good illustration. Paul's thought may be outlined as follows:

Fifteen Vices	Nine Virtues
Now the works of the flesh are plain: immorality, impurity, licentiousness,	But the fruit of the Spirit is love, joy, peace,
idolatry, sorcery,	
enmity, strife, jealousy, anger, selfishness, dissension, party spirit, envy,	patience, kindness, goodness, faithfulness, gentleness,
drunkenness, carousing, and the like. I warn you, as I warned you before, that those who do such things will not inherit the kingdom of God.	self-control; against such, there is no law.

We can see three sets of contrast here. First there is "work" standing over against "fruit"; "flesh" over against "Spirit." The vices result from human inclinations, but the virtues are the products of growth prompted by the Holy Spirit.

Second, vices obviously are set over against virtues. The vices are organized as, first, sexual transgressions (three of them); second, sins involving religion (two are mentioned); third, eight violations against brotherly love, and finally, two examples of intemperate excess. The nine virtues appear to fall into three groups of three, and there may even be some intentional contrasts between these groups of virtues and the groups of vices in the parallel column. For example, "patience, kindness, and gentleness" are antidotes to the kind of poison in a community brought about by "enmity, strife, jealousy, and so on."

Finally, there is the closing contrast between those who espouse the vices and those who practice the virtues. The practitioners "will not inherit the kingdom of God"—a classic understatement probably stemming from Christian catechetical instruction about the kingdom as both an inheritance and yet a demand. In contrast, Paul reminds the Galatians who were being tempted to desert the gospel for a religion of legalism, "Against such [these virtues], there is no law." They are to be heeded.

As might be expected, such virtue-vice lists were common in the ancient world. There are rough parallels in the Old Testament (see Deuteronomy 27:15–26 and Psalm 1). Closer parallels exist in Greek literature, especially in the writings of the Stoic philosophers. Philo, the Jewish philosopher in Alexandria, compiled lists of evils which included as many as 160 items! Such contrasts may also go back to Qumran and even Persian thought.

The significant thing for us to understand is that ethical material of this sort was not uniquely Christian but grew out of the best of the insights of the times. It is true that Christians have often introduced new touches into such directives. For example, in Galatians 5:22, Christians would surely understand the concept of love against the background of God's love for us, and the word for *faithfulness* is the same one that Paul used in discussing "justification by faith." But the implication is that Christians need not reinvent what is already there; they are perfectly free to accept insights for determining moral action from anywhere—so long as the dynamic from which they are viewed and with which they are used is always that of the gospel.

HOUSEHOLD DUTIES

We should probably keep this background in mind as we wrestle with the meaning of certain passages in Bible study for family life today. The tables of household duties in the New Testament are not without their problems in this day of women's liberation. Some leaders would reject the New Testament completely at those points where it admonishes wives to "be subject to your husbands" (Colossians 3:18; Ephesians 5:22; 1 Peter 3:1) and puts women in a category with slaves and children in relation to husbands, masters, and parents.

The words about subjection are certainly part of the New Testament, but it may help to remember they also reflect a social attitude that was widespread in that day in the pagan and especially the Jewish world. They are part of a pattern of thought which says: God is the head of Christ, who is the head of every man, who is the head (as husband) of a wife (1 Corinthians 11:3). Christian theology has seen fit to hold that ultimately Christ

144

is not inferior to God but "is everything the Father is." That could imply that as part of humankind woman too is "everything man is." One can also argue that Paul actually softened the harsh subordination of women known in his day by applying the analogy only to the married woman in relation to her husband (as in 1 Corinthians 11:3).

Colossians 3:18 speaks moreover about being "subject to your husbands, as is fitting in the Lord." And if we want to know what that means, we should look at Ephesians 5 where two points emerge.

1. "The husband is the head of the wife as Christ is the head of the church," and that means in a loving, self-sacrificing way (5:22–33).

2. Both husband and wife are to be subject "to one another out of reverence for Christ" (5:21, italics added). That means a mutual subordination, equality, and respect (see 5:33).

As baptized believers, with the mind of Christ and under the impact of the gospel dynamic, we must think through our own answer of faith.

These New Testament ethical admonitions still have significant meaning if they are not read out of context with no regard for their background. Perhaps what they tell us most of all with regard to the ethics we need in home, society, and world is that first, like the New Testament writers, we need to listen to the best insights of our day. Second, as baptized believers, with the mind of Christ and under the impact of the gospel dynamic, we must think through our own answer of faith.

Some persons may not like working with virtue-and-vice lists. Some find it difficult to work with tables of familial duties. Even so, most of us have a fondness if not an outright yearning for such guidance. The Boy Scout laws are an example. Religious groups stressing discipline, even mind-control, have struck a responsive chord among a large segment of young people in the 70s. There are also approximations of Paul's list of virtues in Galatians 5:22–23 (see Wooden's Triangle).

With such virtues we touch the enduring characteristics of the human spirit at its best. Christianity recognizes these characteristics as important for life. Without making them into a law to be obeyed whereby we can earn salvation or confusing them with the good news, Christianity allows them to play a role in shaping life in the world under the dynamic of the gospel.

145

SOME PASSAGES TO STUDY
AND THINK ABOUT

The gospel of the Triune God provides the basic dynamic for Christian behavior. Scripture, the traditions surrounding it, and the best insights of the world of the day all help Christians to work out appropriate patterns of ethical response.

Throughout the New Testament are many signs of Christians hard at work building bridges between faith and life.

The task was made particularly difficult by the uncertainty about how soon Christ would return. If his absence were brief there was little need to struggle with ethical problems and implications for the future. In spite of such problems we read of the concern of families for creating Christian homes. Love and fellowship within the Christian community are stressed time and again. So is the thorny question of how to relate to a society untouched by the gospel. What was one's proper response to the changing face of the Roman government? (See Romans 13:1-7, and the Book of Revelation.) What was to be the church's response? (See Acts 5:29; 16:35-39 and Paul's other experiences with Roman officials.)

A high spot of New Testament teaching about living the Christian life is 1 Corinthians 13. Often called Paul's "Hymn to Love," it is not so much a hymn as a rhythmic exhortation to Christians about loving one another. It assumes God's love toward us in Christ and goes on to show what is "a still more excellent way" for congregational upbuilding in Christ. This loving way is to be preferred over any of the other charismatic gifts the Corinthians possessed (see 12:31 and 14:1). Read the chapter, if possible in several translations, keeping its outline in mind. The passage is divided into "strophes," which are units composed of two or more repeated lines.

Strophe I (vv. 1-3) is a series of "if" clauses. "If I do thus and so but fail to exhibit love, then I am (or gain) nothing." Note the progression from "speaking in tongues" to sacrificing self or property. None of it matters without love.

Strophe II (vv. 4-8) attributes some fifteen qualities to love. Some like to say they describe what Jesus Christ was like, others that they mirror the divine nature we should imitate.

Strophe III (vv. 9-13) tells of the imperishability of love. It endures even after hope is fulfilled and faith turns to sight.

One might well extend this study by reading all of 1 Corinthians, looking for ways love was brought to bear upon the various ethical problems that arose in that congregation. For the Christian today who lives "in Christ" the principle and dynamic of love for others is still the guiding star.

A second study in New Testament ethics might be Philemon. Read this twenty-five verse book and see what it says about a runaway slave. The traditional reconstruction of events described here is not hard to follow.

146

Onesimus is a slave belonging to Philemon, a Christian of Colossae. Onesimus runs away and meets Paul. The apostle converts Onesimus. Onesimus helps Paul in one of Paul's periods of imprisonment. Paul then sends Onesimus back to his owner. But Onesimus, though still a slave, is now a brother.

Some people today resent the fact that Paul did not strike a harder blow at the institution of slavery, inhumane and cruel as it was. Paul, of course, believed the end of the world was at hand. He probably thought slaves and people in general should therefore stay as they were until God intervened to set things straight (1 Corinthians 7:20–24).

Whatever the reasons for Paul's handling of the situation, we need to remember our own shortcomings before lashing out at him. Chattel slavery is gone today, but there are other forms of economic and social slavery about which Christians today are doing all too little.

Moreover, espousing the cause for ending slavish subservience of individuals or groups ought to lead us to draw out implications about women in the same passages on household duties. Perhaps a century after recognizing the need to end the slave-master relation of the ancient world we are ready to see that the subjection-of-women theme is not all that there is to biblical teaching about male-female relationships.

A third topic in the pages of the New Testament worth examining has to do with the development of the church's understanding of its role in society and the world. Throughout much of the first century the church seemed on the defensive. It was a tiny movement, struggling to exist, scarcely able to touch society at all. But the Epistle to the Colossians begins to set forth that concept of the church as mission which the Book of Acts so artfully dramatizes. The church is the missionary body of Christ, seeking "to make the word of God fully known, . . . to make known . . . among the Gentiles Christ . . . the hope of glory. Him we proclaim, warning every man and teaching every man in all wisdom, that we may present every man mature in Christ" (Colossians 1:25–28). The Epistle to the Ephesians lifts this thought to its most exalted level, with a vision of the church ever growing and expanding in the world on the basis of the witness of Paul and the ministries of countless others (see Ephesians, especially 2:13–22, and 4:11–16).

. . . Living the Christian life is both an individual and a corporate story. We are bidden to live for others, but "in him."

The New Testament reflects a healthy interest in the principle and practice of love among peoples, its application to the knottiest problems of life, and its spread through Christian witness into the world. In tackling the complexities of ever-changing family life, community relationships, and social issues, it absorbed the newest wisdom and the oldest insights

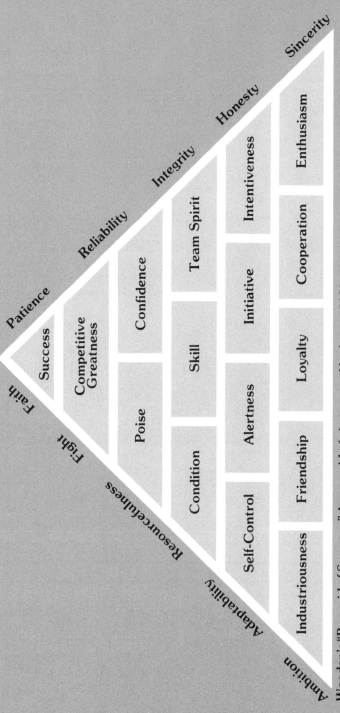

Wooden's "Pyramid of Success." A pyramid of virtues used by former UCLA basketball coach John Wooden to mold and motivate his players, winners of several national championships. Compare the lists with the lists of virtues in the New Testament at Galatians 5:22–23; Ephesians 5:9; 1 Timothy 4:12; 6:11.

from any and all sources. But throughout the New Testament teaching is shaped and directed by the gospel dynamic.

Here then is the pattern that directed the church's first involvement in God's world and has gone on from New Testament times to our own day. Sometimes the church has retreated from the world and ethical concerns, other times it has plunged in with reckless abandon. But its calling remains to live in Christ where it is, facing situations there and applying the gospel as well as common sense. So too for every Christian.

Perhaps what we need as much as anything is the gift of reading the Scriptures with greater sensitivity to our own situation and to our world and with greater ethical concern. The Parable of the Good Samaritan in Luke 10:30-37 provides a good illustration. It has become so familiar we seldom appreciate the shock that must have gone through the Jewish audience when the Jewish preacher Jesus coupled with the hated term *Samaritan* the possibility that such a person might be "good."

Traditionally the Good Samaritan story has been read as an example story. As he did, we should "go and do likewise." That interpretation is all for the good; it has inspired much noble conduct. But what if we do not drain from the story its power to draw us in as participants, and what if we allow it at the outset to compel us to identify not with the fourth man coming along the road but the first one—the victim who was thrown into the ditch, beaten-up, half dead (10:30)? Can we sense from his ditch-level view the failure of all too many from whom one ought to be able to expect help? Can we put ourselves in the shoes of a faithful Jew and recoil from receiving the needed aid from a Samaritan? What a reversal of values! But it enables one to see life anew and challenges us to take it from there. The coming of the kingdom upsets our usual views and liberates us to venture in new directions once we have been ministered to by Jesus or by his Samaritan.

Christians are people who have been ministered to by God and his people in so many ways. Their eyes are opened by the inbreaking of the kingdom to look for new ways in which to serve, shaped by the gospel dynamic of love. Individually and corporately they are bidden to live for others, ministering to them.

References and More Information

Biblical references: Romans 9—16, Philemon, James

Metzger, Bruce M. and Isobel M., editors. *The Oxford Concise Concordance.* See the following entries: minister, ministry

Reumann, John. *Jesus in the Church's Gospels.* Philadelphia: Fortress Press, 1968. See Chapter 10, pages 296–334.

Richardson, Alan. *A Theological Word Book of the Bible.* New York: The Macmillan Company, 1962. See the following entries: laying on of hands, family, marriage, minister, thank

28. The Church: God's People in in Pilgrimage

Bible study all too frequently overlooks "the church" as a theme in the New Testament. But then the churches all too frequently through the centuries have overlooked what Scripture has to say about that institution we call "the church." In this chapter we shall survey what the Bible says about the community "in Christ" as the people of God.

To do this we shall have to examine a number of books as we did in dealing with ethics. The biblical teachings about the church are not concentrated in just one or two Epistles or Gospels, but run through almost every book in the New Testament. We shall concentrate, however, on just four glimpses of the church. They are those seen in the writings of Paul and in James, 1 Peter, and Hebrews. In so doing we shall inevitably encounter related themes. And, as in other studies like this, we should sense a course of development in the New Testament idea of the church.

We shall see God's Christian people of the first century on the move in pilgrimage. That pilgrimage stretches on to our own day. From what the first Christians experienced of God's program for the church we can gain direction for our pilgrim path and for the churches in which we worship and work and into which we seek to win others.

HOW THE EARLY CHURCH DEVELOPED

Cynics have said, "Jesus came preaching the kingdom of God, but the world got the church instead." As we have seen (*UB I*, Chapters 1—2), Jesus did cast his gospel primarily in terms of the kingship of God. It is also true that a church later emerged in which Jesus Christ was Lord (see

From what the first Christians experienced of God's program for the church we can gain direction for our pilgrim path and for the churches in which we worship and work and into which we seek to win others.

The church was "on the way"—literally on the way on Roman roads like the Appian Way near Rome and figuratively on the way of discipleship.

Chapter 12 in *UB I* on "Jesus Is Lord"). But we have also seen something of the continuity of this development. For when God raised Jesus from the dead and made him Lord, the good news inevitably took a new form we have called the Easter gospel. As the witnesses to Jesus shared their story in the Gentile world, the message about the kingdom tended to be misunderstood. New ways of presenting the gospel of the goodness of God the King had to be found. That was the achievement of Paul and John. They viewed the gospel as justification, reconciliation, or eternal life in Christ.

The course of development for the church itself runs something like this.

1. According to the Gospel records, Jesus of Nazareth did not establish what we think of as a church during his lifetime. There is no passage which says the church existed prior to his death and only two verses where the term *church* is used at all. (Both are in Matthew and will be considered in more detail in the next chapter; 18:17 deals with rules for discipline in a community and 16:18 envisions a worldwide church built on the rock of Peter and his confession of Jesus as Christ. Apart from the debates over Peter, both verses have been questioned as sayings of the historical Jesus. And in 16:18 we have a future tense. Jesus says, "I will build my church," meaning later, after the Resurrection.)

2. Although there is nothing in the Gospels about the founding of a separate church outside Judaism before Easter, there are clues to what Jesus intended. It does seem he expected a religious community to result from his ministry and work. The whole background of Israel as a people points in this direction. Those who have had a similar experience of God's lovingkindness and rescuing actions tend to band together. In choosing twelve from among his followers (Mark 3:13-19), Jesus seems to have been prompted by the idea of the twelve tribes in Israel. When he taught his disciples a prayer of their own (Luke 11:1-4), he was marking them as a special group. In identifying with the baptism by John, Jesus and his followers, who had formerly been a part of the Baptist's movement, were stamping themselves as a "remnant" within Israel. When Jesus, in the Upper Room at Passover, gave new meaning to the bread and wine they ate and drank, he was constituting his little group as a fellowship which viewed God and his actions in new ways. The seeds were sown out of which would grow the church.

3. After Easter the Jesus movement took further shape. Emerging at first within Judaism, this movement was scarcely aware of being the beginning of what would become a worldwide church. The Jerusalem converts still went up to the Temple for prayer and continued their Jewish customs and ways (see Acts 2:46; 3:1; 3:11-16; 4:1-4). But the impact of the fact that "they had been with Jesus" (Acts 4:13), and the power of the Resurrection message moved them to go beyond where they had been. "The sect of the Nazarenes" (Acts 24:5), as it came to be called, grew and

expanded. It became "the Way" to life and God for increasing numbers within Israel. Paul spoke of it as "the Way, which they [in official Judaism] call a sect [and in which] I worship the God of our fathers, believing everything laid down by the law or written in the prophets, having a hope in God . . . , that there will be a resurrection of both the just and the unjust" (Acts 24:14–15).

Others drew their own conclusions from some of Jesus' teachings about God as Father and from his actions in eating with publicans and sinners. They began to share the good news with Jews who spoke Greek and followed Greek customs ("the Hellenists," mentioned in Acts 6:1). When persecution drove them from Jerusalem, they shared their message first with the Samaritans and then with people from far-off lands who had embraced Judaism, such as the Ethiopian official (Acts 8:26–39). Eventually the Gentiles were brought into the fellowship of Jesus Christ. According to Acts 10, it was Peter who first took this step. Guided by the Holy Spirit (10:44), he preached to and baptized a Roman centurion and all his household. So the gospel about Jesus spread to Jews and Greeks alike (Acts 11:19–20).

4. Long before Paul wrote any letters and even before his own missionary career began (see Acts 13), there were small groups, cells, fellowships, and house churches of "Christians," as they came to be called (Acts 11:26), meeting in private homes or in public throughout the eastern Mediterranean. In some areas these Jesus chapels or conventicles took the Jewish name of "synagogue" (literally, a "gathering together") or "assembly" (in Greek, *ekklesia,* giving us our word *ecclesiastical*). They adopted patterns of social organization which often included elders or presbyters so that a kind of ministry started to develop. These Jesus groups also took over and began to create forms for worship and communal life. We know little about their structure, liturgies, habits of prayer and Bible reading, and works of mercy and witnessing, but we know that in the 30s and 40s such things were already coming into being. By some time in the 40s the movement had reached all the way to Rome.

5. While we have traced the emergence of local groups, each "church" in its local situation must have had some awareness of the existence of other Christian groups elsewhere and a vision of a universal fellowship. This wider aspect of church life was fostered by travel and personal contacts but above all by the concepts of God as a universal king and of Jesus as Lord of the universe. Some New Testament writings, like Colossians and Ephesians, reflect this larger sense of Christianity more than others. But even in so early a letter as First Corinthians, devoted to local problems in Corinth, Paul touched on the "ecumenical" or universal aspects of the Christian movement. Note the salutation, "To the church of God which is at Corinth . . . together with all those who in every place call on the name of our Lord Jesus Christ, both their lord and ours." Note also

the references to "the churches of God" (11:16; also 4:7; 7:17; 14:33). Given a universal Lord, a universal fellowship was inevitable in spite of all the pulls of local or regional concerns.

6. It is well to remind ourselves that all books in the New Testament came from or through this emerging church. That is obviously true of the Epistles and of Revelation with its letters to the seven churches of Asia Minor. But it is also true with respect to the Gospels. Mark, Matthew, and Luke (especially when we consider Acts) each reflect to greater or lesser degrees a doctrine of the church. There is also ecclesiology (theological doctrine relating to the church) in the Fourth Gospel, although in a different key. When it declares of the Word of God, "we have beheld his glory" or "from his fullness have we all received" (John 1:14, 16), the Christian community is offering its testimony. In John 15 the vine and the branches are a metaphor about the church. And no passage in the New Testament lays more emphasis on "oneness" than John 17, the prayer of Christ for unity—oneness between Christ, the disciples, those who will believe through them, and the Father.

THE CHURCH AND THE KINGDOM

There is a connection between the kingdom of God and the church, which that cynical comment with which we began scarcely comprehends. Out of the kingship of Yahweh which Jesus proclaimed there arose a church of Jesus Christ the Lord. But this church is precisely a place where God's kingship is confessed, centered, and in halting ways realized as nowhere else in the world. The church becomes, indeed, a prelude to that final kingdom where God's rule will be "all in all" (1 Corinthians 15:24–28).

Several New Testament passages illustrate this point. James speaks not only of a "royal" or "sovereign" or "kingly" law to love one's neighbor as oneself (2:8), but also of how God has "chosen those who are poor in the world to be rich in faith and heirs of the kingdom which he has promised to those who love him" (2:5). (Verse 5 with its "kingdom for the poor" is very reminiscent of Jesus' first beatitude in Matthew 5:3, "The kingdom of heaven [will belong to] the poor in spirit.") Second Peter also tells of a future kingdom: "Be the more zealous . . . so there will be richly provided for you an entrance into the eternal kingdom of our Lord and Savior Jesus Christ" (1:10–11). Such is the promise whose fulfillment the Christian community awaits (3:12–13). 1 Peter addresses Christians as "a royal priesthood," literally a "kingly body of priests" (2:9). Hebrews contains routine references to Old Testament kingdoms (11:33) and to the scepter of God's kingly power in the hands of Christ (1:8, using a quotation from Psalm 45:6). But it also goes furthest in portraying the kingdom as a possession of God's people in Christ here and now. It invites us to "be grateful for receiving a kingdom that cannot be shaken" and then as the proper response, "to offer to God acceptable worship, with reverence and awe" (12:28).

All this is evidence that the kingdom message was not forgotten in the church and that it was treasured as a future hope and, to some degree, a present reality. It is the Pauline Epistles, however, which make the tightest connection between the kingdom of God and people in the church. According to these letters, evil, unrighteous persons will not inherit the kingdom of God (1 Corinthians 6:9–10; Galatians 5:5). It is those who have heard the gospel of God about Christ whom God calls into his kingdom (1 Thessalonians 2:12) and whom God makes worthy of the kingdom (2 Thessalonians 1:5). This is a kingdom of "righteousness and peace and joy in the Holy Spirit" (Romans 14:17), which is not a bad description of the church! Paul could speak of Christian missionaries as "fellow workers for the kingdom of God" (Colossians 4:11).

Perhaps the most significant phrase in these letters is the reference to "the kingdom of God's beloved Son" into which God has "transferred us" by calling us out of "the reign of darkness" through the gospel and baptism (Colossians 4:11). This identifies the church as the kingdom of the Son, implying both a link with and some distinction from the kingdom of God which is to be our full inheritance later on. But the point is that the kingdom of God does find expression precisely in the church of Jesus Christ.

PAULINE IDEAS ABOUT THE CHURCH

With all these useful insights we are still left wondering how the New Testament church understood itself if it was at least to some degre "kingdom come."

For help here we turn particularly to the Letters of Paul. They were written early, they reflect many different situations, and they are all marked with a strong sense of the church. What stands out first is a strong sense of continuity with historic Israel. Yet there is also the idea of being the "body of the Messiah" which Israel never had. Finally, there is a sense of divine purpose for the church in the world.

We begin with what might be called "Israel terms." These are words and phrases which Paul applies to the community of believers in Jesus Christ but which referred originally to Israel in the Hebrew scriptures. There is a reference to "the Israel of God" in Galatians 6:16 which many take to mean the church, while others suspect it refers to the Jews. "God's people" is not a phrase Paul uses as specifically as in 1 Peter 2:10 to denote the church. Nor is the related Old Testament term *covenant* as common in Paul. But note the phrases which he did employ about the church: "Abraham's offspring" and "sons of Abraham" (Galatians 3:29 and 3:7), emphasizing the promise to Abraham; "commonwealth of Israel" (Ephe-

155

sians 2:12); "Jerusalem" (Galatians 4:26); the "remnant, chosen by grace" (Romans 11:5). There are also such common phrases as "the saints" and "the elect." Both figures of speech at Romans 11:16–24 have Old Testament backgrounds, the dough offered as first fruits (Numbers 15:20–21) and the root and branches of the olive tree (see Hosea 10:1 and Zechariah 4:3). Even the reference to the church as God's "garden" or "field" (1 Corinthians 3:9) reflects Old Testament usage and is not just an agricultural allusion. The "remnant" of Israel is "the planting of the Lord" (Isaiah 61:3).

This identity with the Israel of the past provided the early Christians with roots and a heritage. It also helped them to hear the Hebrew scriptures speak to them afresh. You are Israel!

The body of Christ

Yet the Christians did not simply think of their community as an extension of God's people of the past. There was also a newness about their self-understanding. The impact of Jesus and the Easter gospel had changed things. The church's consciousness was centered in Jesus Christ. No phrase better clarifies what this meant than in the "body of Christ." It is a key phrase in Pauline writings. Indeed, at times people have made it appear to be the only figure Paul used to describe the church. And at other times it seems to be not a figure of speech at all but a literal statement about reality.

Before we look at what is said about the church as the body of Christ, it is worth pointing out that it is only one of over eighty New Testament expressions describing the church. Moreover, it is an extremely changeable figure with varying meanings. We ought not to overstress it even if it is a favorite of Paul.

We come upon the term "body of Christ" for the first time in an analogy in 1 Corinthians 12. There Paul is trying to stress the oneness of the Christian community in the face of a tendency among the Corinthians to develop splinter groups, each supporting a favorite leader (1:12–13; 3:3–21) or a particular spiritual gift (12:4–11). Appealing to the experience of baptism common to all, Paul writes, "We were all baptized into one body . . . and all were made to drink of one Spirit" (12:13). Then comes his famous analogy which might have been quite familiar from use in Roman history. Menenius Agrippa once persuaded the Plebeians to end a revolt by showing how each group in society has a role, just as different organs do in the human body. Paul compares the differing talents and gifts of Christians to the functions of hands, ears, eyes, the nose, and other parts of the body; each has its function and cannot get along without the others. Like the feet, the head (v. 21) is just another part of the body; neither can say, "I don't need you."

The biggest surprise in 1 Corinthians 12 comes at the conclusion where we might expect Paul to say, "You all are like the parts of a body and must work together." Instead he says, "You are the body of Christ, and individually members of it" (12:27). This should be placed alongside another surprising statement at the beginning of the passage. There instead of "Just as the many members of a body are one, so also with Christians," Paul has written, "Just as the body is one and has many members, and all the members of the body, though many, are one body, so it is with Christ" (12:12). These two statements suggest that the church and its members are intended to be brought together as a body and be ruled by Christ, who permeates the whole. The presence of the risen Jesus in the community makes "body of Christ" more than metaphor.

The sense of this phrase shifts, however, when we turn to the Imprisonment Epistles of Paul, those which indicate they were written while he was in prison. These are Philippians, Colossians, and Ephesians. In the latter two the members of the body are rarely mentioned. Instead, the stress is on Christ as the head of the body, while the body is defined as the church. Colossians 1:18 is a good example of this transition from the earlier use in 1 Corinthians 12 (see also Romans 12:5) to what we also find in Ephesians (1:23; 5:23). A pair of figures graphically depict the difference between the earlier and later use of the term.

1 Corinthians 12	Colossians and Ephesians

As the body and its many members are one, so it is with Christ. You all are the body of Christ.

Christ is the head over his body, the church.

What the two figures have in common, of course, is that Christ rules the body, the church. He works in all its members. The Corinthians passage suggests his presence with each and every woman, man, and child in Christ. The Imprisonment Epistles stress his lordship over all of us in the church. We can grasp here the mutual interdependence and cooperation and coordination with which Christians are to work under their Lord, especially if we add Romans 12:5 to the picture. One can hardly overlook what must have struck the first readers of Paul in Corinth with force: Those who are the body of Christ are precisely those who participate in "the body of Christ," that is, those who partake of the one bread and the one cup in the Lord's Supper (1 Corinthians 10:16–17; 11:26), and those who were nourished by this sacrament were to go and be the body of Christ in the world, using their gifts to serve (Romans 12:1–8).

The church is called upon to proclaim and convey God's work in Christ as good news to and in the world.

But what do the members of the body of Christ do in the world? What is the purpose of the church according to the Pauline Epistles? Paul replies in so many different ways that it is almost presumptuous to suggest a summary. One oft-heard answer that we ought not to accept is to say the purpose of the church is to be "an extension of the incarnation" into the world if thereby we meant that the church on earth is all that Christ was and is. This implies that the church has a savior's role and overlooks the fact that the church, like all its members, is sinful as well as redeemed. It is true that the church belongs to the Lord but in an imperfect way. Christ rules the church but is not identical with it. He always stands over it as Lord. What we can say, of course, is that the church continues the "incarnational principle" in the sense it embodies a humble service in the world, like the ministry of its Lord (Philippians 2:6–11).

Another way to express this would be to say that the church is called upon, first, to proclaim and convey God's work in Christ as good news to and in the world. The church here offers praise to God for this glorious opportunity to serve first of all in proclamation. The church is the missionary body of Christ, making the Word of God fully known to all the world (Colossians 1:21–29). Its gospel is what God has done in Christ.

Second, the church serves by conveying God's work. This means not only witnessing and making available God's forgiveness and justifying grace. It also means serving as a workshop or arena where God is especially at work transforming lives and as a voice crying out for justice and decency in the world. This social-ethical function has become more prominent today than in Paul's day, but the heritage from the Old Testament prophets and certain New Testament dynamics call for the church's involvement here. "No man is an island," John Donne wrote. In the solidarity of humanity, the church is God's spokesperson for the poor, the suffering, and those treated unjustly. "If one member suffers, all suffer together" (1 Corinthians 12:26). The church is that part of humanity whose eyes God has opened to see the vision of the promised new heavens and earth "in which righteousness dwell" (2 Peter 3:13).

Any statement about the purpose of the church that pretends to reflect Pauline thinking cannot overlook its doxological function. The church exists to offer doxologies of God, to sing his praise for mercies granted and opportunities bestowed. It was characteristic of Paul to break out in thanks to God in the midst of the most lofty theological thoughts (see Romans 7:25; 9:5; 11:36; 16:25-27, and the rhapsodic 8:31-39).

The church exists to proclaim; to be a place for God to work; to be a conscience for the world for good; to praise the Lord; and, finally, to be a spearhead of God's plan for humanity. Ephesians, that great epistle about the church, is full of expressions about this task of those who are "in Christ." We might paraphrase 3:7-12 as follows: God's eternal purpose is that, as the church proclaims "the unsearchable riches of Christ," people may see God's plan for their salvation while the angels in heaven look on to see how the ministers of the gospel are advancing the wisdom revealed to them. Or more specifically: the church is the full expression of Jesus Christ; he fills the church, and the church is meant to give full expression to Christ (1:23). Or in more personal terms: the goal of the church is to have every person grow up into Christ, its head, who fills the whole body and gives it growth, working through his various ministers and in all the saints (4:11-16).

The good news here includes the church. The church is not only a vehicle for the gospel but is itself part of it.

THE CHURCH IN JAMES

This sublime picture of the church of Jesus Christ is almost too grand to comprehend. The significance of that comes home to us when we realize that it was worked out by no ivory-tower theologian but a missionary in the midst of hard work and growing pains in troublesome little congregations around the Aegean Sea.

Much more down to earth are the glimpses of the church provided by the Epistle of James, a little sermon or address which has been made into a letter. Perhaps the chief impression it leaves is its blunt concern for living out the social-ethical implications of faith. James undergirds the responsibility of the Christian fellowship to cry out in behalf of justice and decency in the world and especially within its own ranks.

The five chapters in James constitute a New Testament example of "wisdom literature." Just as in ancient Israel so in the "Christian Israel" there is room for expression of the proverbial, that which is the common

159

sense, the plain man's outcry to underscore in simple terms what God wills. James may reflect little of the message that the kingdom of God is breaking in or of the Easter gospel, but it does contain a good many parallels to the teachings of Jesus. Among these are the sayings about perfection (1:4; see Matthew 5:48), hearers and doers (1:22 ff.; see Matthew 7:24 ff.), and peacemakers (3:18; see Matthew 5:9). The Sermon on the Mount lives here as straightforward, practical morality.

The author has traditionally been identified with Jesus' brother who became a follower after Easter. But the book itself refers to the writer only as "a servant of God and of the Lord Jesus Christ" (1:1). There is little of Christology beyond that verse and 2:1, the only places Jesus is mentioned. The *parousia* is alluded to, however, at 5:7-8, and baptism is assumed at 1:8, 21 and probably 2:7. The content seems disorganized, jumping from topic to topic, often via word links. For example, the same word is used in 1:2-4 and 1:13-18. In the first passage it means "trials" in the sense of testings, which can have good effect; in the second it refers to "temptations" to sin, which are bad. We also seem to have polished paragraphs, such as might have been used in a sermon or sermons, to which a vague salutation has been added. ("To the twelve tribes in the Dispersion" [1:1] would be a way of addressing Jews scattered throughout the world. Its use by a Christian author suggests that the church's experience parallels that of Israel.)

One has little trouble absorbing and applying the terse statements and examples about enduring under temptations (1:2-18), profession and practice (1:19—3:18), the condemnation of current abuses (4:1-5, 6), and the closing exhortations (5:7-20). The attack on those who trust in faith and do no works (2:14-26) is what has received attention most often. James has been interpreted as contradicting the Pauline teaching of "justification by faith alone." James calls for works, not faith alone (2:24). But a careful reading will show that what James attacked was a kind of faith that was just a "head trip," mere intellectual belief, the kind even demons can have (2:19). That was never what Paul meant.

James pleads for the kind of faith that goes deeper and expresses itself in a life that is committed and responds in deeds. Paul would have agreed with that although he would have been more careful to underscore that such works cannot save and that the "faith" described as being "apart from works" is unworthy of the name. It has been argued that James was attacking people who had learned Paul's terminology but never understood or practiced it. In that case James could actually be defending Pauline ideas which had gone to seed by using different terms to get at Paul's meaning.

But what does all this tell us about the church or "assembly" (2:2) that James knew? Obviously he is saying that some people in it were prating formulas about faith but not practicing the thing itself. A blunt and straightforward churchman, James, comes out swinging against his opponents. Those who teach are admonished (3:1–5). There are warnings about how we use our tongues (3:6–12), practice wisdom (3:13–18), and get along with others (4:1–12; see 2:8–13). There are also warnings for people who plan without counting God in (4:13–17), especially the rich (5:1–6). Of all this material the most revealing is the scene describing how the rich oppress the poor even in church. James 2:1–7 should be read as a perpetual indictment of any congregation which allows discrimination by one class or group against another. The words in 5:4–6 are reminiscent of an Old Testament prophet inveighing against the privileged who oppressed the poor in Samaria or Jerusalem. And now it was happening in the church! When James says "You have condemned, you have killed the righteous man" (5:6), he may be thinking of the martyrs from Abel to Zechariah (see Matthew 23:35) and perhaps even of Jesus Christ. Today one might include all the martyrs, even those who died in the Nazi holocaust against the Jews and in the tribulations of the Blacks in Namibia and South Africa.

We are to be a church that lines up with the impoverished and oppressed. This, too, is part of the New Testament picture of the church.

The message we thus get is a strong appeal for justice. Do God's will! We are to be a church that lines up with the impoverished and the oppressed. This, too, is part of the New Testament picture of the church. It tells us that some members in this local assembly have failed to act as Christians. And it reminds us that there were voices to speak out, to warn, to condemn, and to recall to Christians the promise of the kingdom (2:5).

1 PETER: THE CHURCH OF THE SUFFERING

The "First Epistle General of Peter," as it is sometimes called, presents us with another aspect of the church in the first century. It touches on one's witness in the face of persecution and possible suffering. Here is an element in Christian identity which has troubled many in the struggles of life over the centuries.

1 Peter is one of the "General Epistles" or "Catholic Letters," so called because they are addressed not to a single church like Corinth or even an area like Galatia but to the church-at-large or a more general audience. (James; 2 Peter; 1, 2, and 3 John; and Jude fit into this same category.) In this case the audience is described as "the exiles of the Dispersion in Pontus, Galatia, Cappadocia, Asia, and Bithynia" (1:1). These were the

161

Christians in pilgrimage in this world who lived in what is now Turkey. "Peter, an apostle of Jesus Christ" (1:1), "a fellow elder and a witness of the sufferings of Christ as well as a partaker in the glory that is to be revealed" (5:1), is mentioned as author. A second shorter letter dealing with false teachers in the church and the delay of the second coming also appears over Peter's name. Probably a majority of scholars agree that 2 Peter was not written by Peter himself and some question that he wrote 1 Peter as well. The date for 1 Peter would fall in the 60s unless it is by someone other than Peter himself. In that case a time as late as A.D. 110 is possible.

One reason for the amount of debate about 1 Peter rises from the kind of theology we find in the book. In content, 1 Peter is really a Pauline letter! That is, much that is said in it is akin to what Paul's letters say. That makes one wonder if it could have been written by the apostle to the Jews whose ideas differed so much from Paul's (see Galatians 2:11 ff.). One answer may be that both 1 Peter and Paul's letters reflect in their points of agreement what must have been common apostolic Christianity.

The other reason for doubts about the date and authorship of 1 Peter has to do with the persecution of Christians reflected in the book. Was it a persecution under the Emperor Nero, A.D. 64–67, which seems to have been limited to Rome? Or was it the more severe persecution under Domitian, about A.D. 96, which we know included the areas mentioned in 1 Peter 1:1? Or was it the persecution which took place in Bithynia (mentioned in 1:1) in the time of Trojan, about A.D. 111? Scholars frankly differ in their judgments. And since Peter was traditionally martyred by A.D. 67 at the latest, any date assigned after 67 means Peter could not have written the document as we have it.

Such matters may be interesting but have little to do with understanding what 1 Peter says about the church. Believers face suffering. To be a witness for Christ exposes one to the possibility of reproach, slander, opposition, and even suffering. How do the five chapters of 1 Peter encourage and equip the suffering saints for their stewardship of God's "varied grace" (4:10)?

For one thing the letter stresses the future hope. Christians have a great hope for the future (1:3–9). "Set your hope fully upon the grace that is coming to you at the revelation of Jesus Christ" (1:13). Judgment looms (4:17–19), but after suffering will come glory (5:10). This theme of suffering and future glory is also found in the Gospel of Luke (see 24:26, 46).

A second element in the writer's strategy is to underscore Baptism. The sacrament unites believers to Christ and thus not only to his suffering but also to his resurrection and the salvation which awaits us (1:3 ff.). There is baptismal language in 1 Peter, especially at 1:23: "You have been born anew . . . through the living and abiding word of God." Some even find reflections of a service where the Baptism would have taken place between 1:21 and 1:22. In 3:20–21 there is also an elaborate comparison of

Baptism with Noah's ark. Baptism saves us "through water," that is, by means of it; the ark saved eight persons "through water," that is, when the flood threatened.

First Peter also appeals to the common faith of the Christian church. Woven into its text are phrases from early creeds.

> [Christ] was destined before the foundation of the world, but
> was made manifest at the end of the times.
>
> (1 Peter 1:20)
>
> Christ also suffered for you.
>
> (1 Peter 2:21)
>
> He himself bore our sins in his body on the tree,
> that we might die to sin and live to righteousness.
>
> (1 Peter 2:24)
>
> For Christ died for sins once for all, the righteous for the unrighteous,
> that he might bring us to God,
> being put to death in the flesh but made alive in the spirit;
> in which he went and preached to the spirits in prison. . . .
> who has gone up into heaven,
> and is at the right hand of God,
> with angels, authorities, and powers subject to him.
>
> (1 Peter 3:18–22)
>
> [He] is ready to judge the living and the dead.
>
> (1 Peter 4:5; see also 1 Peter 4:17)
>
> [Christ's] glory is revealed. . . . when the chief Shepherd is
> manifested.
>
> (1 Peter 4:13; 5:4)

For centuries Christians have found comfort in hard times in these emphases of hope, Baptism, and Christ.

Here we have God's eternal plan—Christ's passion, atoning death, resurrection, ascension, the judgment, and his *parousia*. The epistle reminds us of what has been done for us in Christ and also of how Jesus himself provides for us an example in suffering (see 2:21–25).

For centuries Christians have found comfort in hard times in these emphases on hope, Baptism, and Christ. But we should not overlook one other element in the letter. After painting that magnificent picture of the church in 2:4–9, filled with Old Testament "Israel" figures, 1 Peter goes on to state the purpose for the people of God in the church, "that you may declare the wonderful deeds of him [God] who called you" and from whom "you have received mercy" (2:9–10). For all its trials and troubles, the church is still to be a missionary fellowship. It is to witness to and in the world even when the world persecutes the people of God.

THE CHURCH IN HEBREWS

At one point in his writing the author of Hebrews wanted to expand his examples of what faith had accomplished in the past. Finding that he was running out of space, he remarked that "time would fail to tell of Gideon, Barek, Samson . . ." (Hebrews 11:32). One has a similar feeling in writing about the church in the New Testament. Time fails us here to tell all one would like to tell. It would be helpful, for example, in our day with its stress on managerial style and organizational development to explore 1 and 2 Timothy and Titus, the Pastoral Epistles. They are rich with pastoral advice on structuring the church, including the offices of the overseer-superintendent or bishop and/or elder or presbyter. We move on to that anonymous document, the Letter to the Hebrews, only because it is even more significant for our purposes.

Hebrews consists of twelve closely knit chapters arguing the superiority of Jesus Christ. A thirteenth chapter is made up of a variety of admonitions. Chapters 1—12 are like a majestic sermon, Chapter 13 is more like the conclusion of a letter, including greetings from "those who come from Italy" (13:24). Hebrews has usually been called an epistle like James. It may be best to call it what 13:22 does, a "word of exhortation." No author is mentioned, and there is no consensus in the guesses of scholars over the centuries. Luther suggested Apollos (see Acts 18:24-28 and 1 Corinthians 3:1-9, 21-23). Others suggest that a woman, Priscilla, along with her husband, Aquila, wrote it (see Acts 18:2, 26; 1 Corinthians 16:19). Note the use of "we" at Hebrews 5:11 and 6:3. We simply do not know. The date could be anywhere between A.D. 55 and 95, most likely between 80-90.

Again the most important thing for interpreting the book is to grasp its setting. Hebrews is addressed to Christians who are veterans in the faith. However, they appear in danger of drifting away from their Christian commitment. That they are at least second-generation Christians is shown by references to their past glorious experiences and "former days" (10:32 36; 13:7). But they have become lethargic and "dull of hearing" (5:11). On the verge of lapsing back into what they were before they accepted Christ, they need to be instructed afresh (see 2:1; 10:23; 12:3, 12-13). So the writer argues, cajoles, and threatens, even to the point of saying that once you fall away from Christ, no renewal ever is possible again (see 6:4-6; 10:26; and 12:17). This idea of "no second repentance" is an example of rigorism in early Christianity. It shocked Luther who knew no such limits to God's love. Actually, the author of Hebrews doesn't quite go this far with his audience. His tone assumes they will return to Christ, hold fast to their newly won faith, and inherit the promises (see 6:9-12; 10:35-39 and the admonitions of 11:1—12:2).

Thus Hebrews confidently attacks a problem which has afflicted the church in every generation from the day it was written to the present—the

164

lack of excitement which sets in among some Christians with the passing of time, so that they grow slack in faith.

If we knew exactly who the people were to whom the letter was addressed, we could understand its method of argument better. Traditionally, the audience has been understood to be Jewish Christians who were drifting back to Judaism as a way of life. More recently there have been attempts to link the book with Christians who had once been part of the Dead Sea Scrolls community at Qumran and who had an intense interest in the priesthood. Yet the book also reflects a Greek way of thinking, such as we find in Plato and Philo. In this kind of thinking there is a heavenly world above to which the earthly realm corresponds as "shadow" does to "substance" (see 8:5; 10:1). That is, the heavenly world is the real one.

The superiority of Christ

Whatever these cultural and religious backgrounds, the author tried to address his hearers in a way relevant to them so as to stress the superiority of Christ and thereby urge allegiance to him in the face of apathy, persecution, or whatever. Note the way the argument was developed.

The Supremacy of Jesus, Mediator of the New Testament Revelation
- Jesus is superior to the angels, through whom the law was given (1:1—2:18).
- Jesus is superior to Moses, mediator of the law (3:1-6) and to Joshua— "Jesus" in Greek (3:7—4:16).

Jesus as Great High Priest, Superior to the Priests of the Old Covenant
- Jesus' qualifications to be high priest (5:1-10).
- Jesus is superior to the priests of the old covenant (5:1—7:28).
- Jesus is also superior to the tabernacle and sacrifices of the old covenant (8:1—10:39).

Hence, we are admonished to be loyal to the great High Priest (10:17-39); to have faith in him (11:1-40); and endurance and holiness (12:1-29). Other injunctions are given at Hebrews 13:1-25.

Interwoven into the argument are a good many early Christian creeds, such as the statement on Christ in creation and his atonement and exaltation in 1:3. The way the argument is developed reflects a dualistic view of things. Nowhere is this better seen than in the way the meaning of Christ's death or his atoning for human sin are described. He "made purification for sins" (1:3). Jesus "suffered outside the gate in order to sanctify the people through his own blood" (13:12). Jesus tasted suffering and death for everyone (see 2:9, 14). The phrases echo the ceremonial language of the Old Testament. In 13:12 "outside the gate" reflects not only the fact that Jesus died outside the gate of Jerusalem (see John 19:17, 20) but also that the ritual sacrifice for the Day of Atonement was to take place "outside the camp" (see Leviticus 16, especially v. 27; and Hebrews 13:13).

Hebrews then goes on to say that after his sacrificial self-offering on Golgotha, Christ, the great High Priest, was exalted to a place of honor with God. This involved passing through the heavens to a "true sanctuary . . . set up not by men but by the Lord" (see 1:3; 4:14; 5:8–10; 6:19–20; 8:1–2). There he ministers for us and to us (see 8:6; 9:11–12; 10:19–22). But while saying Christ is alive and serving as present and eternal mediator for his people, the author of Hebrews is very careful to note that the work of Christ in the heavenly sanctuary is not a duplication of the cross outside Jerusalem. That sacrifice occurred "once and for all," one of the great phrases in Hebrews (7:27; 9:12; 10:10). What the High Priest does is to continue to intercede for sinners, on the basis of the atoning cross (see 7:25; 9:24).

All this is enough to make people cry out in thanksgiving and praise, to spend themselves by sacrificially doing good and sharing all they have with others (see 13:15–16). Christ emboldens us to draw near to God and to live in faith (10:22–25).

The emphasis on Christ and his sufficiency and superiority to all prior arrangements for salvation can also be seen in the way Hebrews handles the theme of "the covenant." Seventeen of the thirty-three New Testament uses of the word occur in this writing. The contrast is between the "first covenant" given under Moses at Sinai (9:18–22; see also Exodus 24:6–8) and the "new covenant" for which Jeremiah hoped (Jeremiah 31:31–34, cited and interpreted at Hebrews 8:8–13). The first covenant has become obsolete (8:13), its offerings and priesthood abolished (10:9). Christ is superior to both Moses (3:1–6) and the Levitical priesthood. The author builds his latter case by linking Jesus to a mysterious priest-king Melchizedek, who had appeared in Genesis 14 in the story of Abraham (see Hebrews 7). Christ has a tabernacle in the heavens, superior to that of the Israelites on earth (Hebrews 9:16). In every way the covenant in Christ supersedes the old.

Again, as in Paul, the basic pattern in Hebrews is one of promise (to Abraham) and fulfillment in Christ. But it also has the added dimension of a heavenly world designed by God and perfect in all respects.

Note that when Hebrews refers to the Old Testament tabernacle or tent (9:2 ff.) it is the portable sanctuary used during the years of wilderness wanderings after the Exodus, not the later temples in Jerusalem. This fact underscores a final important theme in this book and in the Bible as a whole.

THE CONTINUING WILDERNESS JOURNEY

The wilderness traditions of Israel go back to the very roots of God's people. They are preserved especially in Exodus 15:22—17:16 and

Numbers 11—36. Two different understandings emerged. According to the one, the wilderness was a place where Isaac experienced great intimacy with Yahweh. There God cared for his people as almost never before or afterwards. Later generations looked back to these glorious years for a model of the ideal life. This positive estimate seems to have found a place especially in the literature of the Northern Kingdom (see Hosea 2, particularly vv. 14-15; Jeremiah 2; Deuteronomy 8:1-10).

The other understanding of the wilderness years was negative. It recognized that Israel had not obeyed God but had been rebellious. In spite of the Exodus miracle the Israelites wanted to return to Egypt and became impatient not merely on their journey but at both the beginning and end of the journey. It has been suggested that Psalm 78 is a Judean argument against the Northern view that everything had been rosy back in the days in the desert. The truth was that the Israelites in the wilderness had been "a stubborn and rebellious generation" (78:8) who "did not keep God's covenant" (78:10).

Against this background it is surprising that the early Christian church sometimes saw itself very much like ancient Israel during the wilderness period. It has passed through the sea in its exodus and discovered that its experiences paralleled those of Israel. First Corinthians 10:1-11 provides the best example of this kind of thinking. Israel's experience is used there as a warning for the church. Paul saw the struggles of Christians in Corinth as a reenactment of the struggles of the ancient Hebrews as they escaped from slavery only to face further problems and temptations. Paul saw Christian baptism as some sort of fulfillment of the ancient Hebrew experience of passing through the waters of the Red Sea on the way out of Egypt.

The Epistle to the Hebrews picks up this same analogy. The church is the people of God between the "exodus" (Christ's death and resurrection) and the "promised land." Hebrews 4 even tells of a promised "rest" for the people of God. En route in life, like ancient Israel, they too are likely to grumble and complain (Hebrews 3:7-19). But now, as then, God is faithful. He has given us his promises (10:23), and we are to walk by faith until we arrive at "the city of the living God . . . the kingdom that cannot be shaken" (12:22, 28).

Here we see the church as God's pilgrim people journeying toward a goal not yet attained. It is "the wandering people of God" kept by him and empowered by God with a vision of the city they seek (11:10, 16; 13:14). This picture has been recovered in recent biblical scholarship and given new prominence. The Second Vatican Council of the Roman Catholic Church also made use of it. In its "Dogmatic Constitution on the Church" Vatican II deliberately stressed this idea of the church as the pilgrim people of God. It is a healthy counterbalance to the institutional and organizational side of its life (foreshadowed in the Pastoral Epistles) to recall Augustine's words and say that the church "like a pilgrim in a foreign

167

land, presses forward amid the persecutions of the world and the consolations of God, announcing the cross and death of the Lord until he comes"[1] (see 1 Corinthians 11:26). The biblical image has helped renew the concept of the church for many Roman Catholics, and can do the same for other Christians as well. The church is part of God's good news for humanity.

References and More Information

1. Walter M. Abbott, S.J., ed., *The Documents of Vatican II* (New York: Guild Press, America Press, Association Press, 1966), p. 24, quoting Augustine, *Civ. Dei* XVIII, 51, 2, *Patrologia Latina* 41, 614.

Biblical references: Hebrews; 1 Corinthians 12; 1 Peter

Metzger, Bruce M. and Isobel M., editors. *The Oxford Concise Concordance.* See the following entries: joy, love, servant, serve, service

Richardson, Alan. *A Theological Word Book of the Bible.* New York: The Macmillan Company, 1962. See the following entries: joy, love, service

29. The Witness of the Synoptic Evangelists

Telling the story of Jesus never ceased in the early church. We have already seen how Jesus himself had appeared preaching the gospel of God. For our knowledge of his actual ministry we must depend on later reports, accounts, and books. This story of Jesus took a new turn with his resurrection. He is proclaimed Lord. The good news henceforth became an Easter gospel. Jesus Christ was spoken of by faith as mediator of creation. So the story of Jesus went on, always being retold. We have seen how the gospel of John appeared to address the good news to the situation and circumstances of the gospel. We now turn to the other three gospel accounts of the Jesus story in the New Testament. They return us to the heart of Christianity, Jesus Christ. These are the "good news books" which in the early manuscripts go under the titles "According to Matthew"; "According to Mark"; "According to Luke."

SOME BACKGROUND

The term at the head of all those titles is *Gospel,* for each evangelist assumed he was presenting the one and only gospel. Luke, of course, added a second volume, Acts, to continue the story of the actions of the risen Christ through his church. We shall see that to some degree Matthew incorporated this emphasis in the one volume he wrote about Jesus.

But while each evangelist presented the one and only gospel, he always did so in a particular time and place. Hence the situation and needs addressed account for a good many differences when we compare the books by Matthew, Mark, Luke, and John. Actually, today's reader has an advantage which no ancient gospel writer ever had. We can read all four Gospels. There is no evidence or likelihood that any of the evangelists had before him the works of his three colleagues in the Christian canon.

We have already examined John's Gospel. It stands out as a high point in New Testament development. But the other three, so alike in many ways that they have traditionally been called the "Synoptics,"[1] should not be overlooked, for they are significant theological works in their own right. Too often Matthew, Mark, and Luke have been regarded as secondary to the writings of Paul and John. Biblical studies in recent years have helped us appreciate as never before the meaningfulness of the work of each evangelist as a witness to Jesus Christ in his own day.

Mark is generally conceded to have been the first Gospel to be written. For many centuries it was assumed (and still is in the opinion of a few scholars) that Matthew was composed first. Mark is usually dated about A.D. 70 and Matthew and Luke ten to twenty-five years later. To many observers Matthew seems to have appeared earlier than Luke and both of these Gospels prior to John, but we should not be dogmatic about such matters. What seems "earlier" or "later" about a particular Gospel may simply reflect the degree of development in that community for which the evangelist wrote or the sources he employed.

More important is just the idea of writing a Gospel book. So far as we know, Mark was the pioneer who first took this momentous step. Prior to that, there had been many isolated stories circulating about Jesus. There were collections of sayings or teachings, passion accounts, creeds, and hymns in oral or written form. But no one had put this material together as an organized whole to provide an account of Jesus' ministry, passion, and resurrection. Mark led the way in setting a new direction for telling the Jesus story.

The New Testament Gospels are witness literature written "through faith for faith" . . . , that is, by persons who believed, in order to convert others and deepen Christian life with the Christian church.

The Gospels, of course, are not biographies. Who would ever set out to recount a person's life and omit, as Mark did, his birth, childhood, education, family, and the psychological aspects, as well as the climax of the story, in this case Jesus' resurrection appearances and his becoming Lord? Even in Matthew, where something of Jesus' infancy is recounted, and in Luke, where there is more attention to biography and psychology, we do not have a "life" in the strict sense. No Gospel is a "life" such as Suetonius wrote of the twelve Caesars or Plutarch provided about famous Greeks and Romans. The New Testament Gospels are witness literature written "through faith for faith" (Romans 1:17); that is, by persons who believed, in order to convert others and deepen Christian life within the church.

It is often said that in writing the first Gospel, Mark created a new literary form which was different from biography and intended to awaken and nurture faith in his Lord. Actually, there were rough analogies in the

Greek world. There were, for example, writings about philosophers like Apollonius of Tyana who traveled about teaching. Some of these philosophers were even credited with working miracles. In the Jewish world there were the lives of prophets who were said to speak in the name of Yahweh and perform extraordinary deeds. Within the Old Testament the cycle of stories about Elijah and Elisha (see 1 Kings 17—2 Kings 10) can be claimed as precedents.

As we look at the Synoptics we shall assume that Mark was the first whose work is preserved as the pioneer retelling of the fuller Jesus story as good news. To be a little more precise, we should say Mark was the first work of a "Gospel" as we know it. Luke told of having "undertaken to compile a narrative" about Jesus, and said his narrative followed the efforts of "many" who had previously set out to do the same thing (1:1). We have no assurance that the "many" are just Mark and Matthew. Also, we have seen that there may have been other sources behind the Fourth Gospel. Thus Mark, at least in part, may indeed be based on prior written materials, or it may be based entirely on oral tradition reduced to writing for the first time. We cannot know which with certainty.

One other preliminary matter merits attention before we look at the three Synoptics individually. While our evangelists were men of theological insight and amazing ability, we should not expect too much creativity on their parts, as if they invented new materials. In most cases they had oral or written sources which they shaped to fit the situation of their day. To this extent each Gospel is a preaching of the good news to people and situations existent about A.D. 70 or 90. But each evangelist dealt with materials he had received from earlier decades, going back to the time of Jesus.

An illustration or two will help to show how the evangelists worked both with fidelity to traditions they received and with a degree of freedom which may surprise us. We can use two obvious collections of materials in Mark. The first is Mark 1:21-39, which could be called "a day in the life of Jesus." We pick up the narrative directly after the opening prologue and stories about the call of the first disciples. On a Sabbath in Capernaum after sunset, when good Jews no longer felt restricted by Sabbath rules, Jesus healed the sick that were brought to him (1:32-34). In the morning he prayed alone and then moved on in his ministry (1:35-39). After an isolated story about a leper with no indication of time or place (1:40-45), there follows a collection of stories about Jesus' controversies with his opponents. Mark 2:1—3:6 provides us with five incidents in which Jesus was opposed by scribes and Pharisees (2:1-12, 13-17, 18-22, 23-28; 3:1-6). They led to a breach between them so great that his opponents were ready to kill him (3:6).

In reading Matthew, we might be shocked to see how this neat chronological Markan sequence is broken up and distributed into a new arrangement. The details work out in the following way. The best way to see the change is, of course, by looking up the verses or examining them in a synopsis of the Gospels.

	Mark	Matthew
Jesus heals in the synagogue at Capernaum	1:21-28	See 7:28-29 (parallels Mark 1:22); Mark 1:21, 23-28 has no parallel in Matthew.
Jesus heals in Simon's home	1:29-31	8:14-15
Jesus heals at evening	1:32-34	8:16-17
Jesus moves on next day	1:35-38	Omitted
Jesus goes to Galilee	1:39	4:23

Whatever Matthew may have thought of Mark's "typical day" in Jesus' ministry, he had reason to use the stories otherwise. One good reason we discovered earlier in our study is that Matthew liked to collect materials in a neat and orderly way. The two healings thus became part of his collection of ten miracle stories in Matthew 8—9. The other verses he used as part of his concluding comments on the Sermon on the Mount at 7:28-29. Matthew 4:23 and Matthew 7:28-29 provide a frame for Chapters 5—9.

To be sure, someone might want to argue Matthew's Gospel came first, but then, we could face the problem of how Mark managed to put together "a day in the life of Jesus" from such random materials in Matthew 4, 7 and 8.

Our other illustrative block of material in Mark 2:1—3:6 tells of how Jesus handled opposition. It is similarly reworked by Matthew. Without going into detail, the following chart shows the parallels. Luke is included to indicate that here Luke follows the sequence in Mark, as he also does at Mark 1:21-39.

	Mark	Matthew	Luke
Jesus heals a paralytic	2:1-12	9:1-8	5:17-26
Criticism of Jesus for receiving and eating with tax collectors like Levi	2:13-17	9:9-13	5:27-32
Criticism of Jesus' disciples for not fasting	2:18-22	9:14-17	5:33-39
Criticism of Jesus' disciples for plucking and eating grain on the Sabbath	2:23-28	12:1-8	6:1-5
Jesus heals on the Sabbath	3:1-6	12:9-14	6:6-11

Here again one can see that Matthew had a different pattern and actually discern what it is. Matthew inserts Mark 2:1-22 in his collection of ten miracles. If you read Matthew 9:18—11:30, you will find he then brought in other miracles to fill out the collection. From Mark 5:21-43 there are the healing of Jairus' daughter and the woman with the hemorrhage; from Mark 10:46-52 the giving of sight to a blind man. Matthew 9:35 rounds out his structure in 4:23—9:35. Matthew 10—11 presents material from sources other than Mark, before picking up Markan material again (12:1 ff.; Mark 2:23 ff.).

It can be quite fascinating to explore such matters and scholars take great pains to search out the possible meaning of these agreements and varieties within Mark, Matthew, and Luke. Very likely Mark 1:21-39 and 2:1—3:6 were collected units of material before Mark put his book together. We could also spend time exploring the history of each story during the years of its oral transmission and use, as "form criticism" does. We could trace the same story through its use by each evangelist or speculate about differences in meaning the same saying has in different contexts. We limit our studies here to examining each Gospel as it stands in order to get at the particular message of each evangelist.

MARK: GOOD NEWS IN DARK AND CHANGING TIMES

Mark starts his work with the words, "The beginning of the Gospel of Jesus Christ, the Son of God." We have already seen that they may refer to Jesus' initial public appearance and his preaching the gospel about the kingdom in Galilee (1:14-15), to the appearance of his predecessor, John the Baptist (1:4), or to the fulfillment of the Old Testament (1:2-3). In any case, there is little there about a specific background. The emphasis is on Jesus and what he did in his ministry. Perhaps 1:1 is best taken as a title for the entire book, as in the RSV.

To understand Jesus' earthly ministry as "the beginning of the gospel" is substantiated by the conclusion of the book. Mark ends abruptly. In the earliest manuscripts and most modern translations, Mark ends at 16:8. The final scene is Easter morn when three women go to the tomb in order to anoint Jesus' crucified body. They find the tomb empty and are told by a "young man . . . in a white robe" that "Jesus has risen, . . . go tell his disciples and Peter that he is going before you to Galilee; there you will see him, as he told you" (16:5-7; see 14:28 for Jesus' promise).

The underlying assumption of this scene at the empty tomb, indeed, of the whole Gospel, is that this Jesus of whom Mark tells is risen and exalted as "Christ" and "Son of God." The good news for Christians begins with this story of how, in fulfilling Old Testament promises, God "anointed

173

Jesus of Nazareth with the Holy Spirit and with power; how he went about doing good and healing all that were oppressed by the devil"; how God was with him even after his death at Jerusalem and raised him up to be Lord and Christ (Acts 10:38–40; 2:32–36). What the sermons in Acts tell in a few proclamatory phrases Mark depicts quite vividly with stories, dialogue, and drama. What the witnesses in Acts tell with their mouths (10:39) Mark relates with pen and papyrus.

Mark's version of the gospel has a certain "pell-mell" quality about it. One event follows hard upon another. "Immediately" is a favorite word (e.g. 1:10, 12, 18, 20, 21). There are few efforts at precise chronology. Mark 1:21–39 has already been mentioned as a time sequence but just when the momentous Sabbath and Sunday occurred is not specified. Dating the Transfiguration (9:2) as "after six days" is unusual; only the Passion narrative contains such chronological concerns. But even here we are left to guess, "Six days after what?" (Presumably it is Peter's "confession," 8:27–30.) The geography is often just as vague. A classic example is at 7:31. Geographers still struggle to trace the route laid out here. "Dalmanutha" at 8:10 remains unknown and some manuscripts substitute other names.

All this suggests that Mark's chief concern was to concentrate on Jesus and his story as the beginning of the Gospel and to tell it with a sense of excitement and urgency. An outline of the book follows.

Prologue (1:1–15)

We are told who Jesus is, what his message is about, and that God is with him.

Jesus ministers in Galilee and beyond (1:16—9:50)

It is difficult to get at the exact structure of these chapters. There are different ways of dividing up the material. The chapters report limited excursions outside Galilee, enough to assure the reader that Gentiles heard "the good news according to Mark" and that their inclusion in the kingdom was foreshadowed in the ministry of Jesus. The following sections and units stand out:

- The call of the first four disciples to become "fishers of men" (1:16–20). Here the phrase seems to mean "to evangelize people," not secure them for the judgment, as in Jeremiah 16:16.
- A "day in the life of Jesus"—teaching and working miracles (1:21–45).
- Controversy between Jesus and his opponents (2:1—3:6). Jesus' growing ministry (3:7–35), involving the recruitment of twelve specially appointed disciples (3:14–19) and the opposition of friends (3:20) and family (3:31–35).
- A collection of three parables about the kingdom (4:1–34).

174

- Two cycles of stories about Jesus' sea miracles related to the healing and feeding:

Stilling the storm at sea (4:35–41)	Walking on the sea (6:45–52)
The Gerasene demoniac (5:1–20)	The blind man of Bethsaida (8:22–26)
Jarius' daughter raised, and the woman with a hemorrhage healed (5:21–43)	The Syrophoenician woman (7:24–30)
	The deaf mute (7:31–37)
Feeding of the Five Thousand (6:34–44)	Feeding of the Four Thousand (8:1–10)

- References to the Twelve sent forth to witness (6:7–13, 30–33) and, more ominously, the rejection of Jesus in his home synagogue (6:1–6) and the martyrdom of John the Baptist (6:14–29). These are entwined with the miracle stories.

- Brief summaries of Jesus' ministry (6:6, 53–56) and one discourse on freedom from Pharisaic and Mosaic laws (7:1–23). This is almost in the spirit of Paul. Or is Paul in the spirit of Jesus on this point? Mark 8:11–21 sums up the "signs" (miracles) which Jesus has been performing and the disciples' lack of understanding. He will give "no sign . . . to this generation" (8:12). They "do not yet understand" (see 8:17–18, 21).

- Peter's confession of Jesus; "You are the Christ" (8:27 ff.). This is surprising in the light of what precedes. Since Jesus turns the conversation in the direction of "the Son of man" and suffering (8:31), one might well judge Peter's use of the term *Christ* at this point a misunderstanding calling for Jesus' correction. But the situation provides Mark the opportunity to use a favorite pattern:

  Christology—having the right view of Jesus as suffering Son of man.

  Discipleship—getting a right view of what it means to follow Jesus, denying self, confessing Jesus, bearing a cross (8:34–37).

  Eschatology—understanding the times. The kingdom is near, our fate when the Son of man returns to judge will depend on our response to Jesus (8:38—9:1).

- The Transfiguration, where Jesus appears transformed with Elijah and Moses and God, bears witness again to him (see 1:11). Here is another clue as to who Jesus is and will be; God is with his Son (9:2–8).

- The dialogue "on the way" (a Markan phrase, 8:27—9:33). Jesus intersperses teachings with another healing story (9:14–29). The Twelve still do not understand the meaning of discipleship (9:33–50) or Jesus' talk about his impending death (9:9–13, 30–32).

- Occasional references to Gentiles are scattered throughout this section. Several teachings and activities suggest Jesus came not only for

175

the Jews. There is the bold teaching that it is the things within the heart of a person which defile, not the foods we eat (7:14-23). Jesus makes an excursion into the region of Tyre and Sidon and heals a Greek woman (7:24-30) as well as Legion (5:1-20) and a deaf man (7:31-36). This fulfills the dream of Isaiah for restoration in the time of the Exile (see 7:37). The important events of 8:27 ff. also occur on a pagan site north of Israel.

Jesus goes up to Jerusalem (Mark 10—13)

"On the way" (apparently down the east bank of the Jordan, 10:1) provides opportunity for more ethical teaching (10:2-31). There is a final miracle (10:46-52), where the man healed then follows Jesus "on the way" (10:52). The disciples still do not understand (10:35-44). Again the passion is emphasized (10:32-34, 45).

After Jesus enters Jerusalem and cleanses the Temple (the next day), we have a series of controversies with chief priests, scribes and elders, Pharisees and Sadducees. The stage is set for his death. "Have faith in God," Jesus counsels (11:22). In some ways the controversy stories and teaching materials in Chapters 11—12 remind one of Mark 2:1—3:6.

Chapter 13, the "little apocalypse" may seem like an intrusion. It must have been very important to Mark to give so much space on the fall of Jerusalem (13:1-2, 14-23), persecution for the gospel's sake (13:9-13), and apocalyptic signs of the end of the age (13:3-8, 24 ff.). Whatever in the way of judgment these words spoke to his own day, Mark was also using them just prior to the story of the death of Jesus to provide a ray of hope. Beyond all suffering and catastrophe stands God who is in control (v. 20), will care for his elect (v. 27), and bring salvation (v. 13). Hence the closing admonition is to watchfulness (13:33, 37).

Jesus' passion, death, and resurrection (Mark 14—16)

Now follows the familiar story of the cross. The plot to kill Jesus is set in motion by Judas Iscariot (14:10-11, 43-46) acting in agreement with the chief priests and scribes (14:1-2, 53 ff.). Since Jesus could not be anointed for burial when he was placed in the tomb on Sabbath eve (16:1), Mark tells about a symbolic anointing beforehand (14:3-9) which is made part of the preaching of the gospel "in the whole world" (14:9).

Step by step the events unfold: the Upper Room (14:12-31); Gethsemane (14:32-52); the Jewish trials by night (14:53-65) and by day (15:1); Peter's denial and remorse (14:66-72); the Roman trial (15:2-20); the Crucifixion (15:21-41); the burial (15:42-47); the empty tomb. The enigmatic ending with the women frightened at the news of Jesus' resurrection (16:8) has been interpreted in many ways. Most likely it is a final stroke of irony—frightened by the best news ever about Jesus! To under-stand the outcome one must go back and reread Mark's prologue and the underlying confession in his witness that Jesus is the risen Lord!

Mark's unwritten purpose

Given this content, what are we to make of Mark's Gospel as a whole? A number of fascinating clues have been suggested. One revolves around the title "Son of God" employed in the title and verse, 1:1. Three times there are very significant confessions about Jesus using this term (1:11; 9:7; 15:39), and an attempt has been made to line each up with "enthrone-ment rituals" known from the ancient Near East (see *UB I*, pp. 157-158). Surely "Son of God" is a significant title for Jesus in Mark's witness, but there is no suggestion in the text of any threefold progression in such ref-erences. He is also called Son of God at 3:11 and 5:7 by demons. It is doubtful if the structure of Mark is tied to the three citations and any re-lated stages.

Another pattern can be found in the parallelism involving John the Baptist, the forerunner of Jesus, and the disciples.

* John the Baptist preached (1:4) and was arrested (1:14), "delivered up" to prison and death.

* Jesus came preaching (1:14) and was "delivered up" (9:31; 10:33).

* The disciples preach, Christians are to preach (3:13; 13:10; 14:9), and they too as Jesus' followers will be "delivered up" (13:9-13).

The suggestion here is that discipleship involves traveling the way which Jesus and his predecessor went (see 8:34-37).

Still another possible clue to Mark's thought lies in the word *gospel*. Again it is a word in his title (1:1) and prologue (1:14-15). In citing 13:10 and 14:9 we noted that the gospel is something which Mark assumes will go on being preached after Jesus' death and resurrection. Two further ref-erences suggest what Mark means by the gospel. When Jesus talks of "losing one's life" or giving up things "for my sake and the gospel's" (8:35, 10:29), the gospel is plainly identified with Jesus himself. In Mark, Jesus Christ is the gospel. His book which tells the Jesus story is "the beginning" of the gospel. The witnesses are to go on telling it!

What situation or circumstances prompted Mark to put together the good news for his day in the manner he chose? It seems clear that his goal was to combine miracle stories, parables, apocalyptic, and passion materials in a way which makes Jesus the Son of God who was delivered up for us and who is himself good news in that very death and his ensuing lordship. A great deal of our understanding depends upon where and when we assume Mark was written.

Since the second century, it has been traditional to hold that Mark was written for Christians in Rome during the persecution under Nero, around A.D. 66-70. If so, its purpose was, obviously, to offer hope amid suffering.

Others have preferred to correlate the writing of the book with the war going on in Palestine, A.D. 66-70, where the Jews had rebelled against Rome. If circulated among Christians there, it could have encouraged them amid their tribulations (see 13:7-8, 14-23). In that case, Mark 13 would have had special meaning for readers of Mark.

A related view depends on the interpretation of 16:7 (see 14:28). The words Jesus "is going before you to Galilee; there you will see him" need not be taken as a reference to a resurrection appearance—which Mark does not report—but could apply to the *parousia*. In that case the book would be a fervent appeal to flee Jerusalem and get to Galilee where the second coming would occur at any moment. But we can't refrain from asking: Why write a book about "the beginning of the gospel" if the world is soon to come to an end?

All these interpretations make of Mark "good news for dark times."

A more theological interpretation suggests the heart of the book is the Passion story in Mark 14—16, toward which the "Passion predictions" (8:31; 9:31; 10:33 ff.) and the controversies in 2:1—3:6 and Mark 12 all point. If this is true we can see Mark trying to stress the "theology of the cross" in contrast to any view of Jesus as a mere miracleworker or teacher. Even the disciples are guilty of a wrong or one-sided view of Jesus

---

Mark is good news not just for evil days, but also for changing times.

---

when they do not understand his impending death.

Finally, if we were to date Mark after A.D. 70 rather than before the fall of Jerusalem, the message would take on still another dimension. When the war against Rome began, many Christians and as many Jews must have seen signs of "the end of the world." There had been giddy hopes of victory and an independent Jerusalem. Instead the city lay in ashes and Yahweh's Temple had been destroyed. Did that mean all hope was lost and God was dead? No, says Mark, go back to your roots in Galilee where it all began. Think again about Jesus' message that God is king. Recall the power shown in his ministry. Faith still asserts that Jesus is Lord and Son of God. And go, share this good news with the Gentiles throughout all the world.

In these last two cases, Mark is good news not just for evil days but also for changing times. The Gospel points us to what matters in Christianity as a new day began in Galilee, whence the mission to preach Jesus as crucified and risen Lord spread forth.

Whatever the precise circumstances or date he wrote his Gospel (for Mark lets us read these only between the lines, not telling us even his own name since the designation "according to Mark" is only a tradition), Mark has left us a powerful pioneering effort at telling Jesus' story in a holistic way. Both Matthew and Luke were to follow his basic outline.

MATTHEW: STRUCTURING THE TEACHINGS OF JESUS AND THE CHURCH

To see what Matthew has done creatively as a preacher and witness, we can compare his larger book with that of Mark. The Markan outline is preserved by the other Synoptic Gospels.

Mark	Matthew	Luke
		Historical Preface 1:1-4
	Infancy, Chs. 1—2	Infancy, Chs. 1—2
Prologue, 1:1-15	Preparation for the ministry, Chs. 3:1—4:11	Preparation for the ministry, Chs. 3:11—4:13
Ministry in Galilee, Chs. 1:16—9:50	Ministry in Galilee, Chs. 4:12—18:35	Ministry in Galilee, Chs. 4:14—9:50
To Jerusalem Chs. 10—13	To Jerusalem, Chs. 19—20	To Jerusalem, Chs. 9:51—19:44
Passion, Death, Resurrection, Chs. 14:1—16:8	Passion, Death, Resurrection, Chs. 21—28	Passion, Death, Resurrection, Chs. 19:45—24:53

Luke varies most from Mark, but the Markan outline shapes both the Gospels of Matthew and Luke in considerable detail.

The same thing holds true if we attempt to construct a "theological outline" of themes in the first two Gospels. (Luke will be treated later.) Mark, the pioneer Gospel, presents the story in two sections with only brief items about backgrounds or about the church.

The Gospel of Mark

Historical Background	Galilee (Mark 1—9)	To and in Jerusalem	Church
Old Testament fulfillment seen in John the Baptist (1:2-3), occasionally	"The place of beginnings, revelation and salvation" Public ministry Jesus preaches,	"The place of hostile powers and the death of Jesus" Private ministry Fewer miracles. Jesus	Church and mission (see 13:10; 11—13)

Historical Background	Galilee (Mark 1-9)	To and in Jerusalem	Church
through Jesus (see 14:18, 34; 15:24). Little on "Israel"	teaches, does miracles about "the kingdom of God"	speaks more about himself and the future.	
	The disciples respond at first but "do not understand."	The disciples still misunderstand and desert and deny Jesus.	
	Controversy stories (2:1—3:6)	Controversy stories (ch. 12)	
	Passion predictions (8:31; 9:31; 10:33 ff.)	Passion narrative	

Matthew picks up many of these emphases and augments them at a number of places. This can be seen in connection with three prominent concerns: teaching, maintaining continuity with the past, and the church.

A theological outline of Matthew

Matthew puts a far greater emphasis on teaching than did Mark. All too often Mark said, "Jesus taught," but failed to report what h said (see Mark 1:22, 27). Matthew was determined to remedy that by providing more content. He also stressed teaching over preaching and healing (see 4:23) in the ministries of both Jesus and the disciples. His must have been a teaching church in which scribe-like teachers were prominent (see 13:52) and the Great Commission was to spread the gospel by teaching (28:20). Matthew made apparent his emphasis on teaching by concentrating what Jesus said in five great discourses, only two of which have parallels in Mark.

- The Sermon on the Mount: Matthew 5—7
- Missionary instructions for the Twelve: Matthew 10 (see Mark 6:7)
- Parables about the kingdom: Matthew 10 (The three parables in Mark 4 are expanded to seven.)
- Discipline in the community of disciples (or the church): Matthew 18
- Eschatology, Matthew 24—25 (See Mark 13 and note the closing of 24:42-51 where the emphasis is not only on watchfulness but also on good stewardship in the interim.)

Some would add Chapter 23, a collection of "woes" against the scribes and Pharisees.

Matthew also wanted to show the gospel's continuity with the past, particularly the Old Testament scriptures. This can be seen in the way he has Jesus and John the Baptist proclaim exactly the same message (3:2; 4:17). The disciples are also to preach that message (10:7), so that we have another example of the sequence of John-Jesus-disciples which Mark

The starting point for mission in Matthew 28:16 is "the mountain." Some identify this place with Mt. Tabor, whose height rises to 1,300 feet over the Plain of Esdraelon in Galilee.

presented. But Matthew goes further by beginning his Jesus story with a genealogy stretching back to Abraham (1:1-17) and by stressing that Jesus is "Son of David." The very title of his book suggests a link with the first book of the Old Testament. Although we translate 1:1, "The book of the genealogy of Jesus Christ," it means literally, "The book of the genesis of Jesus. . . ." Finally, there is Matthew's use of Old Testament verses with the formula "[This happened in Jesus' life] to fulfill what was spoken by the prophet in the Old Testament" and his insertion of allegorical details into parables which reflect Israel's past history. We can easily reject God's messengers, from the time of the prophets, as the Jews called them, right down to the fall of Jerusalem in A.D. 70 (see 22:1-10, especially v. 7).

The third of Matthew's special interests was the church. His is the only Gospel to use the word (16:18; 18:17). He closes with Jesus sending forth his church to preach in all the world (28:16-20). His discourses in Chapters 10 and 18, along with 5—7 and 23—25, can be read as pertinent to the church of his day. Some of the parables of Matthew 13 certainly have woven into them a doctrine of the church. If all of that is true, Matthew has expanded Mark's range of view to something like the following.

The Gospel of Matthew

Creation		Parousia
Background in Israel	*The Period of Jesus*	*The Time of the Church and of Mission*
Jesus' genealogy, stressing Abraham and David ➔ (1:1-17).	Jesus is the son of David, son of Abraham (1:1).	Go to all the world, Gentiles included (28:16-20).
Old Testament promises are now fulfilled (see ➔ 1:23; 2:6; 4:15 ff.).	Jesus is "the servant" (8:17 repeats Isaiah 53:4) who fulfills Scripture.	New promises made: "I am with you always" (28:20).
The law and the prophets, until John the Baptist (11:12 ff.), are in continuity with Jesus.		The disciples are also to be this continuity.
Israel's past history points to rejection (21:33 ff.; 22:2 ff.).	Jesus calls for righteousness (6:33; 5:20; 5:6; 13:43).	The church is also under judgment, and its members face God's ethical demand (22:11-13; 5:20).
	Galilee (Matthew 4—18) *Jerusalem* (Matthew 19—28)	

Matthew sees continuity between the past and the present. Unlike Luke, he does not write a second volume about the church. Instead he imposes a view of the church and a message for the community of his day on the Jesus story as he tells it. The main section on Jesus' ministry follows Mark's outline as indicated above, and the teaching discourses are built in.

Beneath the design

What sort of situation could have prompted Matthew to tell his story in this way? It is commonly conceded that he wrote some ten to twenty-five years after the fall of Jerusalem, somewhere between A.D. 85 and 90. With the sacred city in ruins a period of reflection had set in. Such a mood of intense expectancy for the *parousia* of Christ as that which had characterized Mark's day and lay behind such Pauline letters as those to Thessalonica—and which would rise again about A.D. 95 until the threat to the faith posed by the Emperor Domitian—had passed. Matthew's job was to sustain the future hope without inspiring unrealistic timetables for the end. Read Matthew 24:12, 26-28, 37-51, and Chapter 25 in the light of this background. All of it is material which Mark does not include.

Coming some 15-20 years after Mark also meant that Matthew faced a time of increasingly sharp demarcation between Judaism and the Christian church. Matthew could speak of "their synagogues" (4:23; 10:17; 12:9), that is, the synagogues of the Jews which were to be distinguished from the local assemblies of Jesus' disciples. After A.D. 80, as Judaism was reconstituting itself after the fall of Jerusalem, there was added to the synagogue prayer a petition which no follower of Jesus could pray: "Let . . . the Nazarenes and the *minim* [apparently references to Jewish Christians, the latter term meaning "sectarian" or "infidel"] perish . . . and be blotted from the Book of Life." Christians, including the author of the Gospel of Matthew, responded with equal vehemence at the parting of the ways. Such passages as Matthew 23:1-36; 27:25; and 22:7-8 reflect these feelings. It is important to read them against the times in which they were written. Twentieth-century Christians are no longer in the same situation in which Matthew's community lived. Hence they dare not let these passages fan the fires of anti-Semitism, always latent in the world, for new attacks on Jews or Israelis.

Matthew faced a situation different from that of Mark on one other score. Matthew's church community was strongly Jewish-Christian in background, whereas Mark's Gospel was composed primarily for Gentiles. Matthew's audience has often been described as a kind of Jewish-Christian enclave within the Jewish ghetto in a city like Antioch in Syria or a city in northern Palestine. Because of the hardening of the lines between Judaism and the emerging Christian church, prospects for gaining new members from Jewish backgrounds became increasingly unlikely. Moreover, the rest of the Christian movement was becoming more and more Gentile. But Greek and Roman members knew little of the Hebrew scriptures, the ethics of the Law, and God's past promises. They couldn't even read Hebrew! Conditions for Matthew's group were much like those of an old German or Swedish Lutheran church in the 1960s in a downtown urban area. The boats crowded with Northern European immigrants had long ceased coming; the neighboring blocks around the church were crowded with Blacks and Hispanics. "Will old Emmanuel Kirche die?"

183

The answer which Matthew gives is, "No!" Mission will go on. It was true that never during his earthly ministry did Jesus evangelize Samaritans or Gentiles (see 10:5). In fact, only rarely did he have contact with "foreigners" (see 8:5-13; 15:21-28). But now, after the Resurrection, the restrictions were lifted. The disciples were told to go everywhere, to *all* peoples (28:19-20).

But that did not mean severing ties with the past. Hence Matthew underscored the continuity between ancient Israel, Jesus, and the church. His "formula quotations" pointed up how past promises were being fulfilled.

Above all, the new situation was not to foster "cheap grace," where anything goes when you become a Christian. In Matthew, Jesus' teachings are laid out clearly and in detail. The kingdom is a gift, but you must seek its righteousness (6:33). Indeed, righteousness itself is a code word for God's righteous will, which Matthew sought to spell out as Jesus proclaimed it. At times Matthew makes Jesus sound more legalistic than do the other Gospels, but his goal is to make sure converts see that responsibility follows upon conversion. The indicative is there, but the imperative which follows even more so.

Two other subjects in Matthew's carefully crafted work that deserve attention are the church and Christ's presence in it. Matthew stresses the church as no other evangelist does. He also links it to the kingdom with equal persistence. While Matthew speaks a great deal of "the kingdom of heaven" (see 4:17; 13:24, 31, 33, 44, 45, 47) and occasionally of its equivalent "the kingdom of God" (see 12:28; 19:24), he also introduces a distinction between "the Kingdom *of the Father*" and "the Kingdom *of the Son of Man.*" He does this in the Parable of the Weeds and Wheat (13:24-30). Note the closing verses of its explanation.

> "The *Son of man* will send his angels, and they will gather out of *his kingdom* all causes of sin and evildoers. . . . Then the righteous will shine like the sun in *the kingdom of their Father.*"
>
> (Matthew 13:41-43, italics added)

The kingdom of the Son of man is something already in existence. Those who do evil will be winnowed out of it before the kingdom of the Father comes. It is attractive to suggest that by "the kingdom of the Son of man" Matthew meant nothing other than the church where God's rule and Jesus Christ are acknowledged and obeyed. The church is that sphere where the kingdom is already present, although Matthew warns that its members will also be subject to a judgment (see 22:11-13; 16:27; 13:47-50). His associating the kingdom with Jesus Christ in this way is paralleled by only a few other passages (see 1 Corinthians 15:24; Colossians 1:13; and Revelation 1:9).

Finally, Matthew stresses the presence of Christ himself with the be-

The starting point for mission in Luke is Jerusalem, specifically the Temple inside these walls where the Word was taught and preached (Luke 24:53; Acts 3:1; 5:42).

lieving community and each member. The promise of *Immanuel* or "God with us" (Isaiah 7:14) is very precious to Matthew, and he sees it fulfilled in Jesus Christ. That is made clear at the conclusion of the book. *Immanuel* is brought to completion when Jesus makes a new promise, "Lo, I am with you always, to the close of the age" [or "end of the world"] (28:20). The promise is echoed at 18:20: "Where two or three are gathered in my name, there am I in the midst of them," a passage that occurs only in Matthew. The presence of Jesus with his people in mission has enabled Christians for centuries to bring the gospel to people everywhere.

LUKE: THE STORY OF SALVATION FOR THE WORLD

A good deal has been said already concerning the "good news book" about Jesus traditionally attributed to the Gentile physician Luke (Colossians 4:14; Philemon 24; 2 Timothy 4:11). He is not mentioned by name in the Gospel according to Luke, but it is usually assumed that he is the author of the "we" passages in the Book of Acts, perhaps quoted from a travel diary (see Acts 16:10–18; 20:5–15; 21:1–18; 27:1—28:16). But some argue that the author of both volumes is an otherwise unknown Greek Christian. We should perhaps note in passing that all the Gospels are anonymous. Only later tradition assigned authors to them.

Luke and Acts are also linked by the fact that both mention Theophilus (Luke 1:3; Acts 1:1). Perhaps this man was the author's patron. If so, then it was through Theophilus's generosity that both the Gospel and the account of the beginnings of the church came into being. Luke and Acts make up twenty-eight percent of the New Testament. In the Gospel, Luke concentrates on the account of Jesus' life beginning with events before his birth and ending with Jesus' ascension into heaven. The result of his efforts has been called by some "the most beautiful book ever written."

What makes Luke unique

For sure Luke was a literary craftsman. His basic outline, already given above, follows Mark to a considerable degree. But the work contains a historical preface worthy of a Hellenistic historian of the day (1:1-4), extensive infancy and childhood accounts (Luke 1—2), and such unique teachings and parables and Resurrection appearances as the Parables of the Good Samaritan (10:29-37) and the Prodigal Son (15:11-32) and the story of the risen Christ on the road to Emmaus (24:13-35). Parts of the first two chapters are studded with hymns and songs which Christians still sing and which sometimes echo in Luke's later chapters (1:46-55, 68-79; 2:29-32; see 2:14 with 19:38).

Behind his work are sources which the author says he was diligent to trace out. Luke also claims to have had the example of the "many" who had undertaken to compile a narrative of the events "which have been accomplished among us" by God through Jesus and in the church (1:1). When we ask just what Luke had at hand when he wrote, we come up with a fourfold answer. First, there was Mark. Second, a collection of Jesus' sayings. Third, a source unique to his work containing many incidents and sayings from Jesus' ministry not used by the other evangelists. Fourth, the Old Testament in its Greek form.

A few scholars think Luke may have had Matthew as a source, but most opt for the collection of sayings indicated above. That collection is identified roughly as the material common to Luke and Matthew but missing in Mark. It is often called Q, from the German word *Quelle*, meaning source. Bible students often use three brief designations for these sources, Mark, Q, and L (Luke's special source).

While it is often assumed that Luke took over Mark and added his other materials to it, there is some basis for supposing that he actually began with L and Q and came upon Mark only later, adding that material to what was already a first edition of his Gospel. Such a theory is especially helpful in explaining why the middle section and the Passion narrative in Luke's Gospel differ so much from that in Mark. Luke 9:51—19:44 constitutes a major section of the Gospel referred to earlier simply under the heading "To Jerusalem," and which some commentators call the Samaritan Section. This material mentions Samaritans several times (9:52; 10:33; 17:16) but does not describe much of the action as occurring in Samaria. It consists almost entirely of material found only in Luke or Matthew, almost never in Mark.

Even better evidence for suggesting that Luke went his own way on the basis of accounts he preferred over what is in Mark is the Passion narrative and particularly the Jewish trial(s). Mark focuses on a trial before the Sanhedrin at night (14:53-64), followed by a brief reference to a second meeting of the council in the morning (15:1). Such a sequence violates what we know of rules for the Sanhedrin with respect to night trials and its power to pronounce and execute a death sentence. Luke has a far superior outline. There is only one Jewish trial session, and it takes place during the day (22:66-71). Luke also specifies the charges against Jesus (23:2) and adds a hearing before Herod Antipas (23:6-12). Of course, Luke could have simply rewritten Mark, adding better information and insights, but the case is strong for supposing he had a different source.

It has sometimes been observed that stories in Luke seem to bear a close relationship with passages in the Gospel of John. Compare the two anointing stories in Luke 7:36-50 and John 12:1-8 in contrast to that in Mark 14:3-9 and Matthew 26:6-13. Only in Luke and John do we find the names Mary, Martha, Lazarus, and Annas (Luke 10:38-42 and John 11:1 and 12:1-3; Luke 16:20 and John 11:2; Luke 3:2 and Acts 4:6 and John

18:13, respectively). These are the two Gospels in which Satan leads Judas to betray Jesus (Luke 22:3; John 13:2, 27), we are told it was a right ear of a servant of the high priest which was cut off by a disciple in Gethsemane (Luke 22:50; John 18:10), and a miraculous catch of fish is described (Luke 5:4–9; John 21:5–11). The interplay among the Gospels, revealed by such evidence, has always intrigued scholars and everyday readers. Most likely John knew Luke's Gospel, or at least they shared some common traditions.

Luke's "times and seasons"

It was the situation in which Luke wrote, however, which affected his way of telling the story of Jesus as much as the rich sources he had at his disposal. As with Matthew, the time is after the fall of Jerusalem. (Luke even uses a different section of material about "Jerusalem surrounded by armies" [21:20–24] in place of the Markan verses on "the desolating sacrilege" standing in the holy place [Mark 13:14; Matthew 24:15]). The date is somewhere around A.D. 90. But the mood is more akin to that in John than to the apocalyptic "dark days" reflected in Mark or the feeling of confrontations with Judaism in Matthew. In particular Luke addressed his story of the good news of Jesus to the Greco-Roman world.

Accordingly, as a Gentile writing for Gentiles, Luke eliminates a good many Semitic expressions. The only foreign word retained is *amen,* when it occurs at the start of a saying by Jesus, often translated "verily" or "truly." Even so, the term is eliminated in Luke's Greek version on all but six occasions. In comparison, Mark has thirteen "amens," Matthew thirty, and John twenty-five (always in a double form: "Verily, verily . . ."). After an initial use at 4:24, Luke seems to use "amen" to call attention to the significance of things Jesus says for future Christianity. That initial use had to do with Jesus' rejection in Nazareth when he spoke of the gospel going to non-Jews.

Even this small example suggests Luke was quite conscious of the audience he wanted to reach. It is exemplified by Theophilus who needed to be buttressed by a clear, orderly account of the things about which he is already somewhat informed.

Thus Luke writes to set forth in narrative form the Jesus story. It is intended for a church growing increasingly universal in its outlook. All men and women in the world are targets for its message. Unlike Matthew, Luke does not have to worry about Jewish rivalry. Debates over the law as in Paul's day are a thing of the past. If Luke has any great concern, it is to convey to the Roman government (some even think Theophilus was a state official) the impression that Jesus and Christianity are no threat to an orderly society. So, according to Luke, Pilate pronounced sentence only at the demand of some Jewish leaders (23:24), it is a Roman centurion at the cross who says, "This man was innocent" (23:47), and later in Acts the Roman officials deal fairly and kindly with Paul (see Acts 13:12; 16:38–39; 27:42–43).

But Luke's chief aim is to lay a groundwork in Jesus' ministry for a gospel which will reach out to all people. The evangelist shows special interest in women (8:1–3; 10:38–42) and concern for the poor. His book has been called "The Gospel According to Thirty-One Women" (the number referred to) and Chapters 15—19 "The Gospel According to the Outcast." He also shows special interest in Samaritans and all humankind in general. Note that the genealogy goes back to Adam (3:38) and that at 3:4 only Luke adds the words of Isaiah that "all flesh shall see the salvation of God" (3:6).

Prayer and the power of the Spirit are two resources for witnessing in the world.

In a very real way Luke's theme is "salvation for all." The frontispiece scene in 4:16–30, which we have already examined, makes that clear. Perhaps it is because of this interest that Luke features "gospel" even more than the "kingdom of God" as a theme for Jesus' ministry. His awareness of how Jesus' followers are to spread that gospel of salvation also prompts him to lay more emphasis on prayer and the Holy Spirit than Mark or Matthew. Prayer and the power of the Spirit are two resources for witnessing in the world (see, for example, 18:1; 11:13; 24:49; Acts 1:14; 2:1–4).

Because of his interest in salvation and in his giving his story a historical setting Luke has probably done more than any other New Testament writer to provide us with a sweeping view of God at work in history to save. Some of his theological ideas are profiled in the accompanying chart.

A Theological Outline of The Gospel According to Luke

The Age of Israel

From creation, through God's Law and the prophets, to John the Baptist. (Read 3:23–38; note 16:16.)

The Age of Jesus as "Salvation Time"

Nothing like it has ever been known: Jesus was on earth ministering! He had Satan under control; he did miracles; he taught; he received the poor, women, and Samaritans. He died a martyr's death to show that God is a loving Father. When Jesus says, "Today fulfillment has come" (4:18), he is referring to that unique time of his earthly ministry in:

Galilee	Travel to Jerusalem	Jerusalem
3:21–22	9:51–19:27	19:28—24:53
4:1–9:50	(Samaria)	(*not* Galilee)

The Age of the Church

(Until the Parousia) Jesus sits enthroned at God's right hand (Acts 7:55). The church, though often hard pressed by enemies, bears witness and seeks to evangelize all peoples. The word of God grows and is spread (see Acts 6:7; 12:24; 19:20).

RESURRECTION

ASCENSION

APPEARANCES

JESUS

These three sections provide something of a parallel to the outline in Acts (see 1:8):

Jerusalem	Judea, Samaria, neighboring parts	Paul goes to Rome
Acts 1:12—8:3	8:4—12:24	12:25—28:31

Three implications

A great many implications can be drawn from Luke's theological view of history, where God has been at work in Israel, through Jesus, and now in the church. Three of these are especially of interest at this point.

First, "the Kingdom of God" is a Lukan theme that appears from 4:43 on. Luke seems to view it as many Christians since his time have thought of it, perhaps because of his influence. The kingdom is that rule of God which drew marvelously near when Jesus was on earth. Thus Luke alone reports the saying, "Behold, the kingdom of God is in the midst of you" (17:21). That means not so much "in your hearts" spiritually as "among you" in Jesus and his mighty deeds—unless the emphasis is on the fact that the kingdom is given as a gift, suddenly, without "signs to be observed" (17:20).

But according to Luke, the kingdom is also a reality that lies in the future. Luke 21:31 suggests that it will come only after certain signs enumerated apocalyptically in 21:25-30 have taken place. We have already seen that this present/future kingdom was continued as good news in the early church. Indeed, the closing words of Acts have Paul preaching it in Rome. But talk about a "kingdom" or "Jesus as king" (Acts 17:7) could be misunderstood in Roman circles. All in all, Luke seems to say that the kingdom was here as never before when Jesus was on earth, and it will arrive in its fullness at the future coming of the Lord in glory.

Second, Luke's *eschatology*, or view of the "last things," is crucial to understanding his thought. He recasts the theme of Mark 13 into two separate discourses (17:22-37; 21:5-33). He indicates the fall of Jerusalem was not the end of the world (21:20). There are still "the times of the Gentiles" (21:24) to be fulfilled. Life will go on (17:26-30) with people eating, drinking, marrying, dying. There are "days of the Son of man" to be lived through (17:22 ff.). God's people in the church should continue to live and witness, pray and watch (21:34-36) till their "redemption" (21:28) comes. With faith and trust they are to continue bearing testimony, knowing they are in God's hands (21:12-19).

Third, we have seen how Luke treated Jesus' message about the kingdom and related it to other gospel themes and how he helped Christians live after Jerusalem's fall without giving up the hope for a future return of Christ. By so doing Luke, perhaps more than any other New Testament writer, set the lines of development for future Christianity. The church-year calendar, with its Ascension Day and Pentecost forty and fifty days after Easter and its Christmas Nativity, is a contribution from Luke. So are his understanding of Jesus' place in the history of salvation and the eschatology of a kingdom that came and will come. Luke's two volumes thus provided the norms for a great deal of Christian life and enabled ensuing generations to keep on living faithfully and applying the good news to the daily round of life.

191

References and More Information

1. The term *Synoptic* implies two things. First, that a similar overall view pervades all three works so that we see Jesus in them in much the same way. Second, that if the three books are printed side by side the sequence of stories and even the actual words line up closely in parallel ways.

Biblical references: Look up the Matthew, Mark, and Luke chapter and verse references as you go through Chapter 29. Read all of Mark.

Ruins of the Inn of the Good Samaritan. The Samaritan parable is part of the rich treasury of Jesus' teaching peculiar to Luke.

PART VII One Gospel, Many Forms

The many forms in which the gospel has been expressed is symbolized by the countless shapes and sizes of churches. In every generation church architecture has provided structures that proclaim the good news in fresh and cogent ways.

30. The Gospel Through the Centuries—and Us

The good news from God to humanity in the Scriptures has taken many forms. In fact, there are so many that those who have worked through the first two volumes of this study may wish at the end that "the real gospel" would stand up and identify itself! How nice if we could have one fixed formula of the good news supported with divine approval to serve for all times and situations. But in giving us the Bible, God has not chosen to work that way. There is no single summary of which it can be said, "This is the one and only way of stating the gospel."

What we can do in surveying Scripture's seemingly bewildering array of ways to express the glad tidings for Israel and the early church is first to sort out some of these forms. Second, we can look at how the gospel message has resounded through the centuries from New Testament times to our own day. While doing both we can also examine how these expressions of the gospel have impact on us and how some of this good news may be carried further into God's world by us.

REVIEW OF THE GOOD NEWS IN THE SCRIPTURES

We have found that "the kingdom of God" is a recurring theme in many parts of the Bible. Its prominence in our study is due to the fact that we started with Jesus as he came "preaching the gospel of God, . . . 'The kingdom of God is at hand . . .'" (Mark 1:14–15). God's kingship breaking in on the world during his own ministry was the central message on Jesus' lips. In making the choice he was playing with dynamite, for to talk of Yahweh's kingship was a dangerous act during the Roman occupation. Jesus had to make it clear that he was no zealous revolutionist, but the proclaimer of God's justice, love, and concern, especially to the outcasts among his people.

Chances are that the same theme, "Yahweh has become king and reigns," would have emerged if we had started with some portion of the

196

Old Testament. Only if we had begun with the New Testament book that follows the first three Gospels would we have found the kingdom to be a peripheral motif in contrast to some other subjects.

So it was in light of the Synoptic Gospels and much of the Hebrew scriptures that we traced the kingdom or kingship of God as a continuing theme. It turned out to be reflected in every aspect of Israel's faith and life, marking the nation as a people under the lordship of God. These people were constituted by his actions and pledged obedience to his will. *God is king* for Israel by virtue of their deliverance from slavery in Egypt, the covenant he gave them, and his promises which carried even into the dark days of exile. *God has been king* since creation. He becomes king again each new year with his enthronement as ruler over all the world. *God will be king,* too, proclaimed the faith of Israel as it looked hopefully toward the future.

Therefore, one way of expressing the good news has been to speak of God's sovereign rule as king:

- In the past—at the Exodus, at creation, and at dozens of other times and places.

- In the present—over the believing community and, according to its assertion, throughout the world.

- In the future—when he redeems his people from misfortunes into which they periodically fall and when he finally winds things up with justice and judgment at the "day of the Lord."

Of course, we also saw how this pervasive theme took a back seat after Easter. It gave way to other expressions of good news, because the ancient Near Eastern idea of God as king could lead to misunderstanding among both Jews and Christians. The Roman Empire was likely to view with disfavor the prayers of a synagogue liturgy that asked for a restoration of "the throne of David" in Jerusalem, for "the horn of freedom," and for "the arrogant kingdom to be rooted out in our days." The Romans also looked on any talk of a kingship in connection with Jesus as a menace. So under Roman rule and with the rise of Christianity came the question: Would the age-old theme of the kingdom of God drop from sight? That it did not we shall see in the following discussion of good-news themes.

More ways to tell the good news

In exploring the kingship of God in Scripture we have also come across related themes which sometimes were lifted up as "the gospel." Historically, two events have been supremely important for Jews and Christians. Both are celebrated at the same time of the year at what the Bible calls Passover time. They are—

- The Exodus from Egypt in which God delivers his "son," Israel, from bondage.
- The resurrection at Jerusalem in which God raises his Son, Jesus, from the dead.

Separated by some twelve centuries, here were two ways of speaking about God's victory. This "victor" theme became especially popular in the early centuries of Christianity when the Church Fathers loved to speak of Christ as "victor over death." It continued the Old Testament motif of Yahweh's victory in the "holy war."

We have also uncovered in both Old and New Testaments other related themes which appear and reappear. They have meant good news to countless thousands over the centuries. One is "the covenant," although we have seen that this is less pervasive in the New Testament than in the Old where it took on a variety of forms. Another is the idea of "lordship," first of God and later of Christ. For many people today, the idea of having someone as lord over them may seem like bad news, but for biblical peoples it was a comforting thought. To know that God was pledged to Israel meant security and confidence. Similarly, to know that someone called Jesus whom you had come to know and rely upon as a companion in Galilee was now "Lord of all" held like implications. Related, too, is the notion of "promise." One can build a life upon the pledges made by one whose word is reliable.

"Kingship" and its related topics may have seemed strange before the in-depth study of these last twenty-nine chapters. If the premise behind the choice was that "Christianity is Christ" and he is himself the gospel, such an expectation has not brought disappointment. We have examined Jesus during his ministry, Jesus exalted by his resurrection as Lord, Jesus the Lord affirmed by faith for his role in the creation and preservation of the world, and the Lord Jesus as Messiah or Christ. As if that were not enough, we have also looked at him in the sermons and faith the apostles preached and in each of the Gospels. If anyone wants to say, highlighting the New Testament, that the gospel is Christ, the evidence is there to do it.

Still other ways have been uncovered to state the good news. "Justification" or "the righteousness of God" has been so used not only in the Epistles of Paul but also prior to that in the Old Testament and in the earliest Christian circles. "Eternal life" has been cited in John and elsewhere. What can be better news for a prisoner on trial than to hear the verdict "acquitted" (or "justified")? Or for a person living in a dying society, amidst soured relationships, or within a shriveled personhood than to be handed the gift of true life from beyond? As a final example, in some segments of the Bible the message from God was that the Almighty, the Holy One, is with his people in their greatest needs or perils and that he sustains them in their pilgrimage and witnessing.

Ethics and church as good news

You probably recall other expressions of good news which surprised and delighted you in working through the scriptural witness. Two which people today might not think can be part of the gospel are "ethics" and "community." Both Testaments insist that these two themes can be designated as good news.

Exhortation and orders hardly sound like good news. More often we associate such terms with the law, with bad news. They represent requirements meant to convict people of their sinfulness or regulations to which we can never conform. Biblical religion reasoned, however, that God's will for us is a good thing. To know that it is from him is even better. And to put it into practice as an obedient response to his deliverance is best of all. This is not to say that people save themselves through the law, but that their response is part of that "obedience of faith" which follows when we have been transformed by the gospel (see Romans 12:1-2). Statements about what God wants us to do are thus part of the good news.

We have seen several examples of good-news ethics. Forms of the covenant include stipulations for the conduct of Israel. Paul's letters regularly include an ethical section about what God wills for us on the basis of what God has already done (see Romans 12:1: "I appeal to you . . . therefore, by the mercies of God"). Matthew very clearly builds God's imperative into his Gospel. Luke provides a striking example when he writes of John the Baptist, "So, with many other exhortations, he preached good news to the people" (3:18). Read the verses that preceded that line and they sound like anything but good news. John talks about judgment (3:7, 17), repentance (3:8), and principles of conduct. Some interpreters suggest Luke's verb means nothing more than "preached" in a broad sense, but the same word is used at 4:18, 43. At 3:18 the TEV therefore correctly renders it, "In many different ways John preached the Good News to the people." What is at stake is the idea that the gospel includes a God-given pattern for people's lives in the new age.

The "church" or the community must also be counted as part of the good news and not just an adjunct to it. The church is not a barrier to the good news as some folks may think. Very often earnest students of the Scriptures have set the Bible and the church over against each other. Some sects, particularly Jehovah's Witnesses, make "the organized church" (as if there were a "disorganized" one!) a favorite whipping boy. The Bible itself shows us that the community of Israel has a high rating throughout the Old Testament. Yahweh created it and delivered and sustained it time and time again. He ordained its worship and sent his prophets to renew it. In hard times he sought to sustain a remnant out of it or to create new shoots and life from "the vine that was Israel" (Psalm 80:9-19). In the New Testament, "the church of the Lord" is something "he obtained with his own blood" (see Acts 20:28). The reference is

199

probably to "the blood of his own Son," meaning "Christ died for the church." However, some commentators think "the blood of God himself" is meant! Christ, the true vine, has "branches," that is, church members who "bear fruit" by living ethically (John 15:1–17). Thus the church does not merely preach the good news, but through its members in Christ, it must live it and be a part of the gospel.

VARIETY YET UNITY

The result of finding within the Bible so many ways of experiencing good news should not be a cause of despair or confusion. It can really be a reason for joy. God has spoken and is speaking to people in different times and places. He has many facets of his truth to convey.

Even the tensions uncovered within such a single biblical theme as the kingdom of God have their purpose. Is the kingdom present or future? When a passage stresses the presence of the kingdom, we are being told that God is doing something then and there—or here and now. When another passage speaks of the kingdom as still to come, we learn that even as baptized Christians we do not have all of God at our beck and call.

There have, of course, often been strong efforts to make one theme from the Bible more central than others. Some of these endeavors have cut across denominational lines and have reflected the spirit of an age or a motif whose time had come. For example, a mission impulse to evangelize the world swept through much of Christendom in the nineteenth and early twentieth centuries. Samuel Wolcott captured it in the words:

> Christ for the world we sing;
> The world to Christ we bring
> With loving zeal.
>
> (*SBH* 311)

Countless missionaries set out "to evangelize the world in this generation." The mission movement arose partly from biblical injunctions, partly as a response to revivalist preaching, and partly because the time was right.

Another example is more recent. In America during the 1960s social justice became the central thrust of faith for many people. Lutherans, Baptists, Catholics, clergy, nuns, and lay people from countless backgrounds marched and prayed together for civil rights for blacks.

More frequently, however, a particular thematic stress found in Scripture has separated people and led to the formation of churches and denominations. Sometimes this has involved an effort to make a particular biblical teaching the norm. The Reformation is a case in point. Generally the reformers sought not only to return to Scripture but also to lift up its central truths. Lutherans in particular stressed "the gospel" and defined it in terms of "justification by grace through faith." Admittedly, this way of putting the good news reflects Luther's own personal struggle to find a gracious God. But expressed in terms of "the righteousness of God," this is a major theme in many parts of the Bible. It is probably the principal means used by Paul to express what God is doing for us in gospel language. Lutherans thus remain that confessional church within the Christian family or that movement within the church catholic which continues to propose justification as the article on which a church stands or falls, the organizing theme for theology, and the gospel basis for life.

Not all Christians, of course, agree on the centrality of justification and regard it as a touchstone for Christianity. Other Christians read the Scriptures in the light of their own unique experiences and heritage. They may well choose some other theme to express the good news. Lutherans should have an interest in all such expressions of the good news as a mark of their ecumenical and witness concerns. They should not insist that every formulation of the gospel must agree verbally with their own wordings. They ought to be ready to examine all formulations of the good news, ancient or modern, to see if they express that message from and about God which justification includes. But to do so would require raising several questions.

1. Is God seen here as working salvation, that is, a right and renewed relationship with himself? Is God seen as doing this for all humankind?

2. Is this action of God wholly of his grace and not somehow partially dependent on human actions or intents?

3. Is an obedient, trusting, loving human response being called forth?

4. Is Christ's cross seen as the means for effecting this renewal?

5. Is sin taken seriously as human selfishness, self-love, disobedience, and lack of fear for God? Is it taken as seriously as in Genesis 1—3 and Romans 1—3?

6. Is there hope that transformation, growth, and ultimate fulfillment will result from what God is doing here?

Some would add a seventh question. Are both the personal and cosmic dimensions included?

If all these emphases are somehow represented, we can say we have a proper expression of the gospel. Lutherans will recognize in this sevenfold list the equivalent expressions of what their own classical theological tradition has called: (1) justification; (2) by grace alone; (3) through faith; (4) for Christ's sake; involving (5) sin and the study of the human condition (anthropology); (6) the doctrine of future things or eschatology; and (7) the aspects of justification which go beyond what happens just in the individual's heart and life. Lutherans do not mean to suggest that the good news can be expressed only in the language of justification, righteousness, or the courts of law. They do say that any expression of the gospel must preserve what justification makes so clear.

Thus do the spirit of an age and a denominational heritage help shape how people have expressed the gospel.

It should also be noted that while we have tried in this study to keep separate the different biblical ways of expressing the good news, Christians through the ages have often mixed and combined them. At times these combinations appear to lack discrimination. Biblical scholars think that the easy interpretation of a verse in Isaiah or Matthew by one in John, and interpretation of both verses by a theme from Paul may be a disservice to all four biblical writers and prevent us from hearing God's Word in its original situation. Yet theology has systematically sought to combine these ideas. Poets, of course, take special license in interrelating images. Note, for example, the variety of themes (italicized) in just one verse of a Pentecost hymn by the American Samuel Longfellow:

> *Holy Spirit,* right divine,
> *King* within my conscience reign;
> Be my *law,* and I shall be
> Firmly bound, for ever *free.*
> (*SBH* 130)

To interpret this author fairly, one should begin by finding out what scriptural and other ideas and experiences he had in mind, not only in this fifth stanza of the hymn but in the other stanzas as well. With liberties granted for artistic creativity, only then should one consider how this holds together as a poetic expression of good news to be sung at Pentecost.

To the large number of biblical expressions of good news, we find we must also add subsequent formulations of the gospel in ensuing periods of history. Various churches have emphasized the gospel in different ways, and Christians have combined images and themes.

The Bible is an inexhaustible well for witnessing and a perpetual source for reading good news from God.

Whoever said the noun *good news* is singular? We often pause in everyday speech wondering whether to use a plural or singular verb with *news*. While we usually say, "The news is good," the word is literally a plural form of what is "*new*," and for several centuries was used in its plural and singular forms. The fact is that in the Bible "good news" is decidedly plural in the forms it takes. Could it be otherwise, if God was to speak to so many different situations? What folly to limit our gospel to just one mode of expression when there are so many needs to which to speak! The Bible is an inexhaustible well for witnessing and a perpetual source for reading good news from God.

Yet no matter what form that news took, readers have always been conscious of certain common concerns or emphases running through it.

202

Above all there is the truly good news that God is graciously at work for good in our world and our lives. We have found that to be so whether "kingdom," "Christ," "justification," or "covenant" language was used to say it. The shorthand way Christians have often used to sum up what is involved in all is to speak of "the gospel," thus reflecting the fact that the Greek and Hebrew terms *evangelion* and *besorah* are both singular.

Gospel is preeminently a New Testament term. The RSV translation employs it only in the New Testament sense. But the Old Testament speaks of "good tidings" of "good." The Christian scriptures specify these tidings as "the gospel of God" (Mark 1:14; Romans 1:1); "the gospel concerning his Son" (Romans 1:3); "the gospel of Christ" (Romans 15:19); "the gospel of your salvation" (Ephesians 1:13); and "the gospel of peace" (Ephesians 6:15). It is an "eternal gospel" (Revelation 14:6) which, in the form of the justification theme, is "the power of God for salvation to everyone who has faith" (Romans 1:16). For all its objective content the gospel of the Scriptures is something to be personally appropriated and expressed as "my gospel" (Romans 16:25; 2 Timothy 2:8). It is the only truly good news; there is no other. A gospel contrary to that which proclaims God's saving work in Christ for us is no gospel at all, says Paul, but only a devilish parody and "bad news" (Galatians 1:6–7). "The gospel is the word" (Acts 15:7; Colossians 1:5) and truth (Galatians 2:14; Colossians 1:5).

Gospel, then, is what gives unity to the many themes and ways of expressing the good news in the Bible and beyond. Inevitably, it takes many forms, but gospel as good news is the unifying thread.

"*The* story" (the big story for us), God's story (His Story) in Scripture, is the gospel. In witnessing, our stories, both yours and mine, must ultimately be under His Story and conform to it if they are to be authentic gospel. But to know the richness of how the gospel has been expressed scripturally is a great help for those testimonies we make.

THE GOSPEL AND THE KINGDOM THROUGH THE CENTURIES

Since the close of the New Testament canon the gospel has continued to be told, proclaimed, and spread in many forms. The good news has had an ongoing history which extends down to our day. That fact is realized every time a sermon is preached, a witness evangelizes someone for Christ, or I tell my "God Story" under the overarching spread of the Scriptures as experienced by me and my church.

In his book *Evangelical Witness*, Ralph W. Quare has a chapter intriguingly titled, "Where Has All the Good News Gone?" Some sects say it disappeared for centuries, until they recovered it in modern times. However, Christians who accept history as an arena of God's activity and treasure the promise that God's Spirit has always been at work and that no age is left without God's witness (see Acts 14:17) must reckon more seriously with these intervening centuries. Lutherans cannot say the gospel was not present in the church of the Middle Ages. The gospel was present even in the period before the Reformation reawakened people to what Scripture said.

And so the answer to Quare's question is that the good news has gone out into the world for centuries in many forms. The scriptural expressions of the good news have multiplied, and taken on the colorings of Europe, Asia, Africa, and the Americas as well as the trappings of the years as the gospel moved on. We do not have time or space here to indicate the many ways Christians have expressed themselves. To detail the entire history would require telling the whole history of the church including the development of its theology and its record of evangelization and witnessing.

What we can do, however, is to describe some highlights of how Jesus' way of asserting the gospel as good news about "the kingdom of God" has continued to inspire people through the centuries. We can show the gospel finding ever new and exciting ways of capturing minds and lives for Christ and God.

We have seen that other ways of stating the gospel tended to replace the gospel about the kingdom after Easter as the church advanced into the Roman Empire, but the "kingdom of God" remained a theme in Paul's letters and elsewhere. At times, the kingdom was placed in tandem with the lordship of Jesus Christ (Acts 28:31). On occasion there was reference to the kingdom of Christ as a future, intermediate age (1 Corinthians 15:24) or to the church as an intermediate stage of the kingdom of the Son of man preceding the future kingdom of the Father (Matthew 13:41; Luke 22:29). In the words of Acts 1:6–8, it was not for mortals on earth to know when the kingdom will be restored to Israel. The important thing was that Christ was empowering apostles to be his witnesses. Some were later to see in this passage authorization for an apostolic government in the church marking the reign of God. And equating the kingdom of God's beloved Son with "redemption" and "forgiveness of sins" at Colossians 1:13–14 was to provide the groundwork for interpreting the kingdom as the rule of God in the redeemed, forgiven human heart.

In all these ways, the New Testament contained the seed for later flowerings of the kingdom theme, enhanced by the innumerable Old Testament references to God as king. Even though the Epistles and other writings (apart from the Synoptics) in the New Testament failed to stress the kingdom of God or of Christ, the idea would continue in Christian thought and life for twenty centuries. In the *Te Deum* it even became a way of stating the Easter gospel:

> Thou art the King of Glory, O Christ; . . .
> When thou hadst overcome the sharpness of death:
> Thou didst open the kingdom of heaven to all believers.
> (*SBH*, p. 133)

If we were to put on parade the references to the kingdom in the second, third, and fourth centuries, the most prominent place would go to those that deal with a visible reign of Christ on earth between his second coming and the last judgment—the kind of millennial kingdom some infer from Revelation 20. There are references in this period to the kingdom as "the perfect reign of God in heaven after the last judgment" or as "the visible church on earth between Pentecost and the parousia." But the notion of a thousand-year kingdom on earth, especially one involving martyrs, exerted the greatest attraction in the Christian mind. In a period of persecution and speculations about "the end," millenialism or "chiliasm" was bound to appeal to people.

AUGUSTINE AND THE KINGDOM OF GOD

The person who changed this direction and gave the kingdom new meaning as "the city of God" was Augustine, Bishop at Hippo in North Africa (A.D. 354-430). A Numidian and kin to the Berbers, he may have had Negro blood in him. Augustine's own story is dramatic. In spite of the prayers of his mother Monica, he avoided Baptism and lived a sensuous life, fathering a son out of wedlock and drifting from one religion and philosophy to another. Himself a brilliant teacher of rhetoric, he was moved by the sermons of Ambrose, Bishop of Milan, and then converted when a voice told him, "Take up and read." The passage to which he opened was Romans 13:13-14: "Not in reveling and drunkenness, not in debauchery and licentiousness, not in quarreling and jealousy. But put on the Lord Jesus Christ, and make no provision for the flesh, to gratify its desires." He was baptized at 33, ordained by popular demand, and served as Bishop of Hippo Reguis, a town west of Carthage (modern Tunisia) from 395 till his death in 430.

Augustine was a deep thinker in an age when much was changing and the church was being crippled by opposing Christian groups and rival theological ideas. In particular, Augustine took a stand against the optimistic views of the monk Pelagius who claimed Adam's sin affected no one but Adam. Because people are born with uncorrupted powers and only later fall into sin, children do not need to be baptized. Augustine opposed Pelagius on all three points (see Genesis 1—3; Romans 1—3) and set the future pattern for Christian theology generally.

It is with what he said about the kingdom of God, however, that we are concerned. Early in his career Augustine held to the prevailing view that the kingdom would come as a thousand-year reign of Christ on earth, but in time he repudiated this as an apocalyptic misunderstanding. He knew of the view that the kingdom would come only after the last judgment as well as the statements which linked but did not identify the present church with the kingdom. He knew, for example, of Cyprian's assertion that "a

205

person cannot hope to reach the kingdom who deserts the church which is destined to reign." What Augustine did was to stake out the church and the whole sweep of its history as the reign or kingdom of God. Of course he qualified it to maintain the distinctions between "the church as it now is" and "the church as it will be," but church and kingdom were identified as they never had been before.

Augustine's greatest exposition of his theme is in a twenty-two volume work which he began in 410 when Rome fell to the Visigoths. He finished the writing in 426, just before the Vandals lay siege to his own city. Pagans had been saying that the fall of Rome was due to the abandonment of the worship of the ancient Roman gods. As a historian, Augustine sought to show that the seeds of decline had been planted prior to and apart from the rise of Christianity. As a Christian, he went on to ponder all history philosophically and theologically. There exist, he became convinced, two opposing "cities" (or "commonwealths"). The "city of God" stands over against "the earthly city," or the kingdom of the Devil. Augustine traces the city of God from creation, through Abraham, Israel, Christ, and the church. The "earthly city" or kingdom begins with the fall of the angels (see Genesis 6:4) and of man (Genesis 3), and is traced through Cain (Genesis 4), the tower of Babel, and the great but sinister empires of Nineveh, Babylon, Persia, Macedonia, and Rome.

In this ancient "tale of two cities" there are a number of contrasting elements:

	The City of God	The City of the World
The foundation:	Love of God	Love of self
Purpose:	Heavenly peace	Mere earthly peace
Resource:	Justice	Justice borrowed from the city of God

Augustine saw two distinct classes of people. There were the elect, citizens of the city of God, and those "disapproved," outside, in the kingdom of the Devil. In his system election and grace reign supreme. The Augustinian synthesis went beyond the biblical imagery to combine elements of the gospel into a new pattern. Its results were to be felt in Luther's day and beyond. More important, he had given new life to the kingdom theme. The church is the kingdom of God made up of redeemed humanity, on pilgrimage until the final promised reign of God. The secular power, insofar as it can be reclaimed from the Devil, becomes an instrument of the church. The stage is set for the church to reign supreme. ment of the church. And at this point the stage is set for the church to reign supreme.

THE KINGDOM IN THE MIDDLE AGES

That is just what happened in the Middle Ages. The kingdom of God was identified not simply with "the city of the saints" but with the church and specifically with its hierarchical structures. Pope and bishops ruled God's kingdom, the church, to which the state and earthly kings were expected to be subservient. Of course, this shift had some basis in historical and sociological facts. Already in Augustine's day, as the Roman Empire broke up and went under, the church became the dominant institution in society. In the Middle Ages the papal hierarchy had become even to a greater degree the embodiment of order and rule in society. This church was equated with the kingdom, especially in the western Mediterranean area where Rome's influence was strongest.

Even in the Middle Ages, however, quite apart from the rumblings of national rulers and princes which would lead to the rise of modern secular states, one can find the voices of protest and alternative views. One of the most interesting presaged an interpretation of God's rule which keeps appearing in our own day. It is in the writings of Joachim of Flore (or Fiore), a monk of southern Italy. Brother Joachim said all history is divided into three periods. First there was the age of the Father extending from Adam to John the Baptist as described in the Old Testament when people lived under the Law. It was a time dominated by married people. Second, there was the age of the Son extending from the birth of Jesus Christ to the year A.D. 1260, when people lived under grace. It was the time of the clerics. (Joachim, who died just a few years after 1200, got the figure of 1260 by multiplying the biblical figure of 42 [generations] in Revelation 11:2 and 13:5 by 30, the average number of years in a generation. See also the 1260 days assumed in Daniel 7:25; 12:7. All such references have long been a happy hunting ground for apocalyptists.) Joachim's third age was the age of the Spirit, when the new religious orders, such as the one Joachim founded, would evangelize the world, and people would live under the freedom of the Spirit. It would be the age of the monks!

Joachim thought he was writing "an eternal gospel" (see Revelation 14:6). Like so many apocalyptic timetables, his called for the end of the world or for a decisive new stage just after the "prophet" made his predictions. Like all such timetables, it proved wrong. But in designating his second period as "the middle age" Joachim gave us our term *Middle Ages.* He also exemplifies the thinking of many subsequent groups such as the Millerites and the Rutherfordites. The former are connected with the Adventists and the latter with Jehovah's Witnesses. Such groups invariably seek to fix the date of the *parousia* or of "the Battle of Armageddon" (Revelation 16:1-16). Joachim's scheme of three "dispensations" is the grandfather of most modern attempts to fix a whole series of dispensations, usually seven in number. The Scofield Reference Bible notes are one of these attempts.

IN REFORMATION TIMES

Reformation treatment of the kingdom of God represents a refreshing return to biblical categories. John Calvin's well-known emphasis on "the sovereignty of God" was a bold effort to put the Old Testament "kingship of Yahweh" into other terms. Calvinistic attempts to translate *theocracy* ("rule by God") into city government in Geneva beginning in 1541 were less successful. It provided for a consistory of clergy and lay people to govern all of life according to a strict moral code. Puritan life-style in New England and "blue laws" in many areas of the United States have roots in this approach to building the kingdom of God on earth by religious control through the civil government. The "Geneva experiment" left its mark but did not succeed.

Reflecting Augustine, the Lutheran confessions relate the kingdom of God to the church in contrast to "the kingdom of the devil"[1] (Articles VII and VIII, 16, of the Apology of the Augsburg Confession; see Ephesians 2:2). These confessional writings are careful to add that the church is not to be equated with the hierarchy but with all believers, and that in this world the true church and its members are "hidden under the cross"[2] (Apology of the Augsburg Confession, Articles VII and VIII, 18). That is, there is no reign in glory as yet but life is discipleship, perhaps even marked by suffering (see Mark's view of Christ and discipleship in Chapter 29). Admittedly, there are mingled together in the church "good seed" and "weeds" (Matthew 13:38). Who are "the wicked" and who "the saved" cannot be seen until God's final judgment. The implication is that we should seek to witness to all, let all grow in the church, recognize that Christianity may involve suffering, and allow God to be the final judge.

Perhaps the best-known use of kingdom imagery for Lutherans occurs in the *Small Catechism* where Luther explains the Second Article of the Apostles' Creed. He describes the purpose of Christ's work for each person with the three phrases (italics added):

> in order that I might be his [Christ's],
> live under him *in his kingdom,*
> and serve him in everlasting righteousness,
> innocence, and blessedness.[3]

Therein lie a host of biblical ideas: "in Christ," the kingdom, the response of service, and the righteousness, and life. The kingdom is where those who belong to Christ live and work, that is, in both the church and the world.

One of the most significant proposals from the Reformation for conceiving of God's rule is the doctrine of the two kingdoms. After all we have seen in the Bible and in the interpretations of the kingdom since Augustine, the term should not sound strange. But Luther and Lutheran theologians following him worked out an understanding about God's reign which has proven very useful in dealing with social problems involving ethics even though many have misunderstood and abused it, and others have rejected it.

At the heart of the two-kingdom view is the understanding of faith that God rules not only in his church but in his world as well. In the former his kingship is confessed but in his world it is usually not acknowledged. Nevertheless, Christians believe that he created the world and still preserves it. The two-kingdom doctrine says that God rules in two different ways or styles in these two realms. In the kingdom on the right (to use language from Matthew 25:33, 34, 41), God rules through love and the gospel. In the kingdom on the left, the world or state, he rules through justice and law. The two ways of governing are to be distinguished from one another and not confused. One should not try to run the state on the basis of the Sermon on the Mount which is intended for the disciples of Christ, not civil servants. At the same time the church and its function are to be distinguished from the United Nations or General Motors.

God Rules All the Universe		
On the left	The world, the state through justice and law as his creation.	The church through love and gospel as his redemption. On the right

This way of thinking frees Christians to participate fully in "worldly" concerns for justice and human betterment with people of all religions or of no religion. The gospel motivates Christians to participate in all kinds of activities in and on behalf of the world. But Christians do not say that those with whom they work to get things done in society must join their church or believe as they do. A common concern for justice is enough.

At the same time the church is allowed to be the church—living for the gospel and proclaiming Word and administering Sacrament without losing its soul in order to serve the world. We can witness for justice on all sorts of bases. We witness to Christ as Lord and Savior on the basis of the Bible's God-Story which we have heard. Witness or evangelism, then, is winning lives to Christ and becoming committed to Christ in his body, in order to serve there and in the world—where as believers we say he reigns also as king.

THE KINGDOM TODAY

Coming closer to our own times, we find the kingdom of God has received still other interpretations. Perhaps the one most congenial to Americans and favored by them has involved "the Social Gospel." It was popularized by Walter Rauschenbusch (1861–1918), the son of a German Lutheran who became a Baptist. Rauschenbusch began his ministry in the "Hell's Kitchen" section of New York City with people "out of work, out of clothes, out of shoes, and out of hope," yet living in the shadow of great wealth. He became convinced that God was at work in the social struggle and that the kingdom is "the energy of God realizing itself in human life." Christians must therefore join the struggle for justice to bring about the kingdom on earth. As preacher and seminary teacher in Rochester, New York, Rauschenbusch, with passionate conviction, strove to get faith into action. He worked for settlement houses, urban causes, and the improvement of working conditions. In later decades his disciples would add civil rights and crusades against multinational corporations.

Many traditionalist Christians, usually among the "haves" and not the "have-nots," oppose such efforts as unworthy of the church or they sense in the Social Gospel a human scheme to build what only God can bring about, that is, the kingdom. Undoubtedly many who supported the Social Gospel naively felt they were creating utopia on their own. But Rauschenbusch showed that the age-old symbol could fire the imagination anew. It served a similar purpose among the freedom riders in the 1960s and those who have thought of the church as politically activist, a kind of "avant-garde of the new regime" (Harvey Cox).

Returning to biblical texts in the face of all these inter-relations about the kingdom at the turn of the last century, some New Testament scholars set a new current in motion by stressing the apocalyptic or eschatological side of the kingdom of God in Jesus' teachings. The nineteenth century had pretty well been given over to views of the kingdom or "dominion of God" in an ethical sense. The kingdom "consists of those who believe in Christ, inasmuch as they treat one another with love without regard to differences of sex, rank, or race, thereby bringing about a fellowship of moral attitudes and moral properties extending through the whole range of human life," said Albrecht Ritschl. Adolf Harnack agreed by saying the kingdom is "the rule of the holy God in the hearts of individuals," a matter of "God and the soul, the soul and its God." Given an ethical or an individualist interpretation, the kingdom became something we build, develop, or cultivate. According to such a point of view even Transcendental Meditation could achieve the reign of God!

While some in pietistic sects had always kept alive an apocalyptic view of the kingdom of God's work, it took the New Testament critics, often of a radical bent, to turn the tide. These people began to see that the New Testament simply did not support what their age was saying about the kingdom of God. Ritschl's own son-in-law, Johannes Weiss, wrote in 1892 that the kingdom in Jesus' preaching is not a gradual, evolutionary achievement, but solely and only the activity of God. No one, "not even Jesus can bring, establish, or found the kingdom of God; only God can so do." Weiss saw that such a conclusion from the Bible might make Jesus'

210

Although *Augustine* was first attracted to Christianity by Ambrose, Bishop of Milan, it was his study of Paul's Letters, and especially Romans, that led to his conversion in 386. He became the leading churchman in North Africa and decisive spokesman for orthodox theology in councils and synods. His writings clearly undergird the doctrines of sin and grace enunciated by Luther centuries later.

Lutherans know how important "justification by grace through faith" was to *Martin Luther*. In a time when biographers tend to root that emphasis largely in Luther's personal experience, we need to discover anew its basis in the Scriptures. For the reformer, the final determinative force was always the Holy Spirit touching his life through the Word.

Harry Emerson Fosdick once called Walter *Rauschenbusch* "a major prophet of God's righteousness to his church and nation." Whether we agree or not, Rauschenbusch's influence ran wide and deep, extending beyond racial and national barriers, and continues into our times. Few present-day social activities know how deeply they are indebted to this turn-of-the-century gospel interpreter.

view of the kingdom irrelevant for most people in his day, so he simply admitted that "this conception of ours [of the kingdom as the Highest Good and the supreme ethical ideal] parts company with Jesus'" eschatological view.

The man who carried this finding to its logical outcome and whose name became almost a household word was Albert Schweitzer of the University of Strasbourg. Schweitzer applied this apocalyptic understanding of Jesus' view of God's kingdom not only to Jesus' preaching but to everything Jesus did or said. The result was a Jesus who believed at first that God would inaugurate his kingdom during his own lifetime, probably while the Twelve were on a mission tour (Mark 6:7–13; Matthew 10). But that proved wrong. No Son of man appeared on the clouds of heaven. According to Schweitzer, Jesus then decided that he himself must die. Then the Son of man and the kingdom would come. He died, but still no Son of man, no kingdom. In Schweitzer's view, Jesus died a disappointed eschatologist, and Jesus' teachings which were meant for only that brief interval before the kingdom comes have no lasting value. Having decided this, Schweitzer went off to French West Africa to labor heroically as a medical humanitarian. (*Missionary* may be too strong a term since his ethics and life view leaned increasingly toward Stoicism and oriental religions.)

Schweitzer did recapture the eschatological side of the kingdom, and no one since his day has been able to ignore it. But he made it so one-sidedly apocalyptic that if we agree with him the kingdom has little value apart from being a noble idea to be filled with new content, primarily ethical.

Of course, the story of the meaning of the kingdom is not over. Bible students have faced the fact that all predictions of the end of the world, even those in the New Testament, proved wrong, and so they have gone back to Jesus' words to find some other abiding value in the kingdom. One suggestion came from Rudolf Bultmann who died in 1976. He said that for Jesus the kingdom was a future power which was already determining the present. What it did was force people to come to a decision about God and his rule and about themselves and life. Hence what really matters is the way human existence is conceived of here and now. The announcement of the kingdom is a call for us to turn, repent, and come to "authentic existence" of life in faith. The kingdom proclamation is a summons to live depending on God as a power outside ourselves. This is an existentialist interpretation, that is, one that applies to human existence and uses the language of existentialist philosophy.

Thus, in the long history of its use, extending over more than a thousand years in the Bible and twice that number since Christ, the kingdom of God has had dozens of interpretations and new twists of meaning. We can view it as—

• Otherworldly and future.

• This-worldly and present—individually or via social action.

- A path through history, opposed to the Devil's earthly kingdom, leading to a heavenly realm.
- A stage or dispensation in history.
- The area, the church, where God's rule is confessed, as opposed to the world where he also rules in other ways but is unacknowledged.
- This—worldly but future—to be achieved by God or us or both.
- Any combination of the above!

Needless to say, all the chapters in this study about Jesus' view or Paul's usage or Matthew's have been written with an awareness of this history of interpretation. And the debate goes on. We have suggested some of the biblical content to be examined in connection with God's kingdom (Chapters 1—29). In this chapter we have also looked at some post-biblical interpretations. The one thing that has become abundantly clear is the staying power of this theme as a symbol for something central in the Bible and in Christianity.

Yet one must admit it has been a symbol with not one fixed meaning exhausted when its time has come and gone but a set of meanings which continue to project new insights to inspire and lead the people of God.

This pervasive symbol of the kingdom has thus had a tremendous history stretching from the ancient Near East and its mythological usage to Jesus and beyond. The psalmist caught the vision of what the kingdom of God means when he wrote:

> All thy creatures praise thee, Lord,
>   and thy servants bless thee.
> They talk of the glory of thy kingdom
>   and tell of thy might.
> They proclaim to their fellows how mighty are thy deeds,
>   how glorious the majesty of thy kingdom.
> Thy kingdom is an everlasting kingdom,
>   and thy dominion stands for all generations.
>   (Psalm 145:10-13, NEB)

Anonymous writers between the Old Testament and the New kept the hope alive during dark days, as when the author of the *Assumption of Moses* wrote that God's kingdom shall appear "throughout his creation, and then shall Satan be no more, and sorrow shall depart. . . ." Then came Jesus, and the kingdom was at hand. Ever since, believers have been trying to let the promise for which they pray "Thy kingdom come" reach fulfillment. Luther explained this petition very "existentially" by saying, "To be sure, the kingdom of God comes of itself, without our prayer, but we pray . . . that it may also come to us." Then he added that this happens when "the heavenly Father gives us his Holy Spirit so that by his grace we may believe his holy Word and live a godly life, both here in time and hereafter forever."

213

To express the kingdom meaningfully as gospel in Christ is our task as witnesses.

A Christian in the second century perhaps summed things up well in the succinct sentence, "In the gospel, the kingdom of God is Christ himself." Origen, a theologian of the next century, said it similarly, "Christ is himself the kingdom." The symbolism of the kingdom with God as Lord, breaking into human life supremely in Jesus Christ, has been inserted into the world by Scripture in a rich way. The gospel is the norm which defines the kingdom as good news. Since Easter, Jesus is increasingly its content. God's rule in every life and land and age is the goal. To express the kingdom meaningfully as gospel in Christ is our task as witnesses.

The Bible gives us many ways to grasp hold of the message about the kingdom. The kingdom of God is but one way of expressing the gospel. Witnesses to true life must themselves experience kingdom, justification, Christ, and gospel before they can talk much about them with others. But as they speak and live they will also find God and Christ, the kingdom and the gospel possessing them! In telling the God story, we not only come to know him better; we come to be known by him (Galatians 4:9).

We recall the Hasidic tale of Rabbi Zusya who said of his judgment for the next world he would not be asked why he had not been Moses, but "Why were you not Zusya?" Christians are accustomed to the necessity of being themselves, witnessing where they are, and developing their own gifts and talents. But again, there is that sense in which they must also answer differently because they and their story are never just of themselves but also of their Lord. They are "in Christ" and must live in him.

We come to the zenith of Bible study when we know the God stories of Scripture and the Christ reports so well that they are told with our own accents, comfortably and familiarly; when our stories are each subordinated to his deeds, glory, and might; and when we listen to others to discover what God is saying or wants said through them. Then we are beginning to have the eyes and ears of faith to see and hear the kingdom of God and Christ taking shape in human existence as good news. Word has become our witness and our witness is the Word of God.

References and More Information

1. Apology of the Augsburg Confession, from *The Book of Concord,* trans. Theodore G. Tappert (Philadelphia: Muhlenberg Press, 1959), p. 170.
2. Ibid., p. 171.
3. Ibid., p. 346.

214

Metzger, Bruce M. and Isobel M., editors. *The Oxford Concise Concordance.* See the following entry: earth

Richardson, Alan. *A Theological Word Book of the Bible.* New York: The Macmillan Company, 1962. See the following entries: call, free, inherit beliefs — way you conduct yourself in society